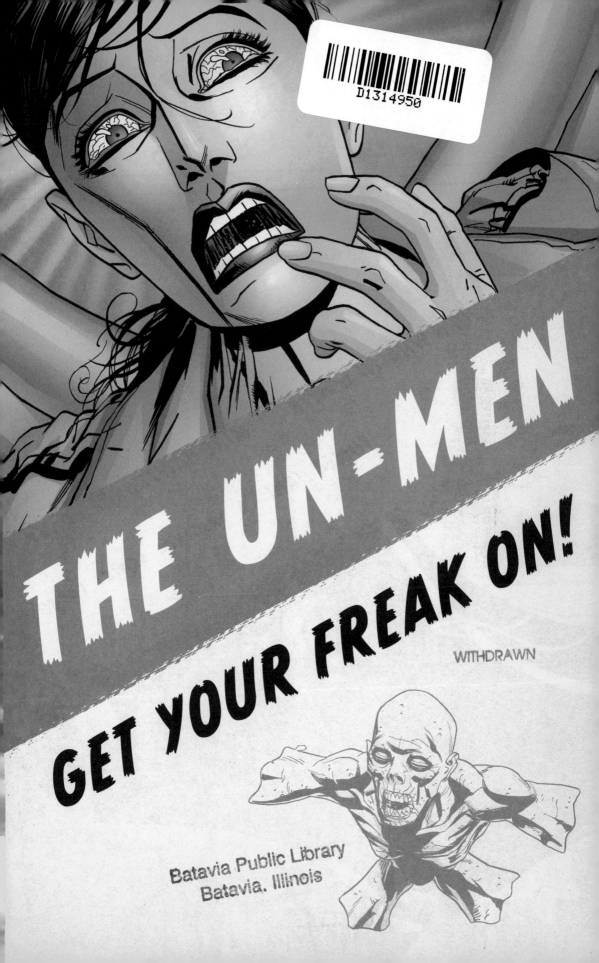

THE UN-MEN

GET YOUR FREAK ON!

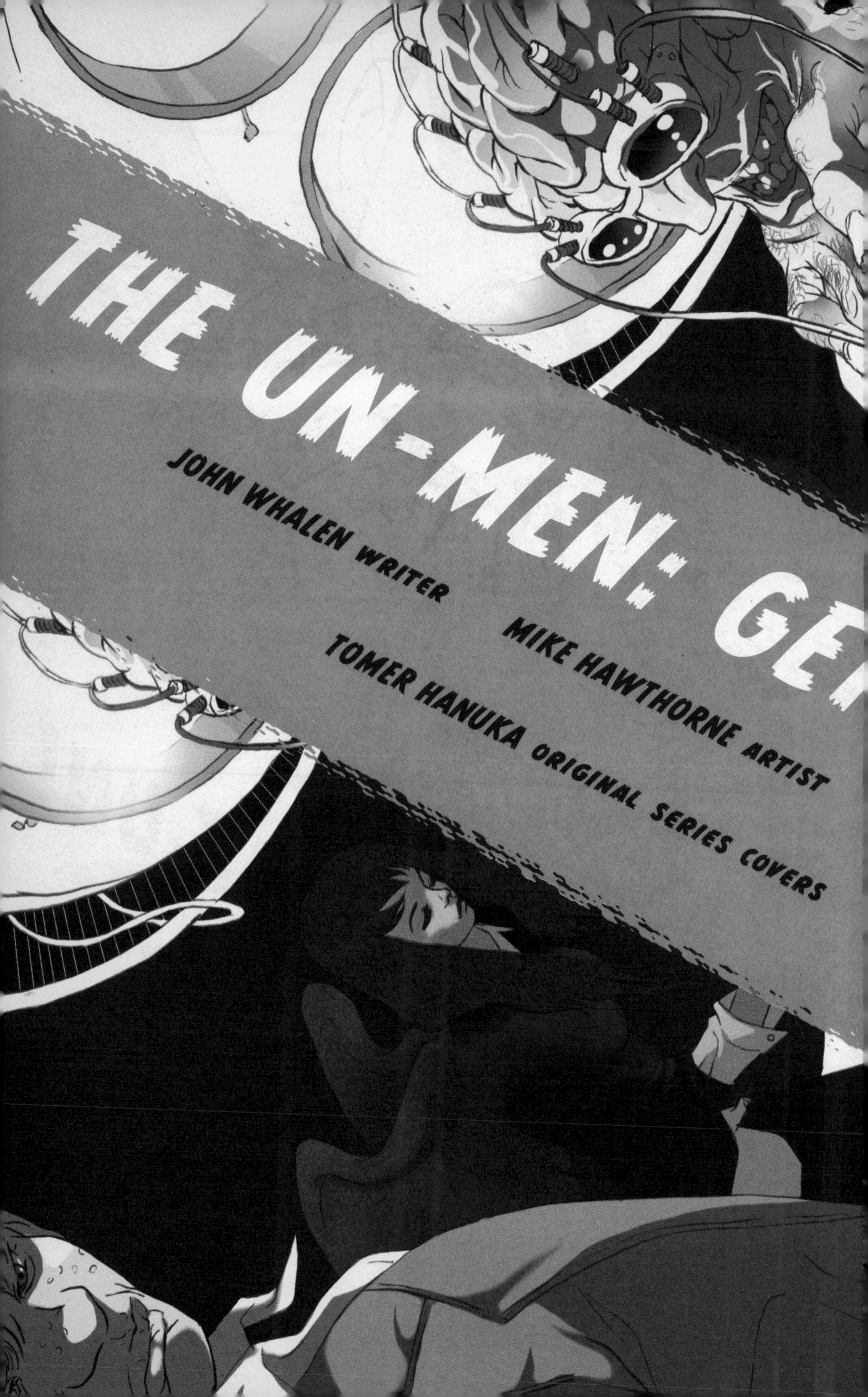
THE UN-MEN: GE
JOHN WHALEN WRITER
MIKE HAWTHORNE ARTIST
TOMER HANUKA ORIGINAL SERIES COVERS

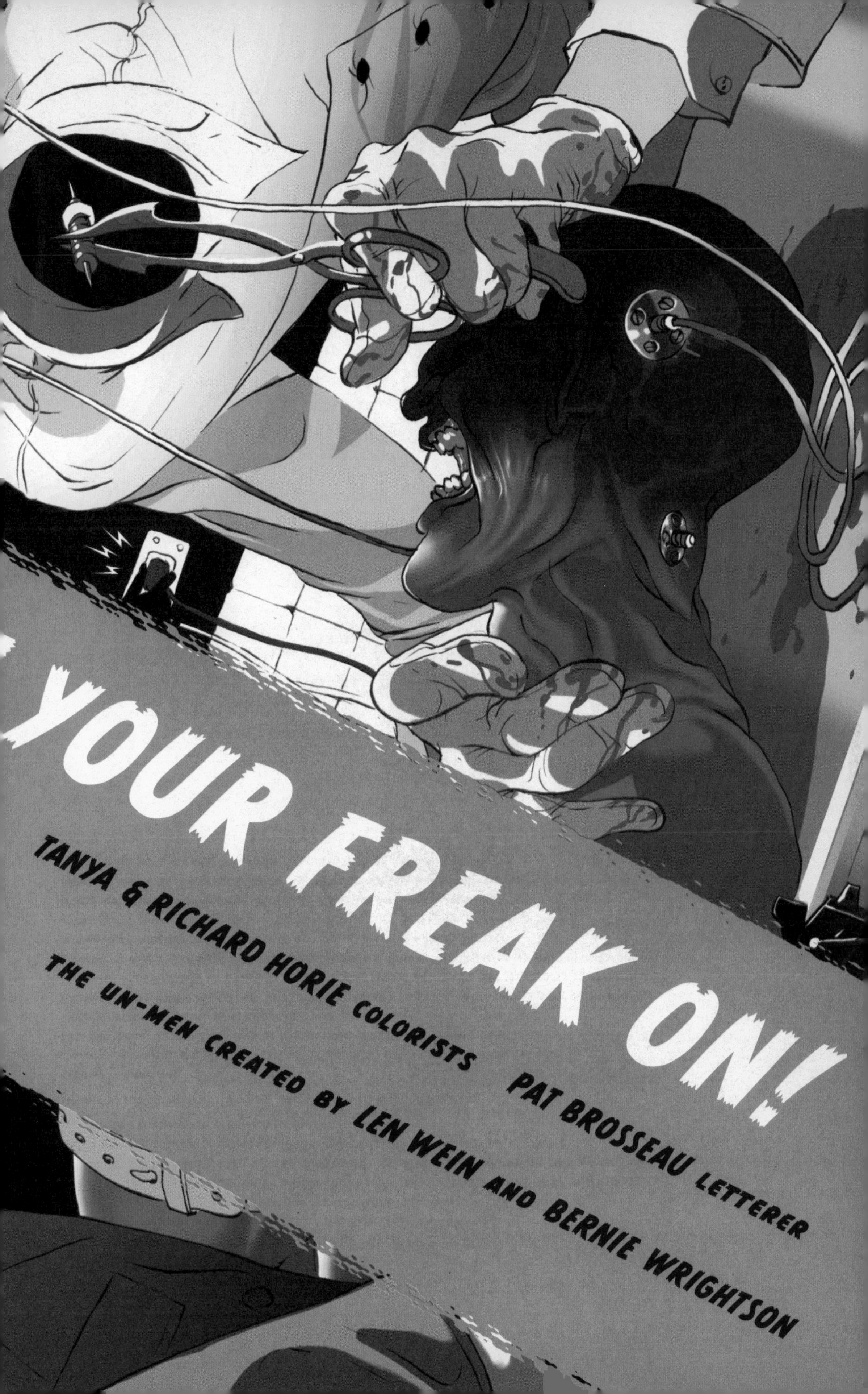
YOUR FREAK ON!
TANYA & RICHARD HORIE COLORISTS PAT BROSSEAU LETTERER
THE UN-MEN CREATED BY LEN WEIN AND BERNIE WRIGHTSON

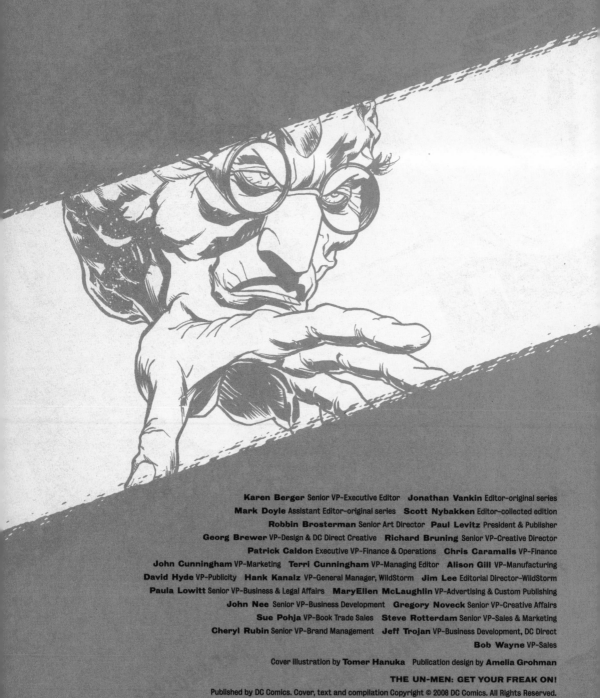

Karen Berger Senior VP-Executive Editor   **Jonathan Vankin** Editor-original series
Mark Doyle Assistant Editor-original series   **Scott Nybakken** Editor-collected edition
Robbin Brosterman Senior Art Director   **Paul Levitz** President & Publisher
Georg Brewer VP-Design & DC Direct Creative   **Richard Bruning** Senior VP-Creative Director
Patrick Caldon Executive VP-Finance & Operations   **Chris Caramalis** VP-Finance
John Cunningham VP-Marketing   **Terri Cunningham** VP-Managing Editor   **Alison Gill** VP-Manufacturing
David Hyde VP-Publicity   **Hank Kanalz** VP-General Manager, WildStorm   **Jim Lee** Editorial Director-WildStorm
Paula Lowitt Senior VP-Business & Legal Affairs   **MaryEllen McLaughlin** VP-Advertising & Custom Publishing
John Nee Senior VP-Business Development   **Gregory Noveck** Senior VP-Creative Affairs
Sue Pohja VP-Book Trade Sales   **Steve Rotterdam** Senior VP-Sales & Marketing
Cheryl Rubin Senior VP-Brand Management   **Jeff Trojan** VP-Business Development, DC Direct
Bob Wayne VP-Sales

Cover illustration by **Tomer Hanuka**   Publication design by **Amelia Grohman**

THE UN-MEN: GET YOUR FREAK ON!
Published by DC Comics. Cover, text and compilation Copyright © 2008 DC Comics. All Rights Reserved.
Originally published in single magazine form as THE UN-MEN 1-5 Copyright © 2007, 2008 DC Comics. All Rights Reserved.
VERTIGO and all characters, their distinctive likenesses and related elements featured in this publication are trademarks
of DC Comics. The stories, characters and incidents featured in this publication are entirely fictional.
DC Comics does not read or accept unsolicited submissions of ideas, stories or artwork.

DC Comics, 1700 Broadway, New York, NY 10019. A Warner Bros. Entertainment Company.
Printed in Canada. First Printing. ISBN: 978-1-4012-1702-0

INTRODUCTION BY LEN WEIN

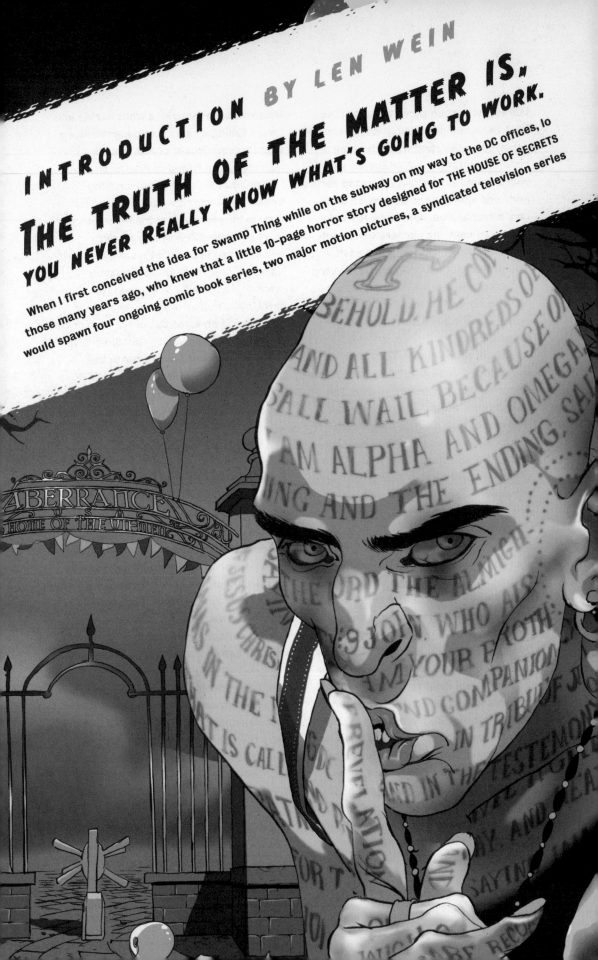

THE TRUTH OF THE MATTER IS, YOU NEVER REALLY KNOW WHAT'S GOING TO WORK.

When I first conceived the idea for Swamp Thing while on the subway on my way to the DC offices, lo those many years ago, who knew that a little 10-page horror story designed for THE HOUSE OF SECRETS would spawn four ongoing comic book series, two major motion pictures, a syndicated television series

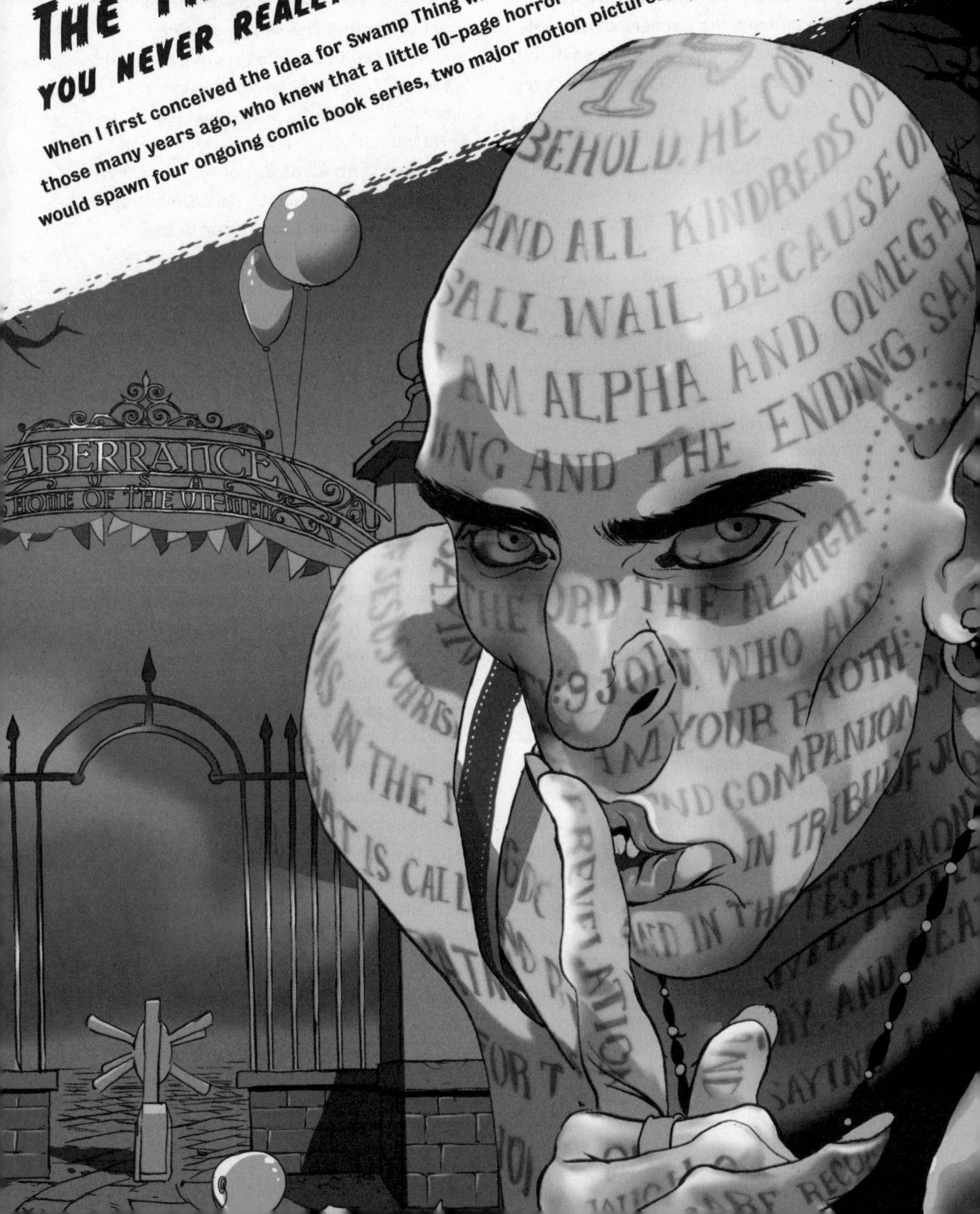
ABERRANCE
U S A
HOME OF THE

lasting more than three seasons (the first two seasons of which were recently released on DVD, and which feature a hopefully entertaining interview with your humble scribe), an animated series and Lord alone knows how much ancillary merchandise. Who knew it would help to cement the careers of not only artist Bernie Wrightson and myself, but also of the vast majority of the writers and artists who have followed in our footsteps over the decades? Anyone here ever hear of a guy named Alan Moore, for example?

You just never know what's going to click with an audience. When the classic TV series *Happy Days* premiered, the character of Arthur Fonzarelli was a throwaway with a single line of dialogue; when the series ended a decade later, Fonzie was the undisputed star of the show. When the sitcom *Family Matters* introduced über-nerd Steve Urkel, he was supposed to be a one-shot joke; by the end of that season, he had taken over the series.

And then there are the Un-Men.

When I created them way back in the second issue of the SWAMP THING ongoing series, the Un-Men were intended to be little more than cannon fodder, something for Swampy to pound on for a few pages to generate some action until we got to the real meat of the story and introduced sorcerer/scientist Anton Arcane. But then Bernie's pencilled artwork arrived, and when I got a good look at the marvelous monstrosities his twisted mind had envisioned, I knew there was a whole lot more to those grotesque freaks than I had originally thought. Suddenly they were real to me. They had attitudes, personalities. Frankly, they scared the hell out of me.

Which was perfect since what Bernie and I were telling was a classic horror story slightly reminiscent of H.G. Wells's legendary *The Island of Doctor Moreau*.

In point of fact, all of our original SWAMP THING stories were inspired by classic horror icons. In his meandering journey around the world, Swampy encountered everything from a Scottish werewolf to a Frankensteinian man-monster to a family of witches to M'Nagalah, a mind-numbingly hideous cancer-god straight out of H.P. Lovecraft (and recently revived by Gail Simone to wreak all sorts of havoc over in the pages of THE ALL-NEW ATOM). I make no apologies for this. These were the kinds of stories Bernie and I wanted to tell, the kinds of stories that had terrified and influenced and molded us when we were younger. That was precisely the sort of legacy we hoped to pass on to the next generation.

But that was then and this is now. The world has changed a great deal in the past three decades. Today's monsters aren't generally covered in coarse hair or sewn together from leftover body parts. They don't lurk in the bowels of Gothic castles. Today's monsters wear Armani suits and lunch at the Palm and keep offices on the penthouse floor and are generally a great deal more worried about the bottom line and their golden parachute than they are about whether their hunchbacked assistant will bring them the correct brain to implant.

And that is the world into which writer John Whalen (late of DC's THE BIG BOOK OF THE WEIRD WILD WEST) and artist Mike Hawthorne (of Vertigo's THE EXTERMINATORS fame) have injected my precious Un-Men. A world of political correctness and social expediency. A world where "freak"

is still a dirty word unless a freak is the one who says it. A world where the freaks shall inherit the Earth. Or, at least, one small irradiated patch of it.

So welcome to Aberrance, USA, the freakiest place on Earth, now home to my errant Un-Men. If you've read the original SWAMP THING stories, there are faces (such as they are) that you may recognize here. The delightfully disgusting Cranius is back to run the show (though when he developed that Teutonic accent I'll never know). Janus, clearly evolved from the creature who once rowed Swampy ashore to a Balkan castle, is now the public face of the Un-Men. And there's even a tip of the hypothetical hat to hypnotic, serpentine Ophidian.

But there's new blood here as well: the multi-limbed Tripes, angelic Niko, Inkabod, the tattooed word made flesh. Oh, and of course there's Federal Agent Kilcrop, arguably the least freakish freak of all, sent here to solve a simple murder that is anything but simple. New freaks for a new millennium.

So Hurry! Hurry! Step right this way, folks, and buy a ticket to the freak show. You're just in time. The next performance is about to start.

And, trust us, you wouldn't want to miss the opening act.

—Len Wein

January 2008

Veteran comics writer and editor Len Wein is the creator of such memorable characters as Wolverine, the New X-Men and the Human Target, as well as the cocreator (with Bernie Wrightson) of the Swamp Thing and the Un-Men. In his long and prolific career he has written for hundreds of titles, encompassing nearly every significant character in the medium. He has also built a successful career in TV animation, scripting such hit series as X-Men, Spider-Man and Batman: The Animated Series.

"WE ARE NOT ACCIDENTAL FREAKS — NATURE'S PLODDING MISTAKES. NOR ARE WE MEN LIKE YOU. *WE ARE UN-MEN.*"

CHAPTER ONE

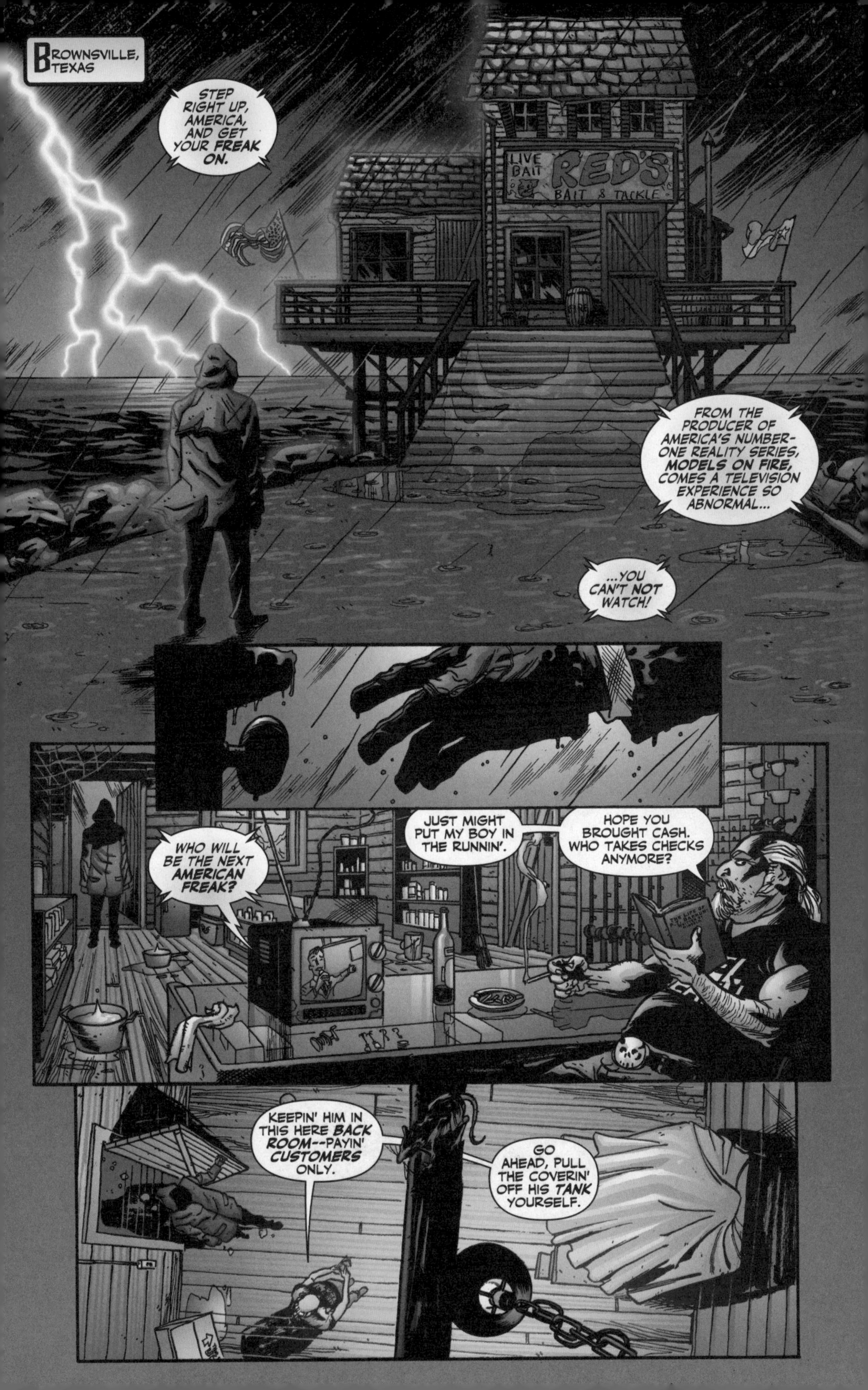
BROWNSVILLE, TEXAS
STEP RIGHT UP, AMERICA, AND GET YOUR FREAK ON.
LIVE BAIT
RED'S BAIT & TACKLE
FROM THE PRODUCER OF AMERICA'S NUMBER-ONE REALITY SERIES, MODELS ON FIRE, COMES A TELEVISION EXPERIENCE SO ABNORMAL...
...YOU CAN'T NOT WATCH!
WHO WILL BE THE NEXT AMERICAN FREAK?
JUST MIGHT PUT MY BOY IN THE RUNNIN'.
HOPE YOU BROUGHT CASH. WHO TAKES CHECKS ANYMORE?
KEEPIN' HIM IN THIS HERE BACK ROOM--PAYIN' CUSTOMERS ONLY.
GO AHEAD, PULL THE COVERIN' OFF HIS TANK YOURSELF.

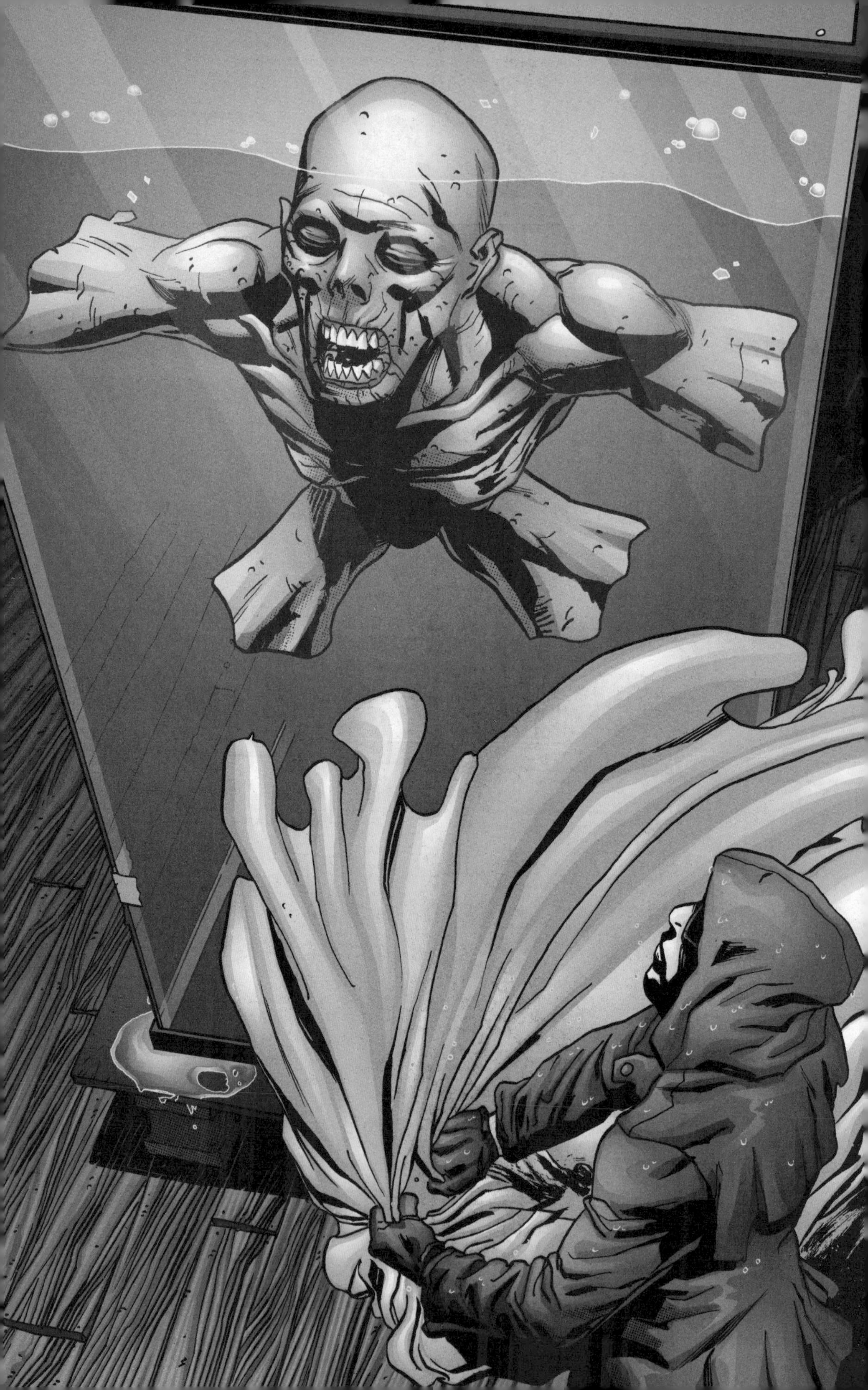

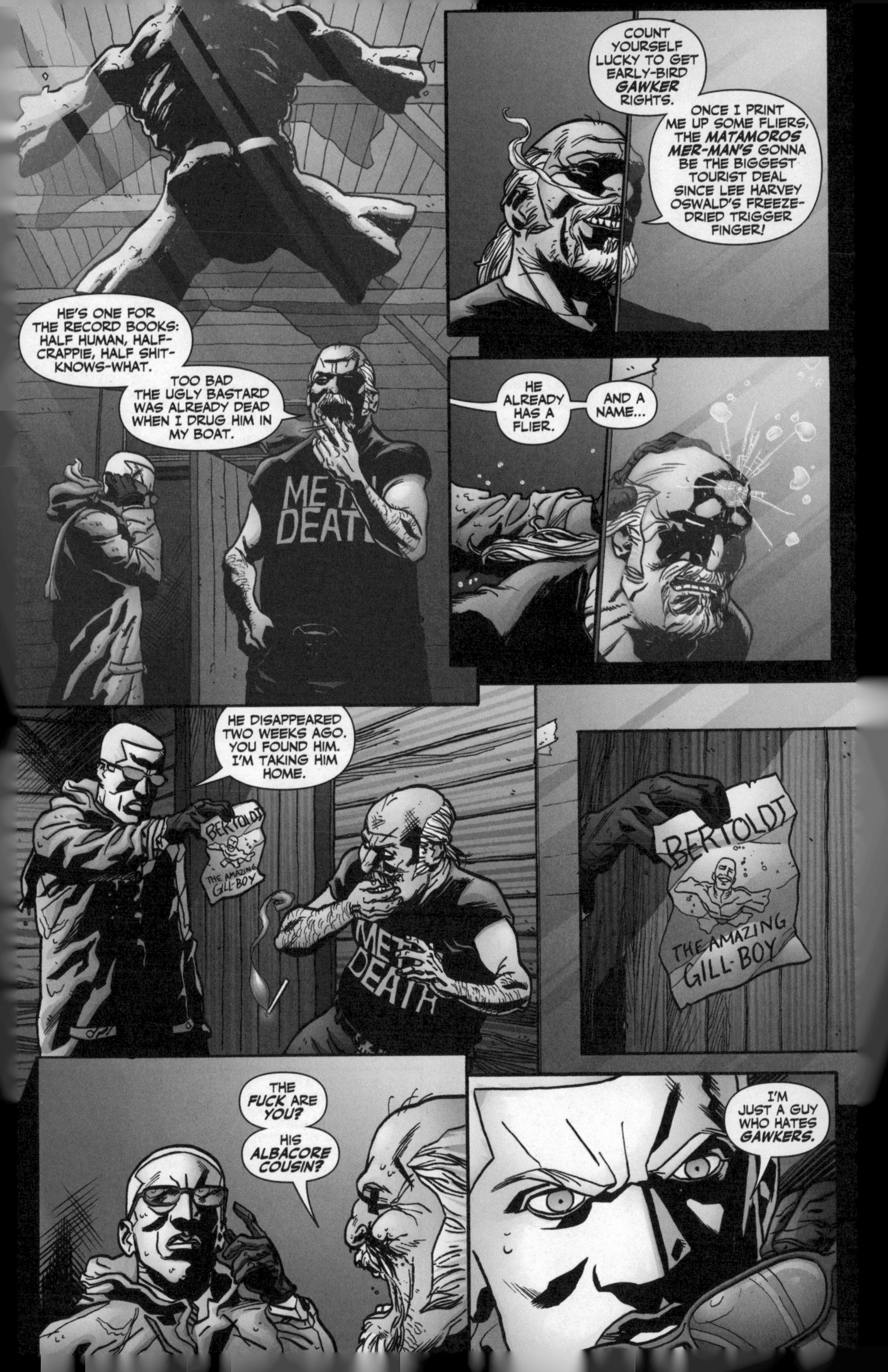
COUNT YOURSELF LUCKY TO GET EARLY-BIRD GAWKER RIGHTS.
ONCE I PRINT ME UP SOME FLIERS, THE MATAMOROS MER-MAN'S GONNA BE THE BIGGEST TOURIST DEAL SINCE LEE HARVEY OSWALD'S FREEZE-DRIED TRIGGER FINGER!
HE'S ONE FOR THE RECORD BOOKS: HALF HUMAN, HALF-CRAPPIE, HALF SHIT-KNOWS-WHAT.
TOO BAD THE UGLY BASTARD WAS ALREADY DEAD WHEN I DRUG HIM IN MY BOAT.
HE ALREADY HAS A FLIER.
AND A NAME...
HE DISAPPEARED TWO WEEKS AGO. YOU FOUND HIM. I'M TAKING HIM HOME.
BERTOLDI
THE AMAZING GILL-BOY
THE FUCK ARE YOU?
HIS ALBACORE COUSIN?
I'M JUST A GUY WHO HATES GAWKERS.

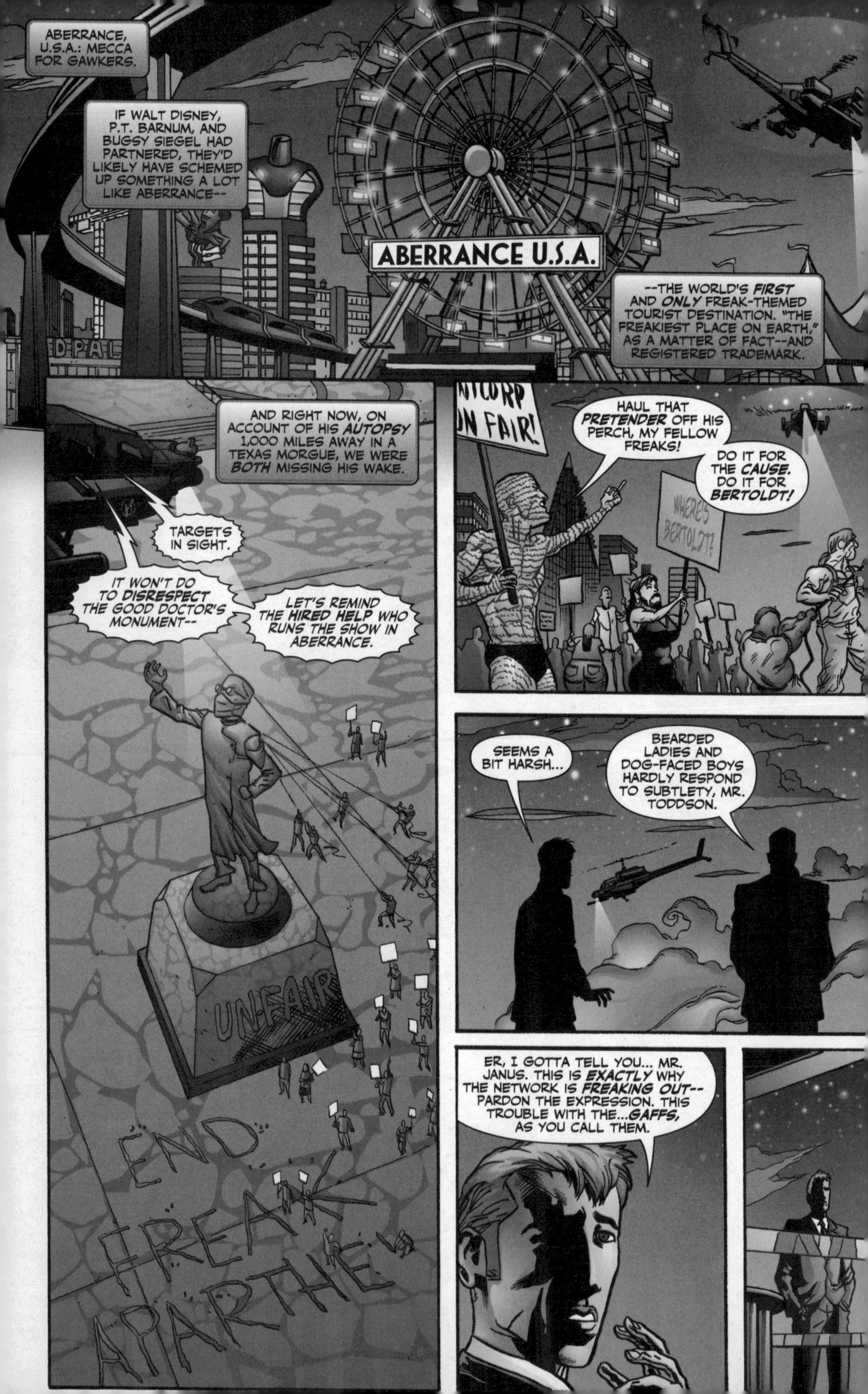
ABERRANCE, U.S.A.: MECCA FOR GAWKERS.
IF WALT DISNEY, P.T. BARNUM, AND BUGSY SIEGEL HAD PARTNERED, THEY'D LIKELY HAVE SCHEMED UP SOMETHING A LOT LIKE ABERRANCE--
ABERRANCE U.S.A.
--THE WORLD'S FIRST AND ONLY FREAK-THEMED TOURIST DESTINATION. "THE FREAKIEST PLACE ON EARTH," AS A MATTER OF FACT--AND REGISTERED TRADEMARK.
AND RIGHT NOW, ON ACCOUNT OF HIS AUTOPSY 1,000 MILES AWAY IN A TEXAS MORGUE, WE WERE BOTH MISSING HIS WAKE.
TARGETS IN SIGHT.
IT WON'T DO TO DISRESPECT THE GOOD DOCTOR'S MONUMENT--
LET'S REMIND THE HIRED HELP WHO RUNS THE SHOW IN ABERRANCE.
UN-FAIR
END FREA APARTHE
ON FAIR!
HAUL THAT PRETENDER OFF HIS PERCH, MY FELLOW FREAKS!
DO IT FOR THE CAUSE. DO IT FOR BERTOLDT!
WHERE'S BERTOLDT?
SEEMS A BIT HARSH...
BEARDED LADIES AND DOG-FACED BOYS HARDLY RESPOND TO SUBTLETY, MR. TODDSON.
ER, I GOTTA TELL YOU... MR. JANUS. THIS IS EXACTLY WHY THE NETWORK IS FREAKING OUT-- PARDON THE EXPRESSION. THIS TROUBLE WITH THE...GAFFS, AS YOU CALL THEM.

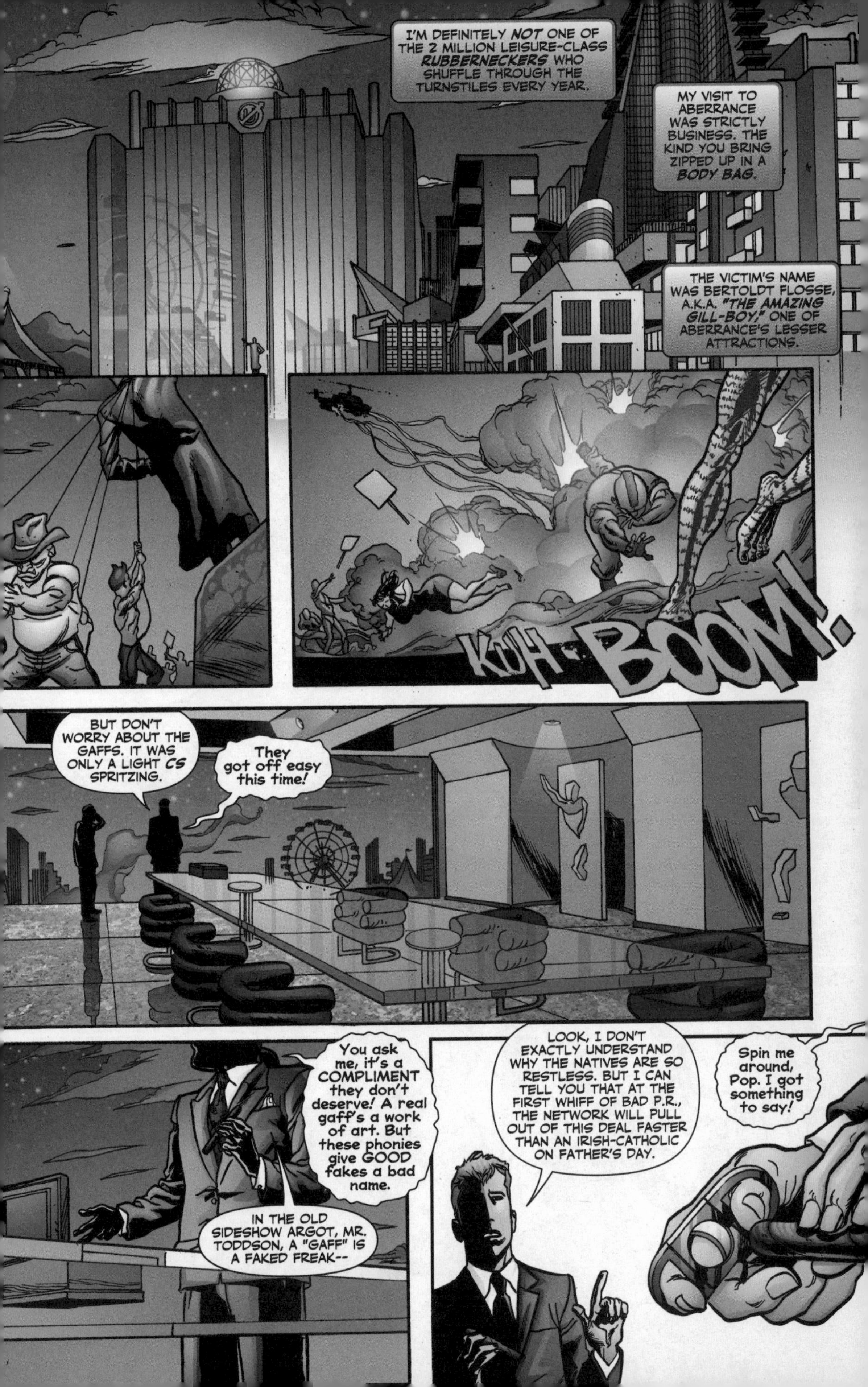
I'M DEFINITELY NOT ONE OF THE 2 MILLION LEISURE-CLASS RUBBERNECKERS WHO SHUFFLE THROUGH THE TURNSTILES EVERY YEAR.
MY VISIT TO ABERRANCE WAS STRICTLY BUSINESS. THE KIND YOU BRING ZIPPED UP IN A BODY BAG.
THE VICTIM'S NAME WAS BERTOLDT FLOSSE, A.K.A. "THE AMAZING GILL-BOY," ONE OF ABERRANCE'S LESSER ATTRACTIONS.
KUH-BOOM!
BUT DON'T WORRY ABOUT THE GAFFS. IT WAS ONLY A LIGHT CS SPRITZING.
They got off easy this time!
You ask me, it's a COMPLIMENT they don't deserve! A real gaff's a work of art. But these phonies give GOOD fakes a bad name.
IN THE OLD SIDESHOW ARGOT, MR. TODDSON, A "GAFF" IS A FAKED FREAK--
LOOK, I DON'T EXACTLY UNDERSTAND WHY THE NATIVES ARE SO RESTLESS. BUT I CAN TELL YOU THAT AT THE FIRST WHIFF OF BAD P.R., THE NETWORK WILL PULL OUT OF THIS DEAL FASTER THAN AN IRISH-CATHOLIC ON FATHER'S DAY.
Spin me around, Pop. I got something to say!

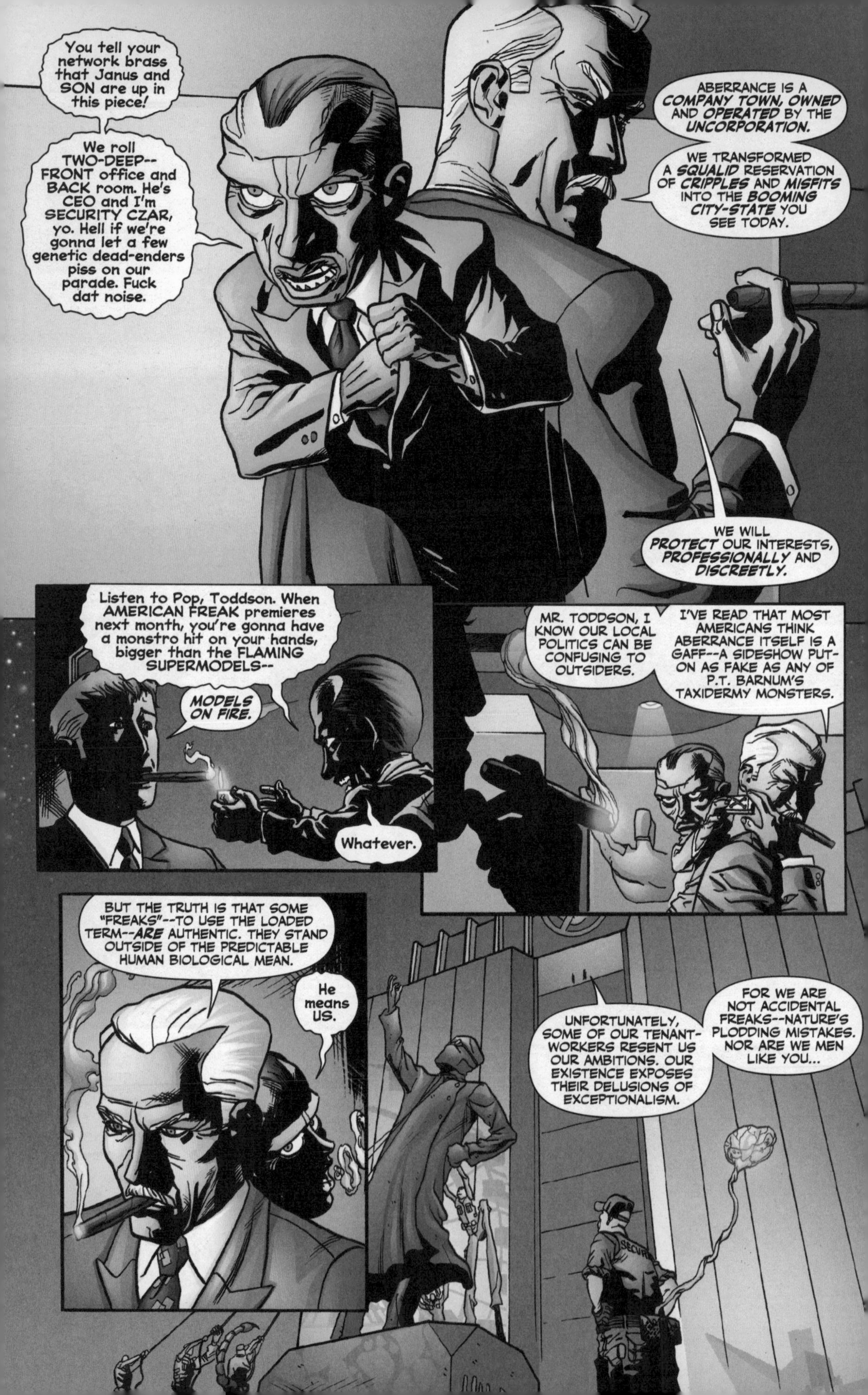
You tell your network brass that Janus and SON are up in this piece!
We roll TWO-DEEP-- FRONT office and BACK room. He's CEO and I'm SECURITY CZAR, yo. Hell if we're gonna let a few genetic dead-enders piss on our parade. Fuck dat noise.
ABERRANCE IS A COMPANY TOWN, OWNED AND OPERATED BY THE UNCORPORATION.
WE TRANSFORMED A SQUALID RESERVATION OF CRIPPLES AND MISFITS INTO THE BOOMING CITY-STATE YOU SEE TODAY.
WE WILL PROTECT OUR INTERESTS, PROFESSIONALLY AND DISCREETLY.
Listen to Pop, Toddson. When AMERICAN FREAK premieres next month, you're gonna have a monstro hit on your hands, bigger than the FLAMING SUPERMODELS--
MODELS ON FIRE.
Whatever.
MR. TODDSON, I KNOW OUR LOCAL POLITICS CAN BE CONFUSING TO OUTSIDERS.
I'VE READ THAT MOST AMERICANS THINK ABERRANCE ITSELF IS A GAFF--A SIDESHOW PUT-ON AS FAKE AS ANY OF P.T. BARNUM'S TAXIDERMY MONSTERS.
BUT THE TRUTH IS THAT SOME "FREAKS"--TO USE THE LOADED TERM--ARE AUTHENTIC. THEY STAND OUTSIDE OF THE PREDICTABLE HUMAN BIOLOGICAL MEAN.
He means US.
UNFORTUNATELY, SOME OF OUR TENANT-WORKERS RESENT US OUR AMBITIONS. OUR EXISTENCE EXPOSES THEIR DELUSIONS OF EXCEPTIONALISM.
FOR WE ARE NOT ACCIDENTAL FREAKS--NATURE'S PLODDING MISTAKES. NOR ARE WE MEN LIKE YOU...

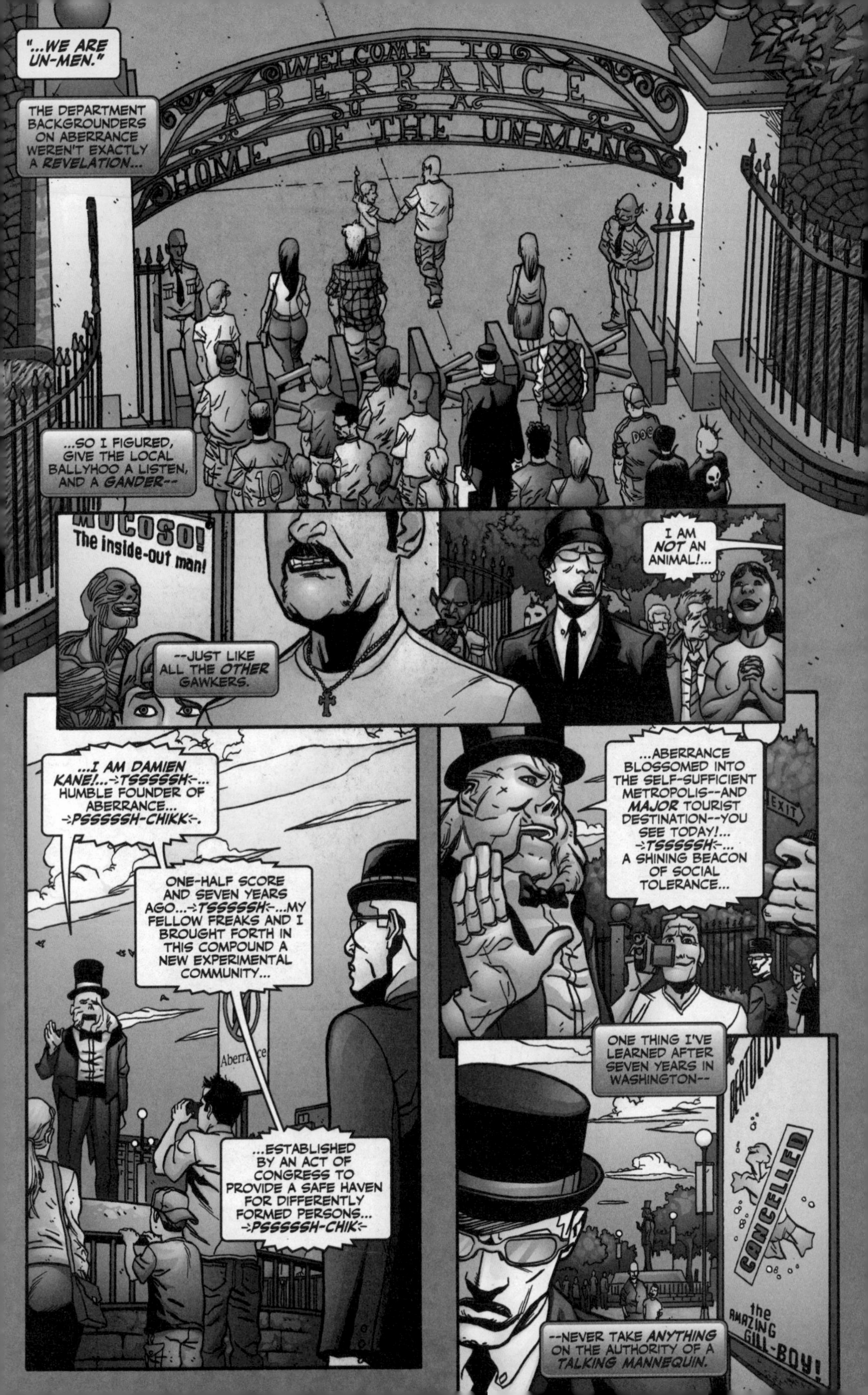
"...WE ARE UN-MEN."
THE DEPARTMENT BACKGROUNDERS ON ABERRANCE WEREN'T EXACTLY A REVELATION...
WELCOME TO ABERRANCE U S A HOME OF THE UN-MEN
...SO I FIGURED, GIVE THE LOCAL BALLYHOO A LISTEN, AND A GANDER--
DOC
MUCOSO! The inside-out man!
--JUST LIKE ALL THE OTHER GAWKERS.
I AM NOT AN ANIMAL!...
...I AM DAMIEN KANE!...→TSSSSSH←... HUMBLE FOUNDER OF ABERRANCE... →PSSSSSH-CHIKK←.
ONE-HALF SCORE AND SEVEN YEARS AGO...→TSSSSSH←...MY FELLOW FREAKS AND I BROUGHT FORTH IN THIS COMPOUND A NEW EXPERIMENTAL COMMUNITY...
...ESTABLISHED BY AN ACT OF CONGRESS TO PROVIDE A SAFE HAVEN FOR DIFFERENTLY FORMED PERSONS... →PSSSSSH-CHIK←
Aberrance
...ABERRANCE BLOSSOMED INTO THE SELF-SUFFICIENT METROPOLIS--AND MAJOR TOURIST DESTINATION--YOU SEE TODAY!... →TSSSSSH←... A SHINING BEACON OF SOCIAL TOLERANCE...
EXIT
ONE THING I'VE LEARNED AFTER SEVEN YEARS IN WASHINGTON--
CANCELLED
the AMAZING GILL-BOY!
--NEVER TAKE ANYTHING ON THE AUTHORITY OF A TALKING MANNEQUIN.

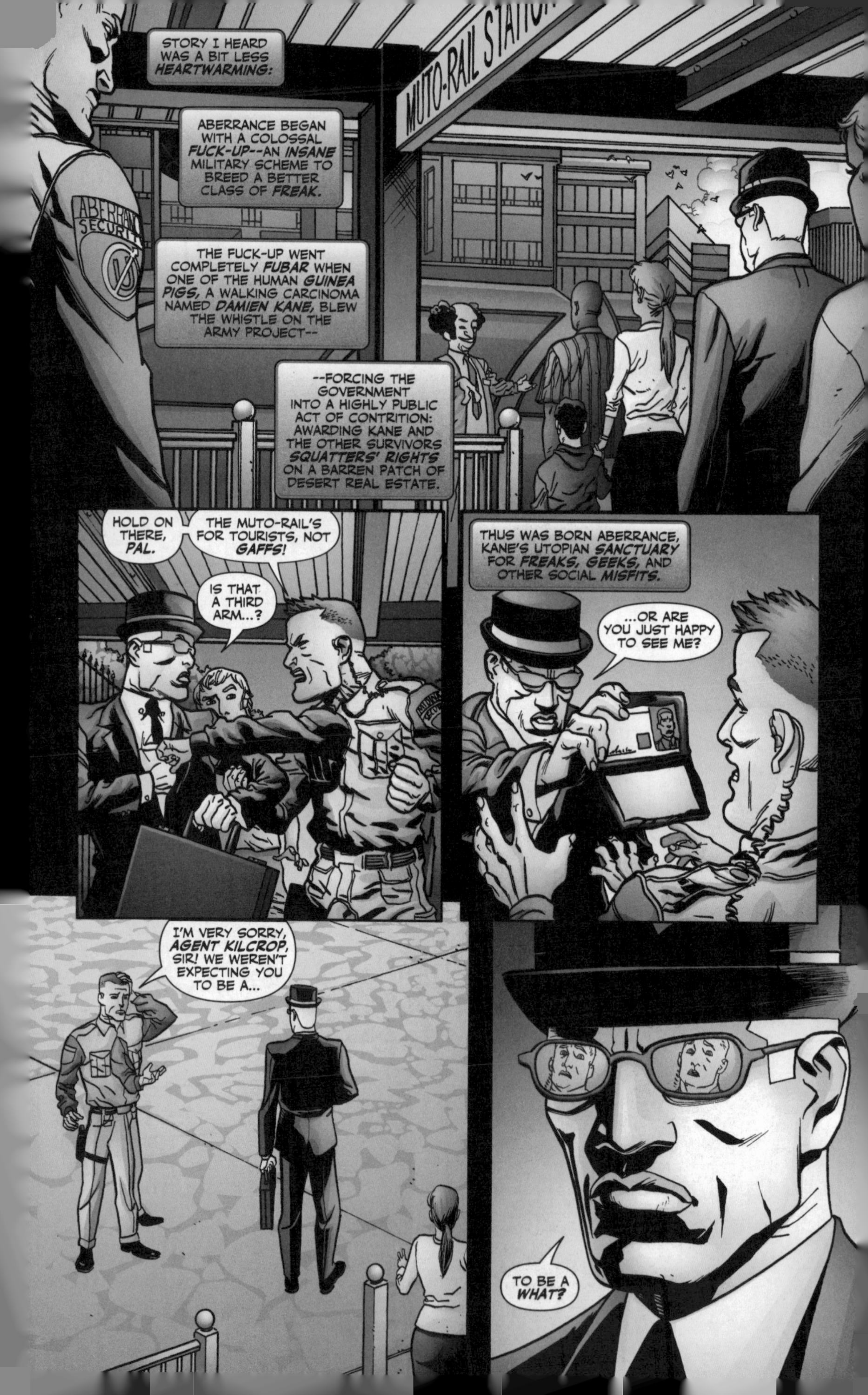

MUTO-RAIL STATION
STORY I HEARD WAS A BIT LESS HEARTWARMING:
ABERRANCE BEGAN WITH A COLOSSAL FUCK-UP--AN INSANE MILITARY SCHEME TO BREED A BETTER CLASS OF FREAK.
THE FUCK-UP WENT COMPLETELY FUBAR WHEN ONE OF THE HUMAN GUINEA PIGS, A WALKING CARCINOMA NAMED DAMIEN KANE, BLEW THE WHISTLE ON THE ARMY PROJECT--
--FORCING THE GOVERNMENT INTO A HIGHLY PUBLIC ACT OF CONTRITION: AWARDING KANE AND THE OTHER SURVIVORS SQUATTERS' RIGHTS ON A BARREN PATCH OF DESERT REAL ESTATE.
HOLD ON THERE, PAL.
THE MUTO-RAIL'S FOR TOURISTS, NOT GAFFS!
IS THAT A THIRD ARM...?
THUS WAS BORN ABERRANCE, KANE'S UTOPIAN SANCTUARY FOR FREAKS, GEEKS, AND OTHER SOCIAL MISFITS.
...OR ARE YOU JUST HAPPY TO SEE ME?
I'M VERY SORRY, AGENT KILCROP, SIR! WE WEREN'T EXPECTING YOU TO BE A...
TO BE A WHAT?

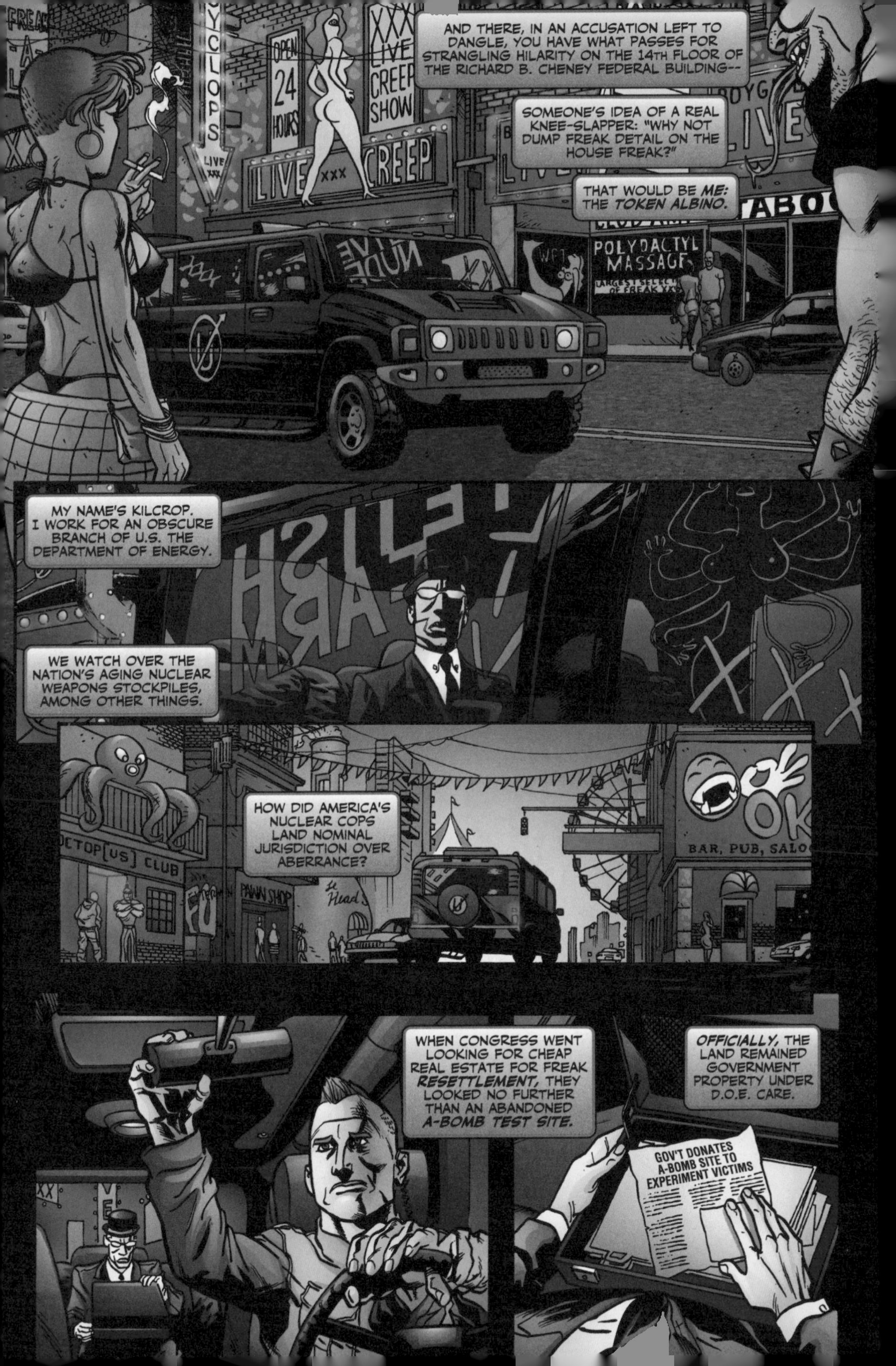
AND THERE, IN AN ACCUSATION LEFT TO DANGLE, YOU HAVE WHAT PASSES FOR STRANGLING HILARITY ON THE 14TH FLOOR OF THE RICHARD B. CHENEY FEDERAL BUILDING--
SOMEONE'S IDEA OF A REAL KNEE-SLAPPER: "WHY NOT DUMP FREAK DETAIL ON THE HOUSE FREAK?"
THAT WOULD BE *ME:* THE *TOKEN ALBINO.*
MY NAME'S KILCROP. I WORK FOR AN OBSCURE BRANCH OF U.S. THE DEPARTMENT OF ENERGY.
WE WATCH OVER THE NATION'S AGING NUCLEAR WEAPONS STOCKPILES, AMONG OTHER THINGS.
HOW DID AMERICA'S NUCLEAR COPS LAND NOMINAL JURISDICTION OVER ABERRANCE?
WHEN CONGRESS WENT LOOKING FOR CHEAP REAL ESTATE FOR FREAK *RESETTLEMENT,* THEY LOOKED NO FURTHER THAN AN ABANDONED *A-BOMB TEST SITE.*
OFFICIALLY, THE LAND REMAINED GOVERNMENT PROPERTY UNDER D.O.E. CARE.
GOV'T DONATES A-BOMB SITE TO EXPERIMENT VICTIMS

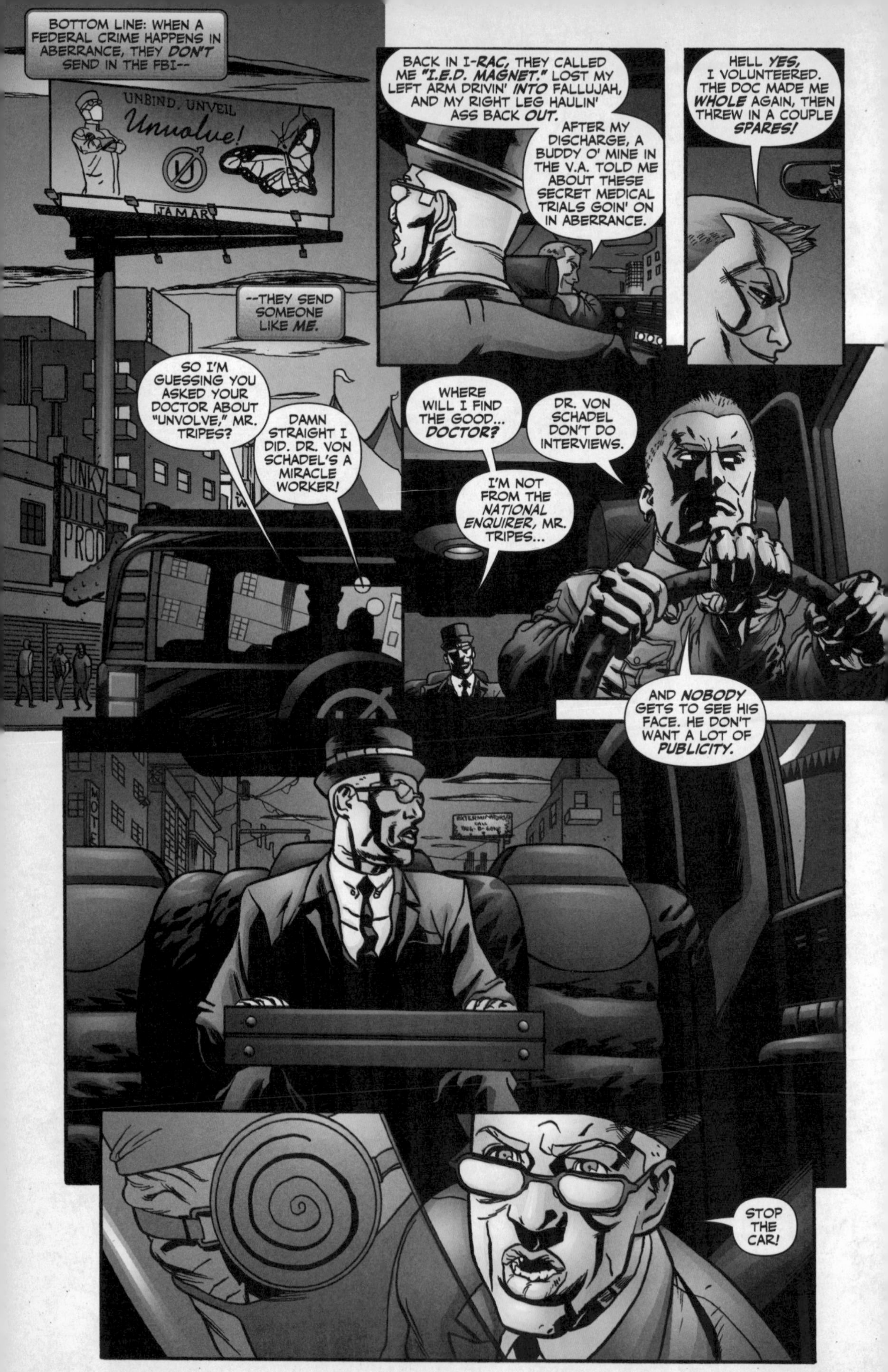

BOTTOM LINE: WHEN A FEDERAL CRIME HAPPENS IN ABERRANCE, THEY DON'T SEND IN THE FBI--
UNBIND. UNVEIL
Unvolve!
JAMAR
--THEY SEND SOMEONE LIKE ME.
SO I'M GUESSING YOU ASKED YOUR DOCTOR ABOUT "UNVOLVE," MR. TRIPES?
DAMN STRAIGHT I DID. DR. VON SCHADEL'S A MIRACLE WORKER!
BACK IN I-RAC, THEY CALLED ME "I.E.D. MAGNET." LOST MY LEFT ARM DRIVIN' INTO FALLUJAH, AND MY RIGHT LEG HAULIN' ASS BACK OUT.
AFTER MY DISCHARGE, A BUDDY O' MINE IN THE V.A. TOLD ME ABOUT THESE SECRET MEDICAL TRIALS GOIN' ON IN ABERRANCE.
HELL YES, I VOLUNTEERED. THE DOC MADE ME WHOLE AGAIN, THEN THREW IN A COUPLE SPARES!
WHERE WILL I FIND THE GOOD... DOCTOR?
DR. VON SCHADEL DON'T DO INTERVIEWS.
I'M NOT FROM THE NATIONAL ENQUIRER, MR. TRIPES...
AND NOBODY GETS TO SEE HIS FACE. HE DON'T WANT A LOT OF PUBLICITY.
STOP THE CAR!

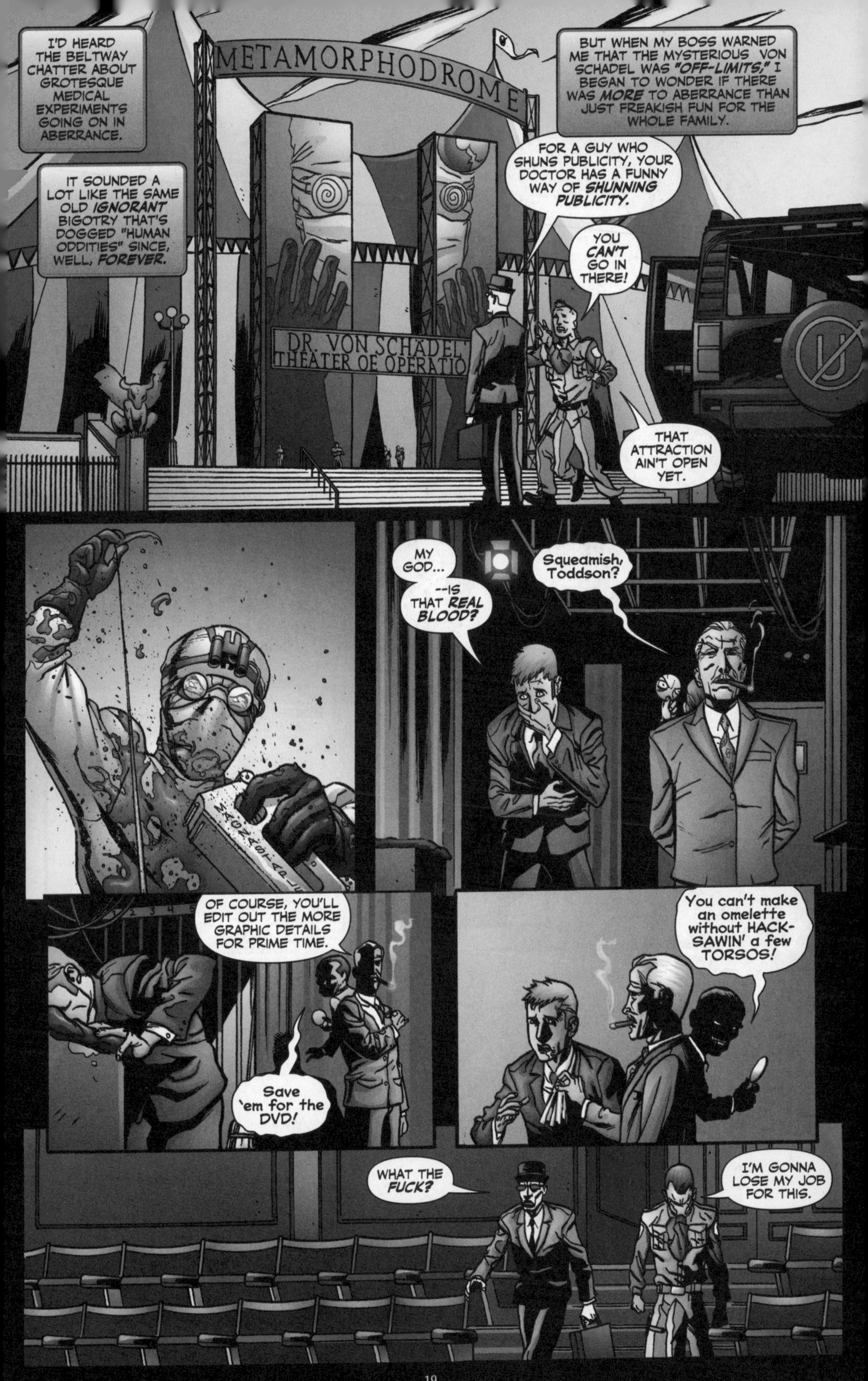
I'D HEARD THE BELTWAY CHATTER ABOUT GROTESQUE MEDICAL EXPERIMENTS GOING ON IN ABERRANCE.
IT SOUNDED A LOT LIKE THE SAME OLD IGNORANT BIGOTRY THAT'S DOGGED "HUMAN ODDITIES" SINCE, WELL, FOREVER.
METAMORPHODROME
BUT WHEN MY BOSS WARNED ME THAT THE MYSTERIOUS VON SCHADEL WAS "OFF-LIMITS," I BEGAN TO WONDER IF THERE WAS MORE TO ABERRANCE THAN JUST FREAKISH FUN FOR THE WHOLE FAMILY.
FOR A GUY WHO SHUNS PUBLICITY, YOUR DOCTOR HAS A FUNNY WAY OF SHUNNING PUBLICITY.
YOU CAN'T GO IN THERE!
DR. VON SCHÄDEL'
THEATER OF OPERATIO
THAT ATTRACTION AIN'T OPEN YET.
MY GOD... --IS THAT REAL BLOOD?
Squeamish, Toddson?
OF COURSE, YOU'LL EDIT OUT THE MORE GRAPHIC DETAILS FOR PRIME TIME.
Save 'em for the DVD!
You can't make an omelette without HACK-SAWIN' a few TORSOS!
WHAT THE FUCK?
I'M GONNA LOSE MY JOB FOR THIS.

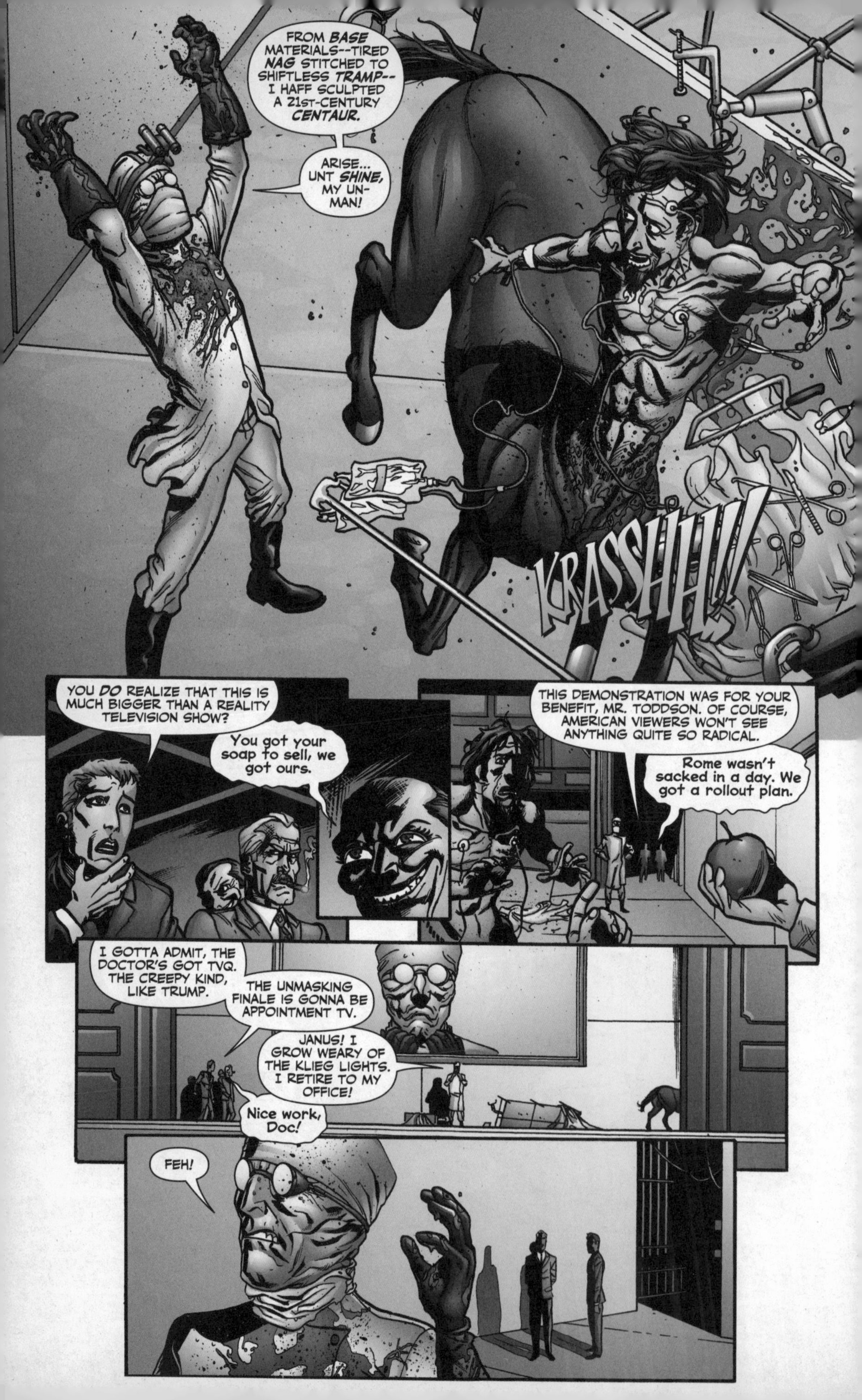
FROM BASE MATERIALS--TIRED NAG STITCHED TO SHIFTLESS TRAMP--I HAFF SCULPTED A 21ST-CENTURY CENTAUR.
ARISE... UNT SHINE, MY UN-MAN!
KRASSHH!!
YOU DO REALIZE THAT THIS IS MUCH BIGGER THAN A REALITY TELEVISION SHOW?
You got your soap to sell, we got ours.
THIS DEMONSTRATION WAS FOR YOUR BENEFIT, MR. TODDSON. OF COURSE, AMERICAN VIEWERS WON'T SEE ANYTHING QUITE SO RADICAL.
Rome wasn't sacked in a day. We got a rollout plan.
I GOTTA ADMIT, THE DOCTOR'S GOT TVQ. THE CREEPY KIND, LIKE TRUMP.
THE UNMASKING FINALE IS GONNA BE APPOINTMENT TV.
JANUS! I GROW WEARY OF THE KLIEG LIGHTS. I RETIRE TO MY OFFICE!
Nice work, Doc!
FEH!

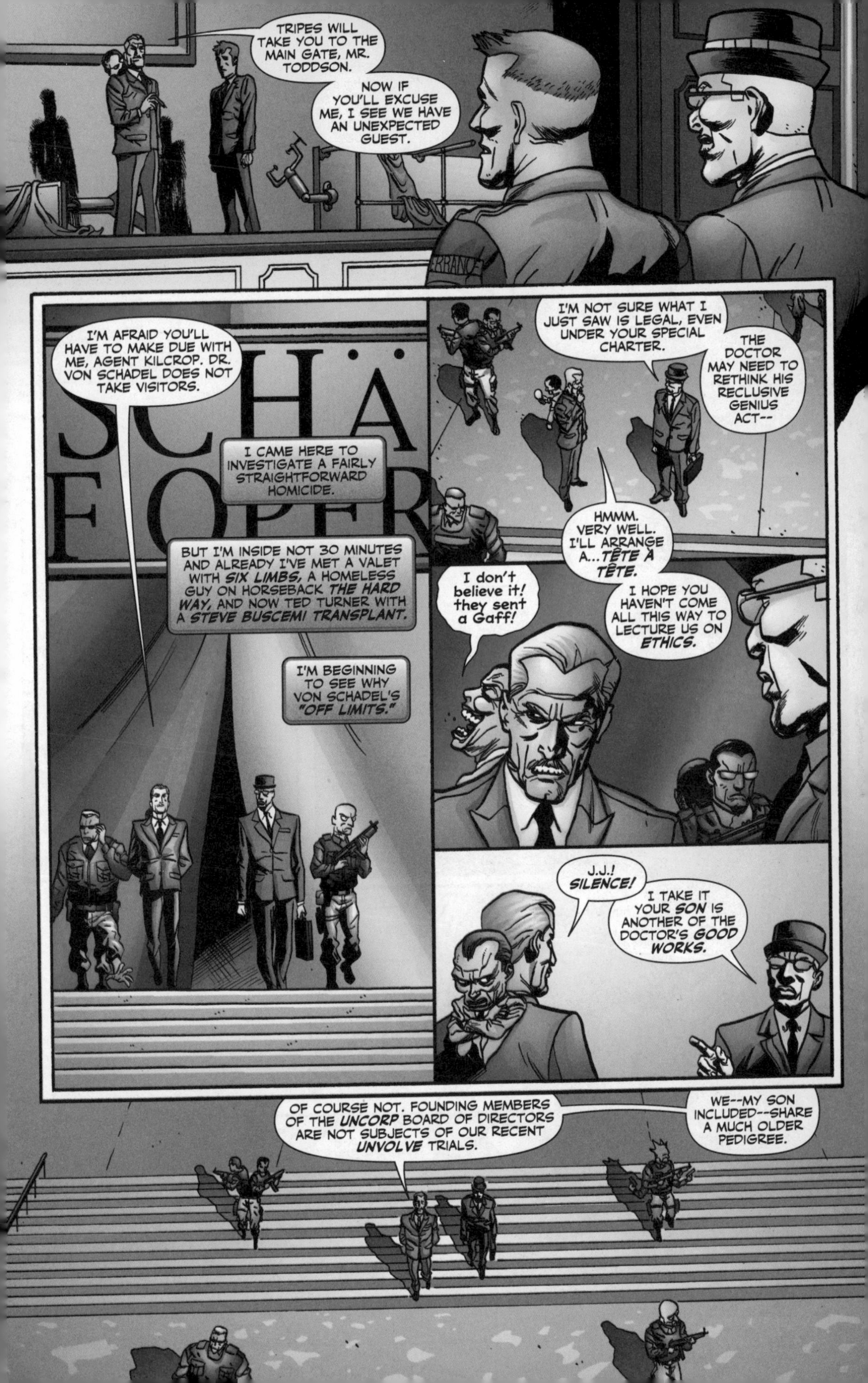
TRIPES WILL TAKE YOU TO THE MAIN GATE, MR. TODDSON.
NOW IF YOU'LL EXCUSE ME, I SEE WE HAVE AN UNEXPECTED GUEST.
I'M AFRAID YOU'LL HAVE TO MAKE DUE WITH ME, AGENT KILCROP. DR. VON SCHADEL DOES NOT TAKE VISITORS.
I CAME HERE TO INVESTIGATE A FAIRLY STRAIGHTFORWARD HOMICIDE.
BUT I'M INSIDE NOT 30 MINUTES AND ALREADY I'VE MET A VALET WITH SIX LIMBS, A HOMELESS GUY ON HORSEBACK THE HARD WAY, AND NOW TED TURNER WITH A STEVE BUSCEMI TRANSPLANT.
I'M BEGINNING TO SEE WHY VON SCHADEL'S "OFF LIMITS."
I'M NOT SURE WHAT I JUST SAW IS LEGAL, EVEN UNDER YOUR SPECIAL CHARTER.
THE DOCTOR MAY NEED TO RETHINK HIS RECLUSIVE GENIUS ACT--
HMMM. VERY WELL. I'LL ARRANGE A...TÊTE A TÊTE.
I don't believe it! they sent a Gaff!
I HOPE YOU HAVEN'T COME ALL THIS WAY TO LECTURE US ON ETHICS.
J.J.! SILENCE!
I TAKE IT YOUR SON IS ANOTHER OF THE DOCTOR'S GOOD WORKS.
OF COURSE NOT. FOUNDING MEMBERS OF THE UNCORP BOARD OF DIRECTORS ARE NOT SUBJECTS OF OUR RECENT UNVOLVE TRIALS.
WE--MY SON INCLUDED--SHARE A MUCH OLDER PEDIGREE.

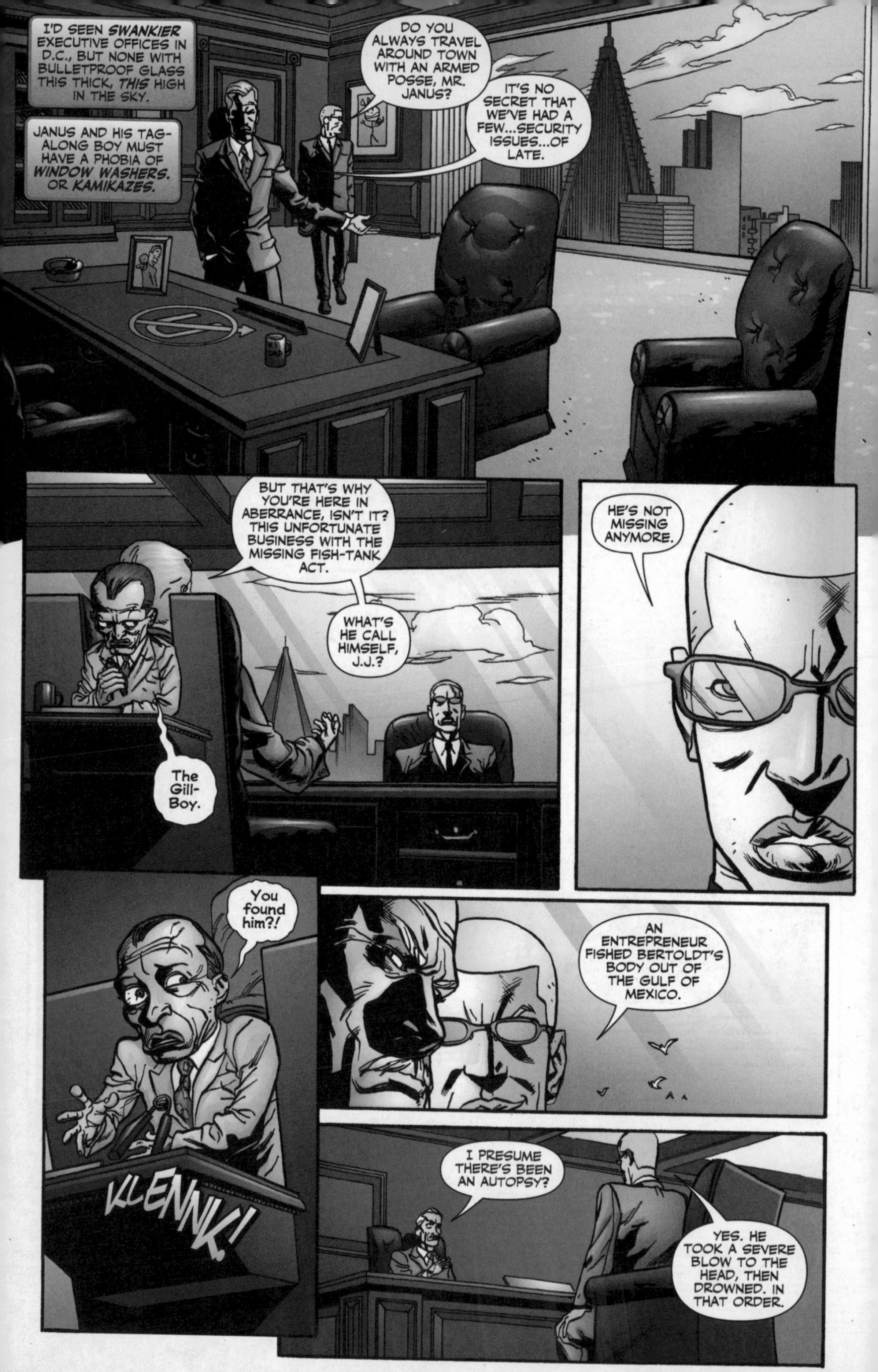
I'D SEEN SWANKIER EXECUTIVE OFFICES IN D.C., BUT NONE WITH BULLETPROOF GLASS THIS THICK, THIS HIGH IN THE SKY.
JANUS AND HIS TAG-ALONG BOY MUST HAVE A PHOBIA OF WINDOW WASHERS. OR KAMIKAZES.
DO YOU ALWAYS TRAVEL AROUND TOWN WITH AN ARMED POSSE, MR. JANUS?
IT'S NO SECRET THAT WE'VE HAD A FEW...SECURITY ISSUES...OF LATE.
BUT THAT'S WHY YOU'RE HERE IN ABERRANCE, ISN'T IT? THIS UNFORTUNATE BUSINESS WITH THE MISSING FISH-TANK ACT.
WHAT'S HE CALL HIMSELF, J.J.?
The Gill-Boy.
HE'S NOT MISSING ANYMORE.
You found him?!
KLENNK!
AN ENTREPRENEUR FISHED BERTOLDT'S BODY OUT OF THE GULF OF MEXICO.
I PRESUME THERE'S BEEN AN AUTOPSY?
YES. HE TOOK A SEVERE BLOW TO THE HEAD, THEN DROWNED. IN THAT ORDER.

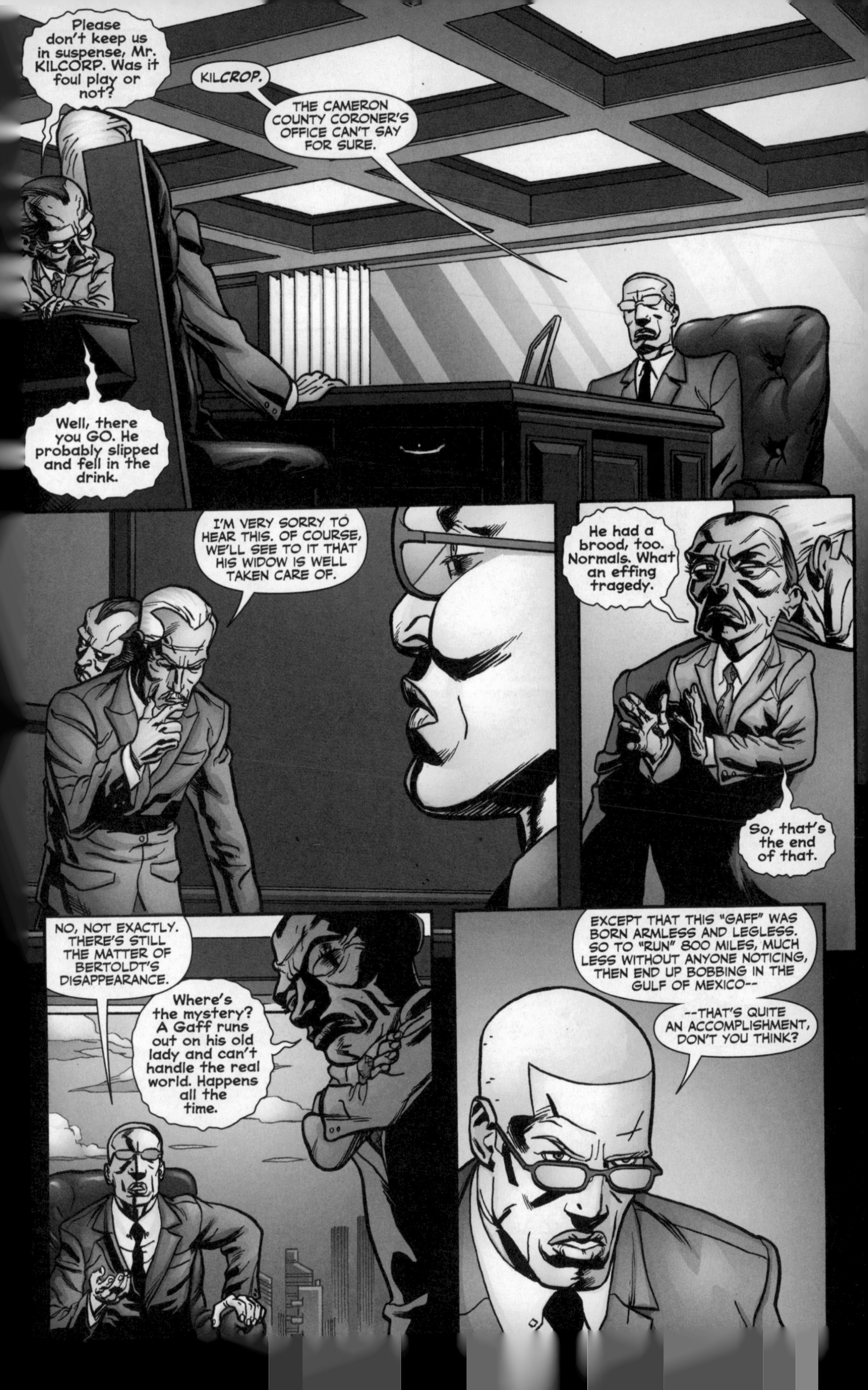
Please don't keep us in suspense, Mr. KILCORP. Was it foul play or not?
KILCROP.
THE CAMERON COUNTY CORONER'S OFFICE CAN'T SAY FOR SURE.
Well, there you GO. He probably slipped and fell in the drink.
I'M VERY SORRY TO HEAR THIS. OF COURSE, WE'LL SEE TO IT THAT HIS WIDOW IS WELL TAKEN CARE OF.
He had a brood, too. Normals. What an effing tragedy.
So, that's the end of that.
NO, NOT EXACTLY. THERE'S STILL THE MATTER OF BERTOLDT'S DISAPPEARANCE.
Where's the mystery? A Gaff runs out on his old lady and can't handle the real world. Happens all the time.
EXCEPT THAT THIS "GAFF" WAS BORN ARMLESS AND LEGLESS. SO TO "RUN" 800 MILES, MUCH LESS WITHOUT ANYONE NOTICING, THEN END UP BOBBING IN THE GULF OF MEXICO--
--THAT'S QUITE AN ACCOMPLISHMENT, DON'T YOU THINK?

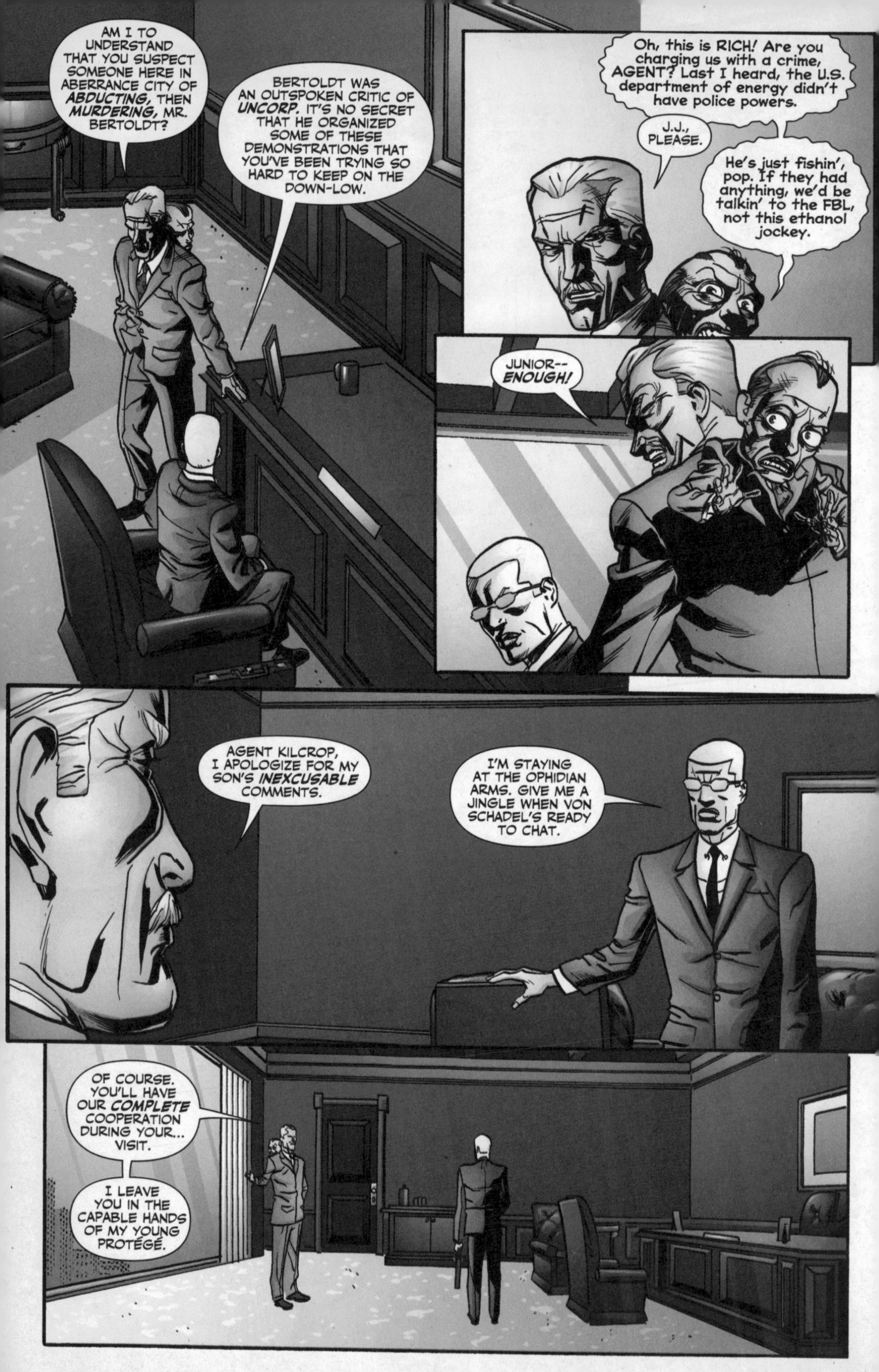
AM I TO UNDERSTAND THAT YOU SUSPECT SOMEONE HERE IN ABERRANCE CITY OF *ABDUCTING,* THEN *MURDERING,* MR. BERTOLDT?
BERTOLDT WAS AN OUTSPOKEN CRITIC OF *UNCORP.* IT'S NO SECRET THAT HE ORGANIZED SOME OF THESE DEMONSTRATIONS THAT YOU'VE BEEN TRYING SO HARD TO KEEP ON THE DOWN-LOW.
Oh, this is RICH! Are you charging us with a crime, AGENT? Last I heard, the U.S. department of energy didn't have police powers.
J.J., PLEASE.
He's just fishin', pop. If they had anything, we'd be talkin' to the FBI, not this ethanol jockey.
JUNIOR-- *ENOUGH!*
AGENT KILCROP, I APOLOGIZE FOR MY SON'S *INEXCUSABLE* COMMENTS.
I'M STAYING AT THE OPHIDIAN ARMS. GIVE ME A JINGLE WHEN VON SCHADEL'S READY TO CHAT.
OF COURSE. YOU'LL HAVE OUR *COMPLETE* COOPERATION DURING YOUR... VISIT.
I LEAVE YOU IN THE CAPABLE HANDS OF MY YOUNG PROTÉGÉ.

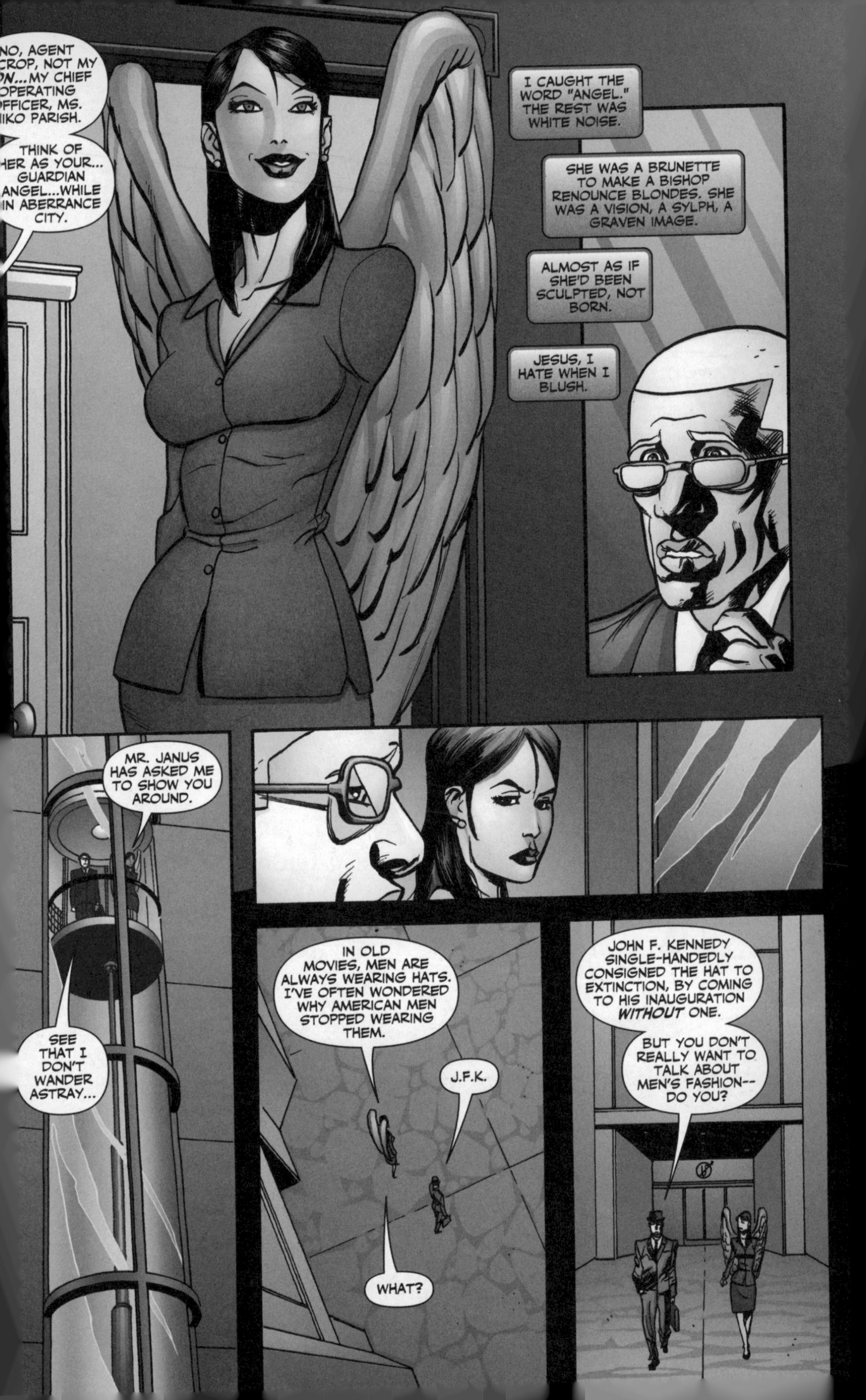

NO, AGENT CROP, NOT MY ON...MY CHIEF OPERATING OFFICER, MS. IKO PARISH.
THINK OF HER AS YOUR... GUARDIAN ANGEL...WHILE IN ABERRANCE CITY.
I CAUGHT THE WORD "ANGEL." THE REST WAS WHITE NOISE.
SHE WAS A BRUNETTE TO MAKE A BISHOP RENOUNCE BLONDES. SHE WAS A VISION, A SYLPH, A GRAVEN IMAGE.
ALMOST AS IF SHE'D BEEN SCULPTED, NOT BORN.
JESUS, I HATE WHEN I BLUSH.
MR. JANUS HAS ASKED ME TO SHOW YOU AROUND.
SEE THAT I DON'T WANDER ASTRAY...
IN OLD MOVIES, MEN ARE ALWAYS WEARING HATS. I'VE OFTEN WONDERED WHY AMERICAN MEN STOPPED WEARING THEM.
J.F.K.
WHAT?
JOHN F. KENNEDY SINGLE-HANDEDLY CONSIGNED THE HAT TO EXTINCTION, BY COMING TO HIS INAUGURATION *WITHOUT* ONE.
BUT YOU DON'T REALLY WANT TO TALK ABOUT MEN'S FASHION-- DO YOU?

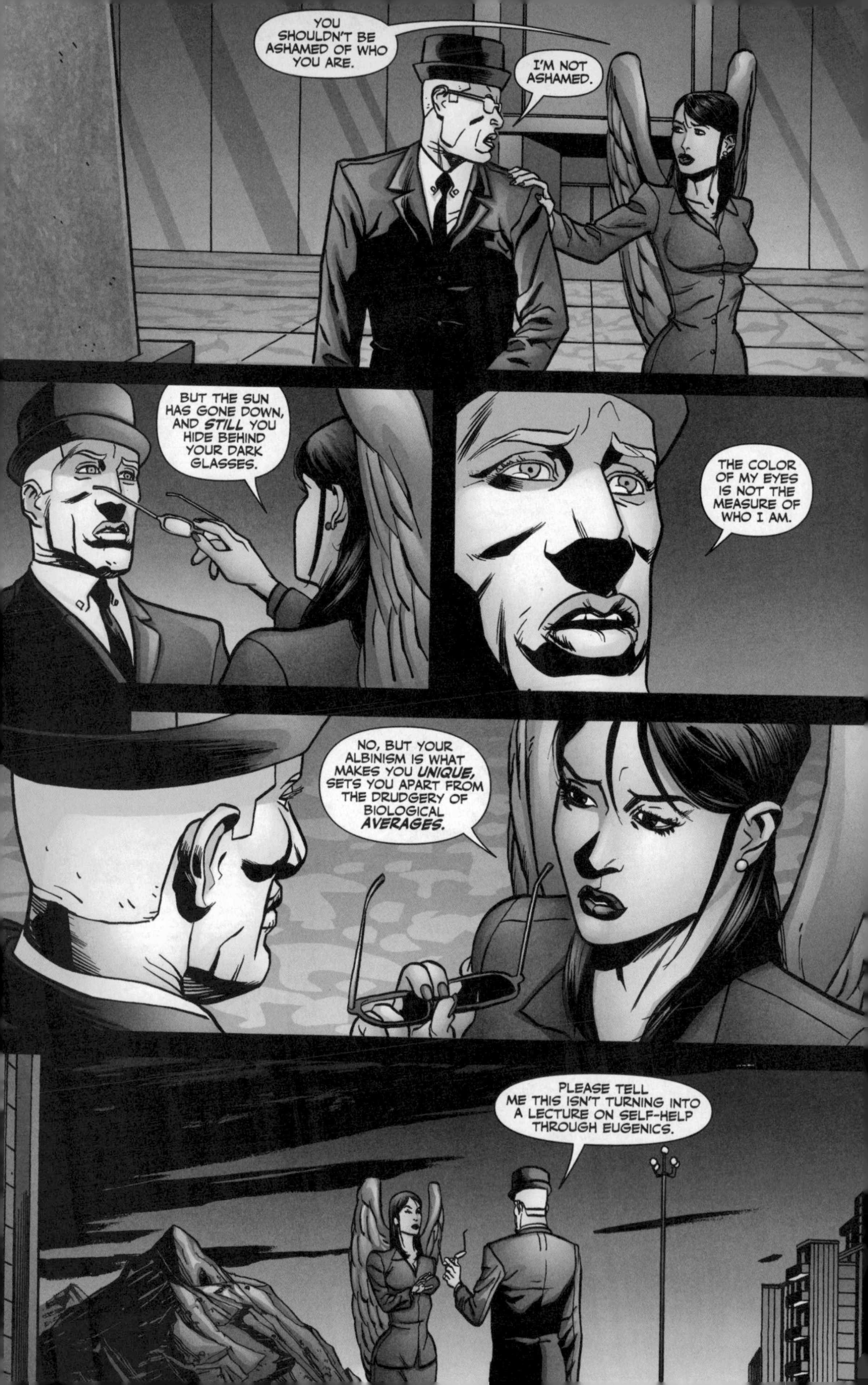
YOU SHOULDN'T BE ASHAMED OF WHO YOU ARE.
I'M NOT ASHAMED.
BUT THE SUN HAS GONE DOWN, AND STILL YOU HIDE BEHIND YOUR DARK GLASSES.
THE COLOR OF MY EYES IS NOT THE MEASURE OF WHO I AM.
NO, BUT YOUR ALBINISM IS WHAT MAKES YOU UNIQUE, SETS YOU APART FROM THE DRUDGERY OF BIOLOGICAL AVERAGES.
PLEASE TELL ME THIS ISN'T TURNING INTO A LECTURE ON SELF-HELP THROUGH EUGENICS.

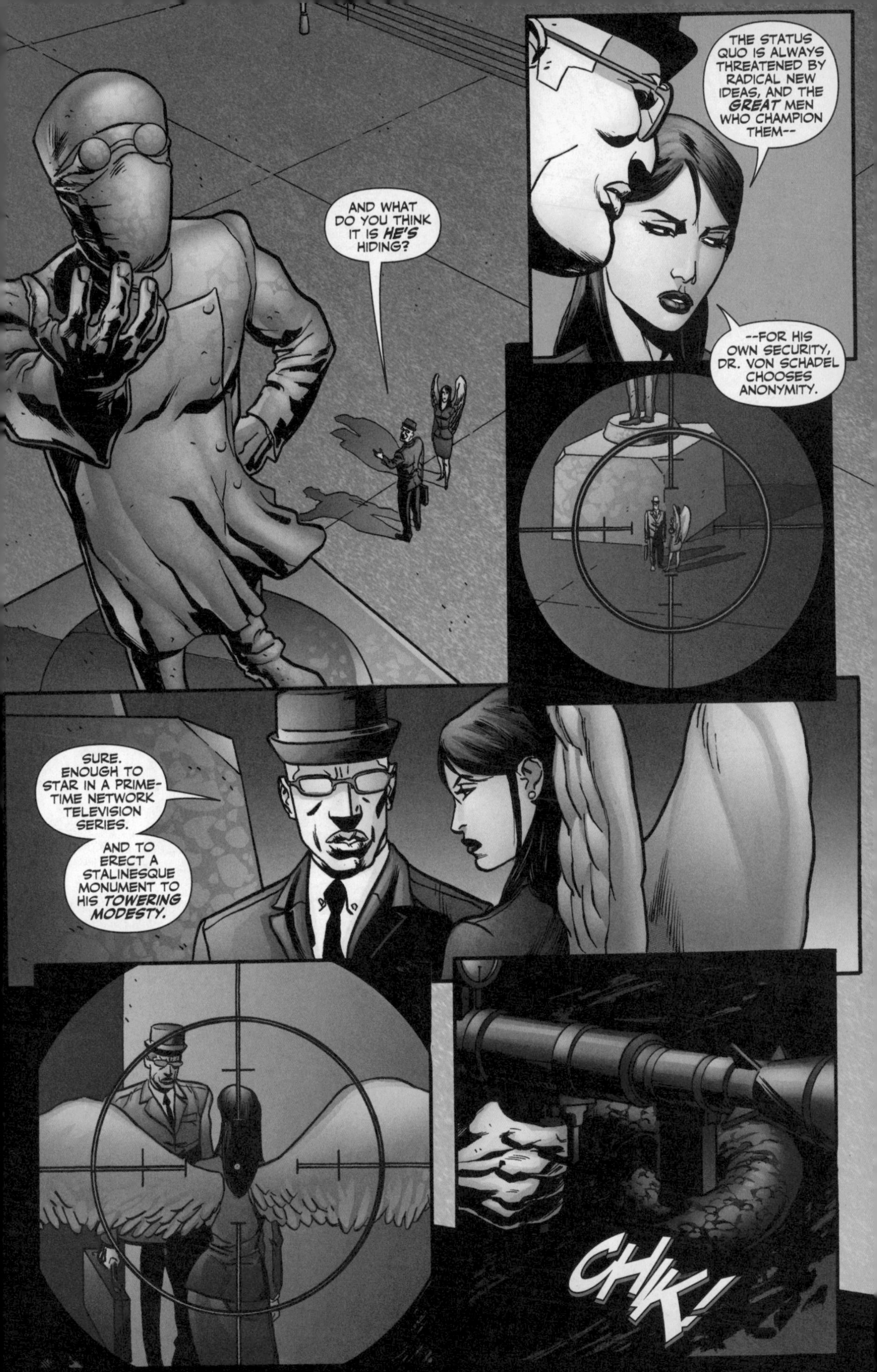

AND WHAT DO YOU THINK IT IS *HE'S* HIDING?
THE STATUS QUO IS ALWAYS THREATENED BY RADICAL NEW IDEAS, AND THE ***GREAT*** MEN WHO CHAMPION THEM--
--FOR HIS OWN SECURITY, DR. VON SCHADEL CHOOSES ANONYMITY.
SURE. ENOUGH TO STAR IN A PRIME-TIME NETWORK TELEVISION SERIES.
AND TO ERECT A STALINESQUE MONUMENT TO HIS *TOWERING* ***MODESTY.***
CHIK!

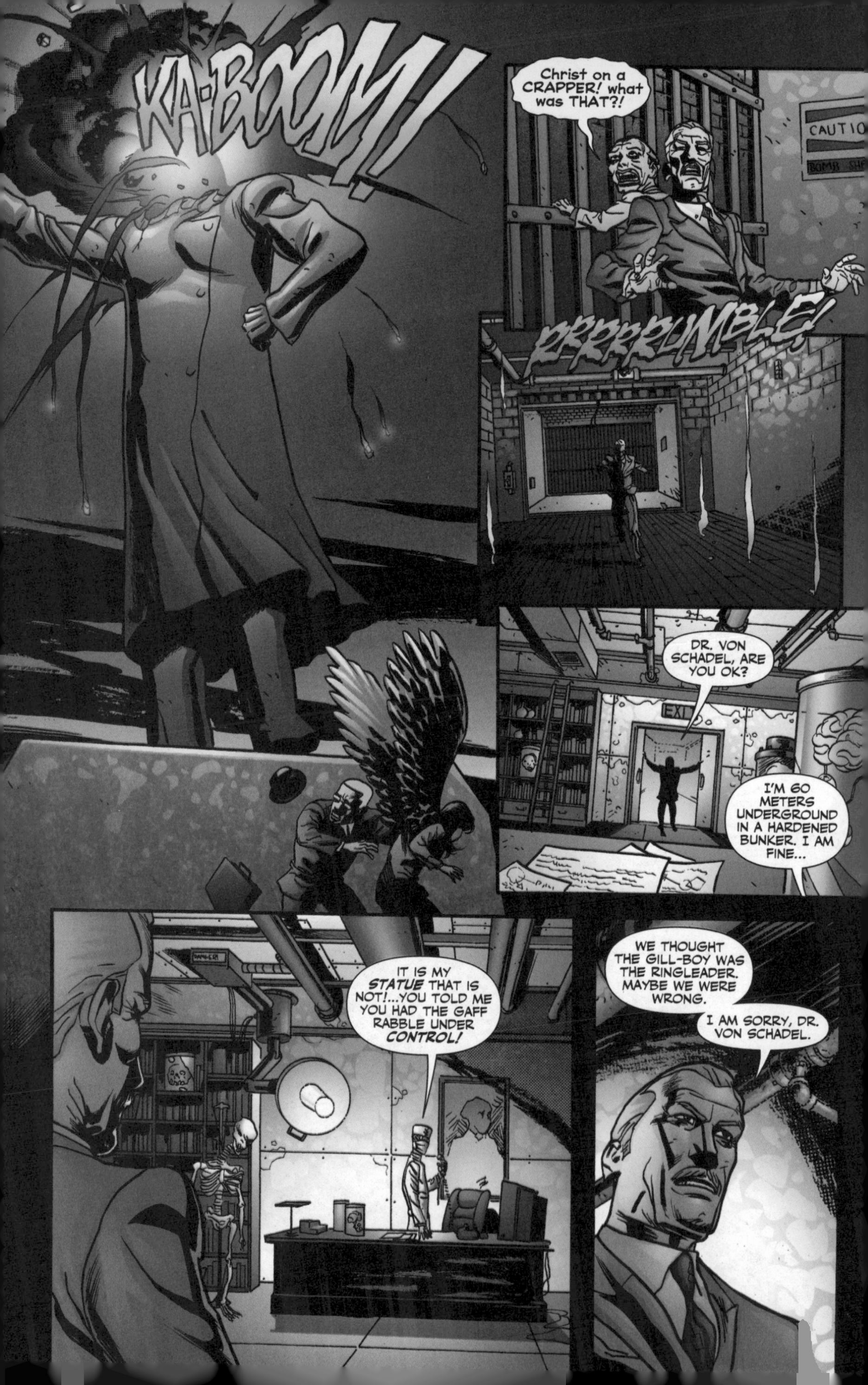
KA-BOOM!!
Christ on a CRAPPER! what was THAT?!
PRRRRUMBLE!
DR. VON SCHADEL, ARE YOU OK?
EXIT
I'M 60 METERS UNDERGROUND IN A HARDENED BUNKER. I AM FINE...
IT IS MY *STATUE* THAT IS NOT!...YOU TOLD ME YOU HAD THE GAFF RABBLE UNDER *CONTROL!*
WE THOUGHT THE GILL-BOY WAS THE RINGLEADER. MAYBE WE WERE WRONG.
I AM SORRY, DR. VON SCHADEL.

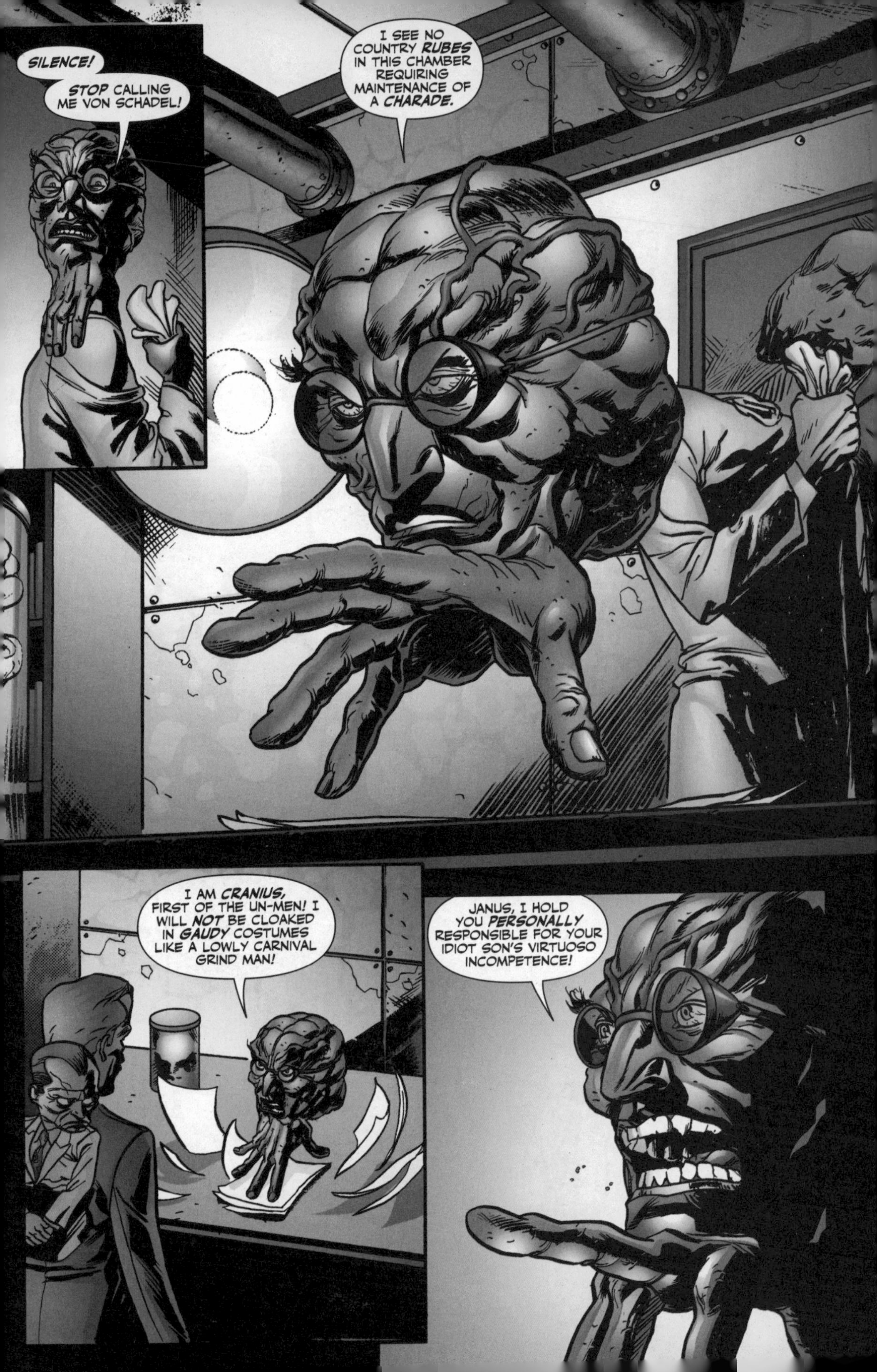
SILENCE!
STOP CALLING ME VON SCHADEL!
I SEE NO COUNTRY RUBES IN THIS CHAMBER REQUIRING MAINTENANCE OF A CHARADE.
I AM CRANIUS, FIRST OF THE UN-MEN! I WILL NOT BE CLOAKED IN GAUDY COSTUMES LIKE A LOWLY CARNIVAL GRIND MAN!
JANUS, I HOLD YOU PERSONALLY RESPONSIBLE FOR YOUR IDIOT SON'S VIRTUOSO INCOMPETENCE!

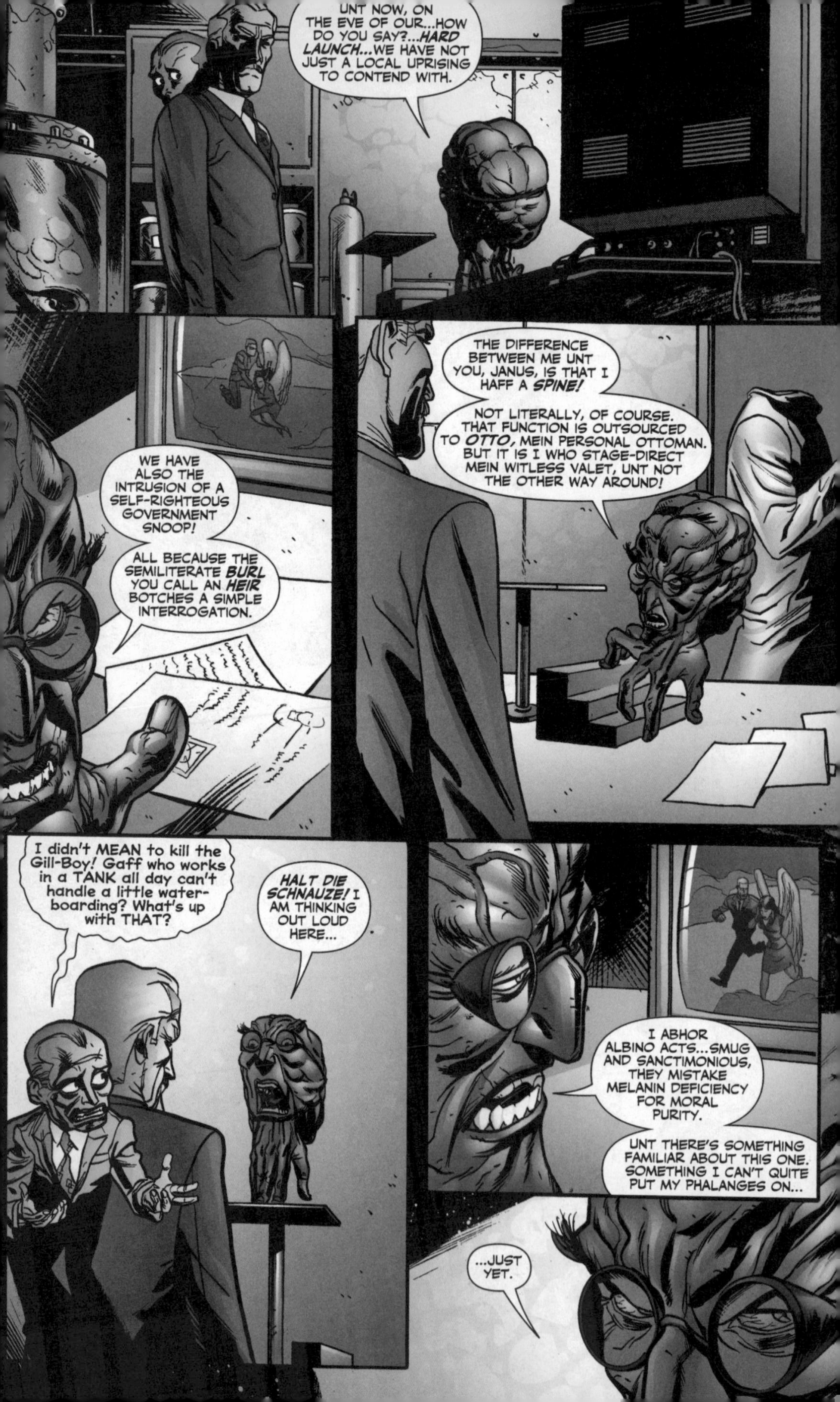
UNT NOW, ON THE EVE OF OUR...HOW DO YOU SAY?...HARD LAUNCH...WE HAVE NOT JUST A LOCAL UPRISING TO CONTEND WITH.
WE HAVE ALSO THE INTRUSION OF A SELF-RIGHTEOUS GOVERNMENT SNOOP!
ALL BECAUSE THE SEMILITERATE BURL YOU CALL AN HEIR BOTCHES A SIMPLE INTERROGATION.
THE DIFFERENCE BETWEEN ME UNT YOU, JANUS, IS THAT I HAFF A SPINE!
NOT LITERALLY, OF COURSE. THAT FUNCTION IS OUTSOURCED TO OTTO, MEIN PERSONAL OTTOMAN. BUT IT IS I WHO STAGE-DIRECT MEIN WITLESS VALET, UNT NOT THE OTHER WAY AROUND!
I didn't MEAN to kill the Gill-Boy! Gaff who works in a TANK all day can't handle a little water-boarding? What's up with THAT?
HALT DIE SCHNAUZE! I AM THINKING OUT LOUD HERE...
I ABHOR ALBINO ACTS...SMUG AND SANCTIMONIOUS, THEY MISTAKE MELANIN DEFICIENCY FOR MORAL PURITY.
UNT THERE'S SOMETHING FAMILIAR ABOUT THIS ONE. SOMETHING I CAN'T QUITE PUT MY PHALANGES ON...
...JUST YET.

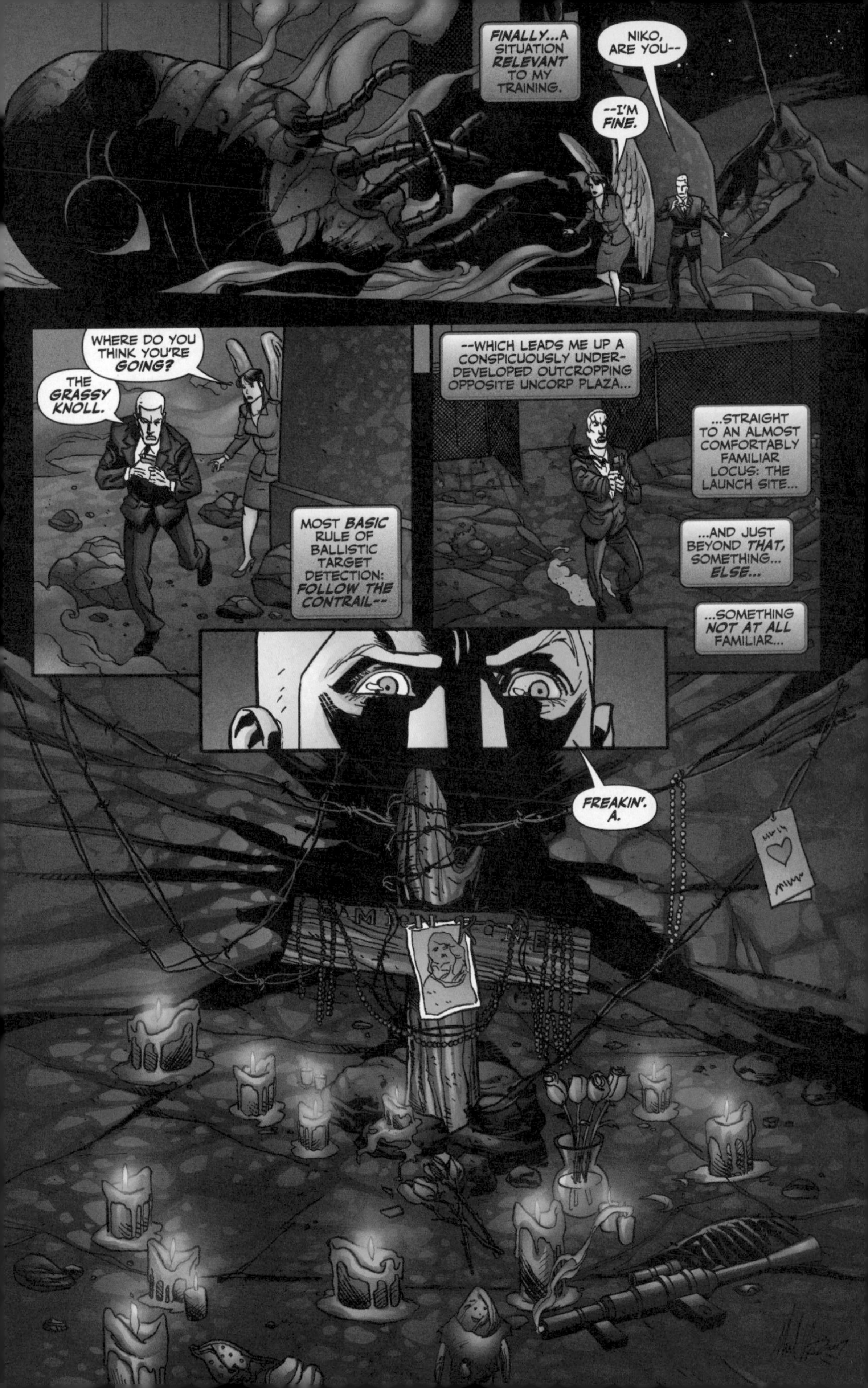
FINALLY...A SITUATION RELEVANT TO MY TRAINING.
NIKO, ARE YOU--
--I'M FINE.
WHERE DO YOU THINK YOU'RE GOING?
THE GRASSY KNOLL.
MOST BASIC RULE OF BALLISTIC TARGET DETECTION: FOLLOW THE CONTRAIL--
--WHICH LEADS ME UP A CONSPICUOUSLY UNDER-DEVELOPED OUTCROPPING OPPOSITE UNCORP PLAZA...
...STRAIGHT TO AN ALMOST COMFORTABLY FAMILIAR LOCUS: THE LAUNCH SITE...
...AND JUST BEYOND THAT, SOMETHING... ELSE...
...SOMETHING NOT AT ALL FAMILIAR...
FREAKIN'. A.

"WE ARE POISED TO UNLEASH A REVOLUTION IN HUMAN TRANSFORMATION!"

CHAPTER TWO

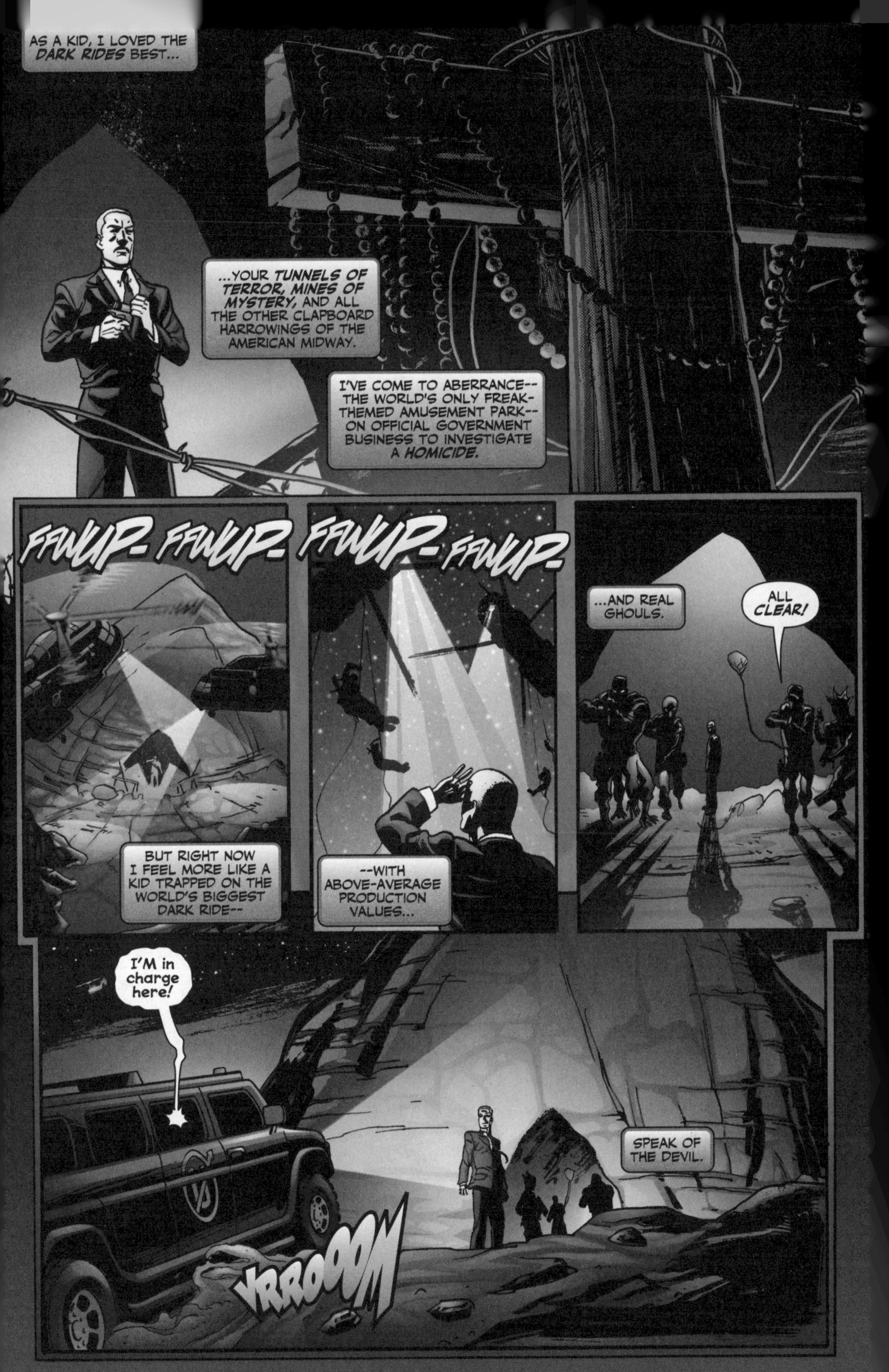
AS A KID, I LOVED THE DARK RIDES BEST...
...YOUR TUNNELS OF TERROR, MINES OF MYSTERY, AND ALL THE OTHER CLAPBOARD HARROWINGS OF THE AMERICAN MIDWAY.
I'VE COME TO ABERRANCE-- THE WORLD'S ONLY FREAK-THEMED AMUSEMENT PARK-- ON OFFICIAL GOVERNMENT BUSINESS TO INVESTIGATE A HOMICIDE.
FFWUP- FFWUP-
BUT RIGHT NOW I FEEL MORE LIKE A KID TRAPPED ON THE WORLD'S BIGGEST DARK RIDE--
FFWUP- FFWUP-
--WITH ABOVE-AVERAGE PRODUCTION VALUES...
...AND REAL GHOULS.
ALL CLEAR!
I'M in charge here!
SPEAK OF THE DEVIL.
VRROOOM

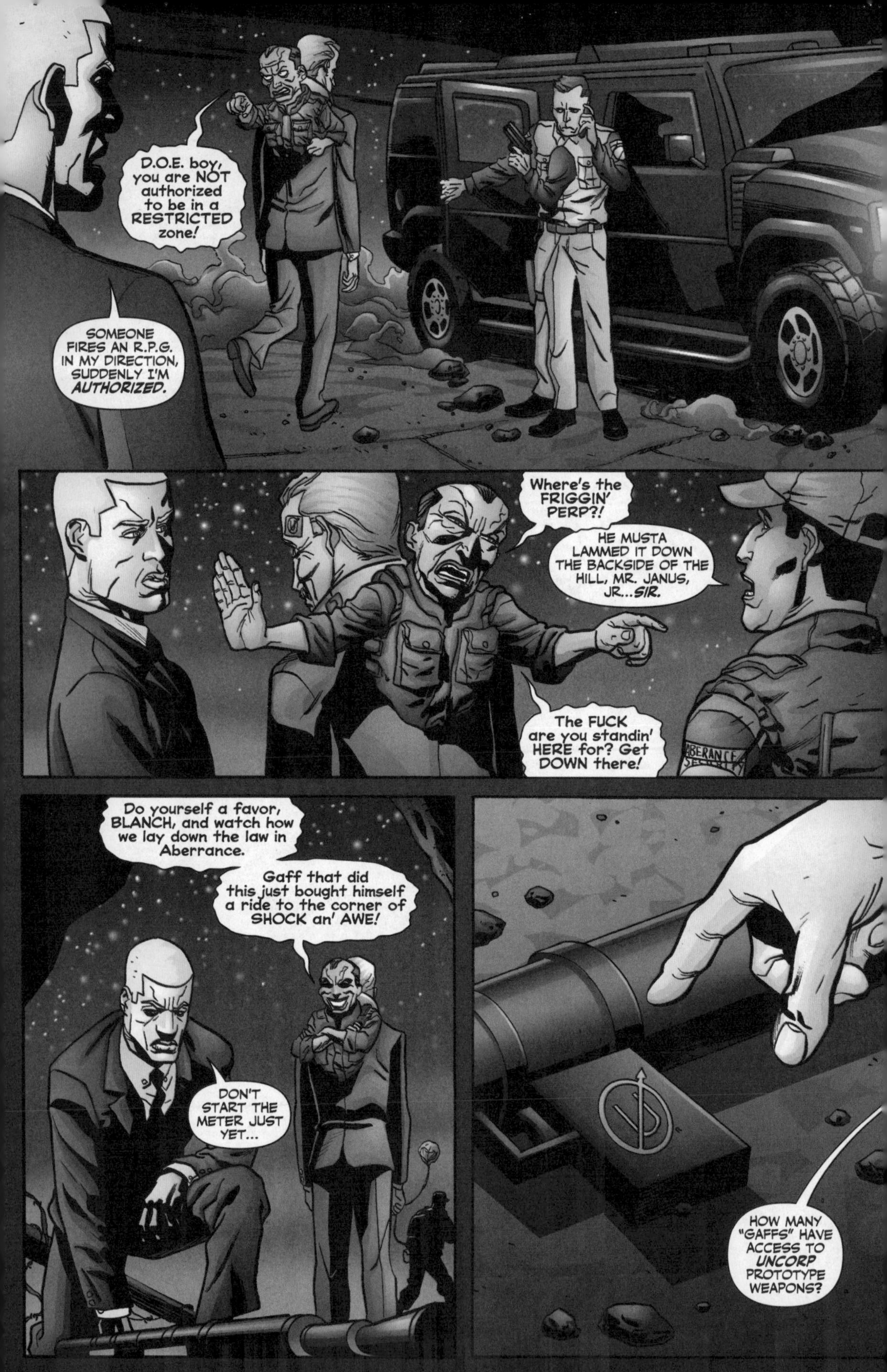
D.O.E. boy, you are NOT authorized to be in a RESTRICTED zone!
SOMEONE FIRES AN R.P.G. IN MY DIRECTION, SUDDENLY I'M AUTHORIZED.
Where's the FRIGGIN' PERP?!
HE MUSTA LAMMED IT DOWN THE BACKSIDE OF THE HILL, MR. JANUS, JR...SIR.
The FUCK are you standin' HERE for? Get DOWN there!
Do yourself a favor, BLANCH, and watch how we lay down the law in Aberrance.
Gaff that did this just bought himself a ride to the corner of SHOCK an' AWE!
DON'T START THE METER JUST YET...
HOW MANY "GAFFS" HAVE ACCESS TO UNCORP PROTOTYPE WEAPONS?

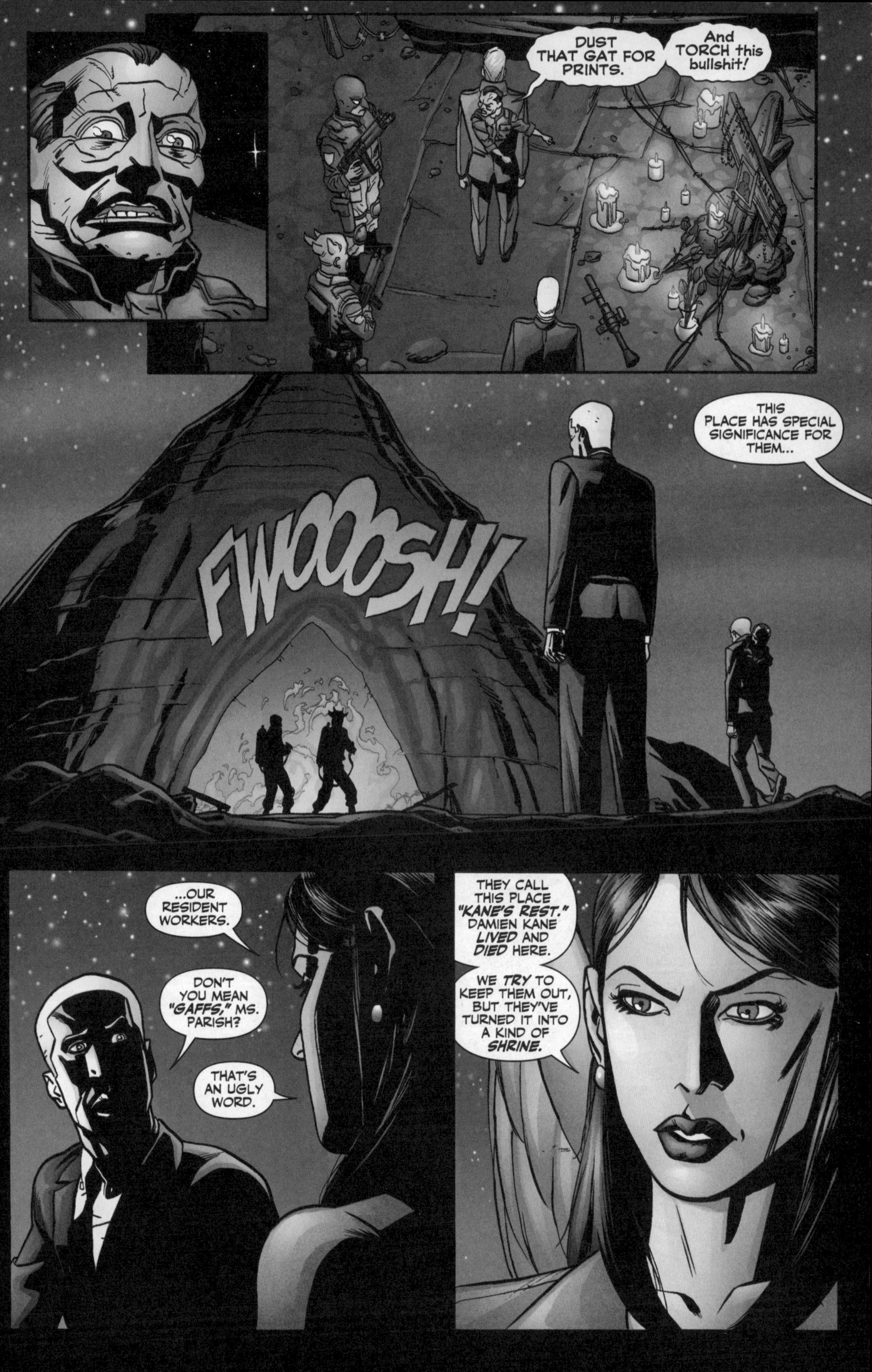
DUST THAT GAT FOR PRINTS.
And TORCH this bullshit!
THIS PLACE HAS SPECIAL SIGNIFICANCE FOR THEM...
FWOOOSH!
...OUR RESIDENT WORKERS.
DON'T YOU MEAN "GAFFS," MS. PARISH?
THAT'S AN UGLY WORD.
THEY CALL THIS PLACE "KANE'S REST." DAMIEN KANE LIVED AND DIED HERE.
WE TRY TO KEEP THEM OUT, BUT THEY'VE TURNED IT INTO A KIND OF SHRINE.

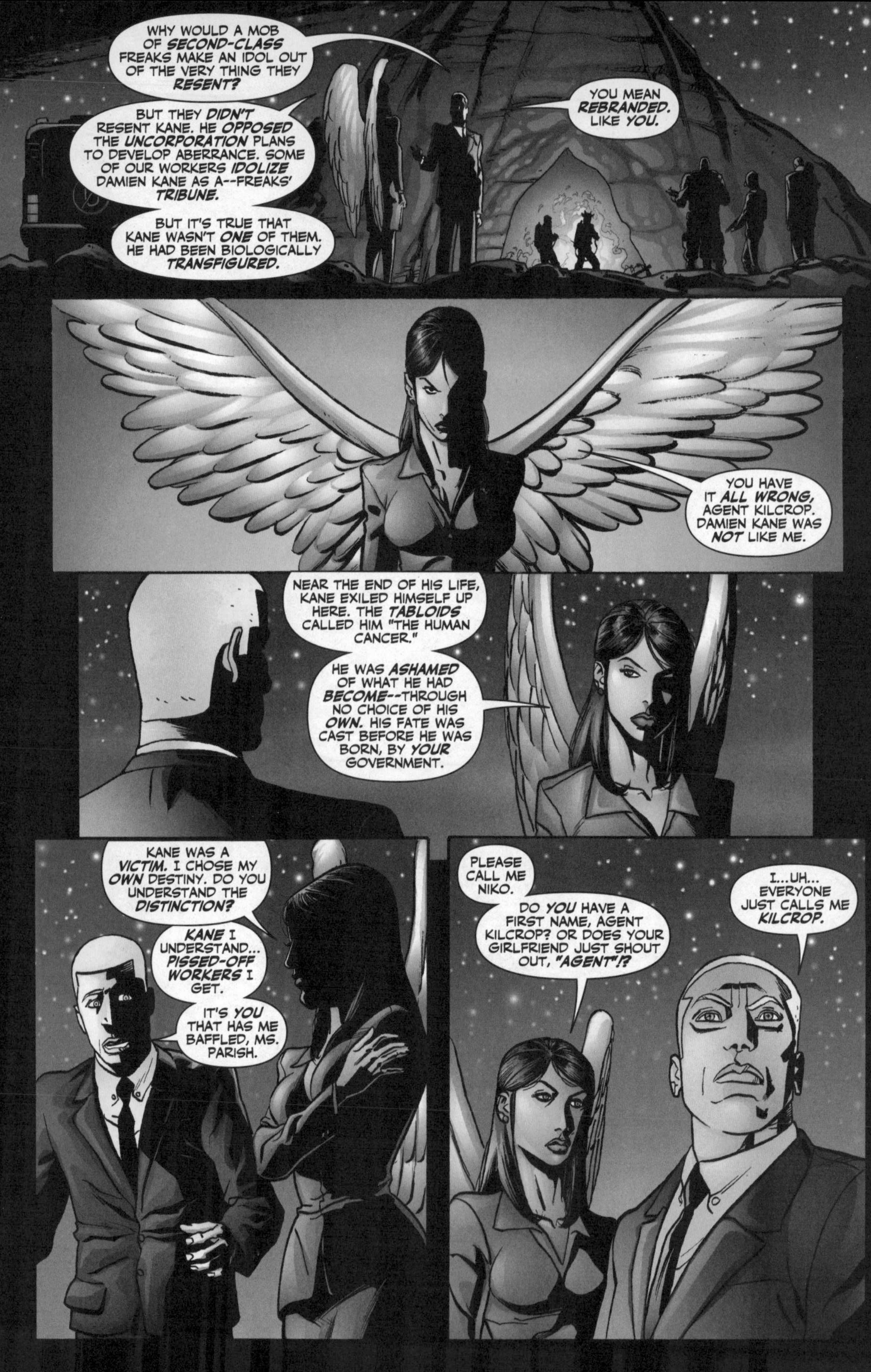
WHY WOULD A MOB OF SECOND-CLASS FREAKS MAKE AN IDOL OUT OF THE VERY THING THEY RESENT?
YOU MEAN REBRANDED. LIKE YOU.
BUT THEY DIDN'T RESENT KANE. HE OPPOSED THE UNCORPORATION PLANS TO DEVELOP ABERRANCE. SOME OF OUR WORKERS IDOLIZE DAMIEN KANE AS A--FREAKS' TRIBUNE.
BUT IT'S TRUE THAT KANE WASN'T ONE OF THEM. HE HAD BEEN BIOLOGICALLY TRANSFIGURED.
YOU HAVE IT ALL WRONG, AGENT KILCROP. DAMIEN KANE WAS NOT LIKE ME.
NEAR THE END OF HIS LIFE, KANE EXILED HIMSELF UP HERE. THE TABLOIDS CALLED HIM "THE HUMAN CANCER."
HE WAS ASHAMED OF WHAT HE HAD BECOME--THROUGH NO CHOICE OF HIS OWN. HIS FATE WAS CAST BEFORE HE WAS BORN, BY YOUR GOVERNMENT.
KANE WAS A VICTIM. I CHOSE MY OWN DESTINY. DO YOU UNDERSTAND THE DISTINCTION?
KANE I UNDERSTAND... PISSED-OFF WORKERS I GET.
IT'S YOU THAT HAS ME BAFFLED, MS. PARISH.
PLEASE CALL ME NIKO.
DO YOU HAVE A FIRST NAME, AGENT KILCROP? OR DOES YOUR GIRLFRIEND JUST SHOUT OUT, "AGENT"!?
I...UH... EVERYONE JUST CALLS ME KILCROP.

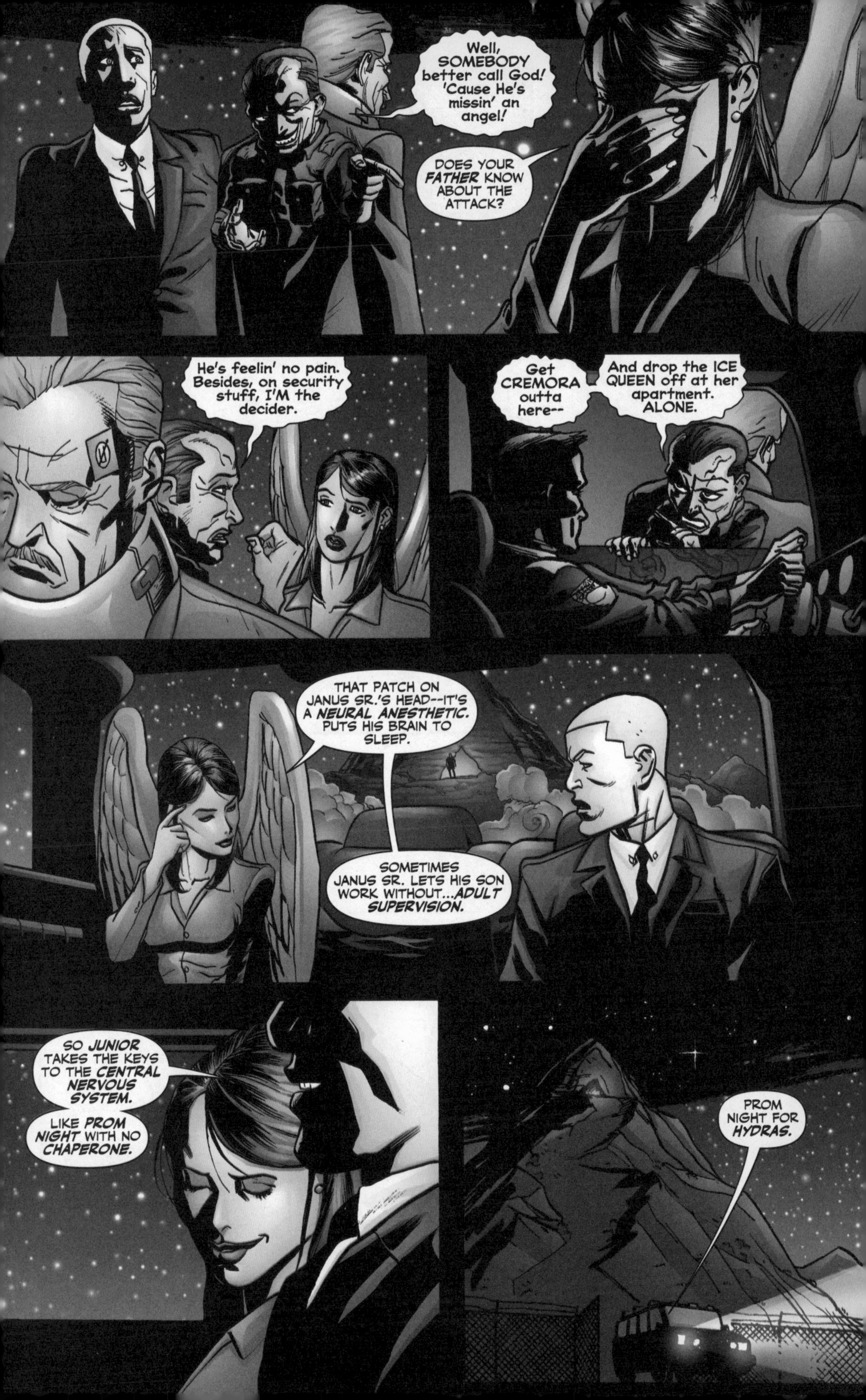
Well, SOMEBODY better call God! 'Cause He's missin' an angel!
DOES YOUR FATHER KNOW ABOUT THE ATTACK?
He's feelin' no pain. Besides, on security stuff, I'M the decider.
Get CREMORA outta here--
And drop the ICE QUEEN off at her apartment. ALONE.
THAT PATCH ON JANUS SR.'S HEAD--IT'S A NEURAL ANESTHETIC. PUTS HIS BRAIN TO SLEEP.
SOMETIMES JANUS SR. LETS HIS SON WORK WITHOUT...ADULT SUPERVISION.
SO JUNIOR TAKES THE KEYS TO THE CENTRAL NERVOUS SYSTEM.
LIKE PROM NIGHT WITH NO CHAPERONE.
PROM NIGHT FOR HYDRAS.

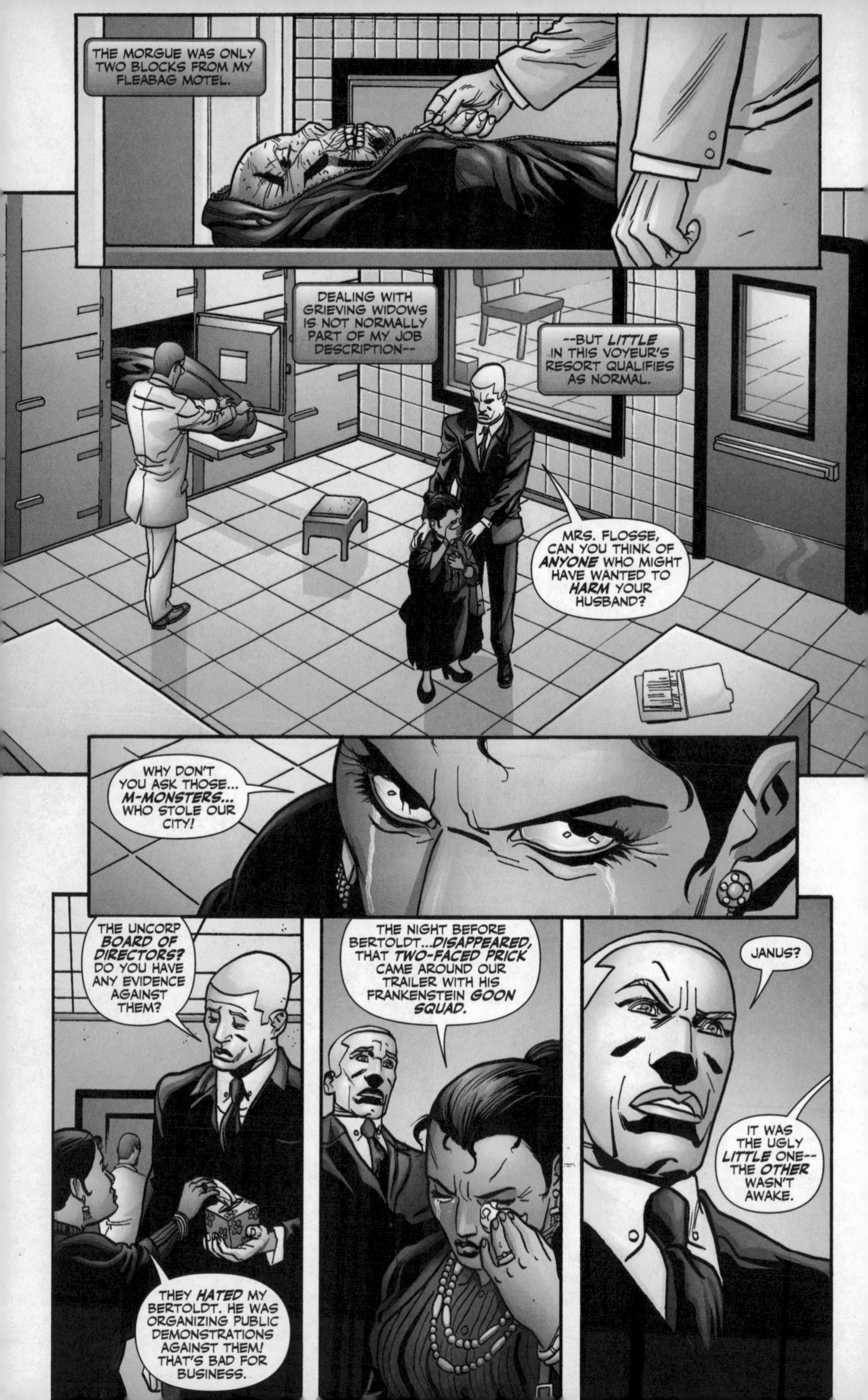
THE MORGUE WAS ONLY TWO BLOCKS FROM MY FLEABAG MOTEL.
DEALING WITH GRIEVING WIDOWS IS NOT NORMALLY PART OF MY JOB DESCRIPTION--
--BUT LITTLE IN THIS VOYEUR'S RESORT QUALIFIES AS NORMAL.
MRS. FLOSSE, CAN YOU THINK OF ANYONE WHO MIGHT HAVE WANTED TO HARM YOUR HUSBAND?
WHY DON'T YOU ASK THOSE... M-MONSTERS... WHO STOLE OUR CITY!
THE UNCORP BOARD OF DIRECTORS? DO YOU HAVE ANY EVIDENCE AGAINST THEM?
THEY HATED MY BERTOLDT. HE WAS ORGANIZING PUBLIC DEMONSTRATIONS AGAINST THEM! THAT'S BAD FOR BUSINESS.
THE NIGHT BEFORE BERTOLDT...DISAPPEARED, THAT TWO-FACED PRICK CAME AROUND OUR TRAILER WITH HIS FRANKENSTEIN GOON SQUAD.
JANUS?
IT WAS THE UGLY LITTLE ONE-- THE OTHER WASN'T AWAKE.

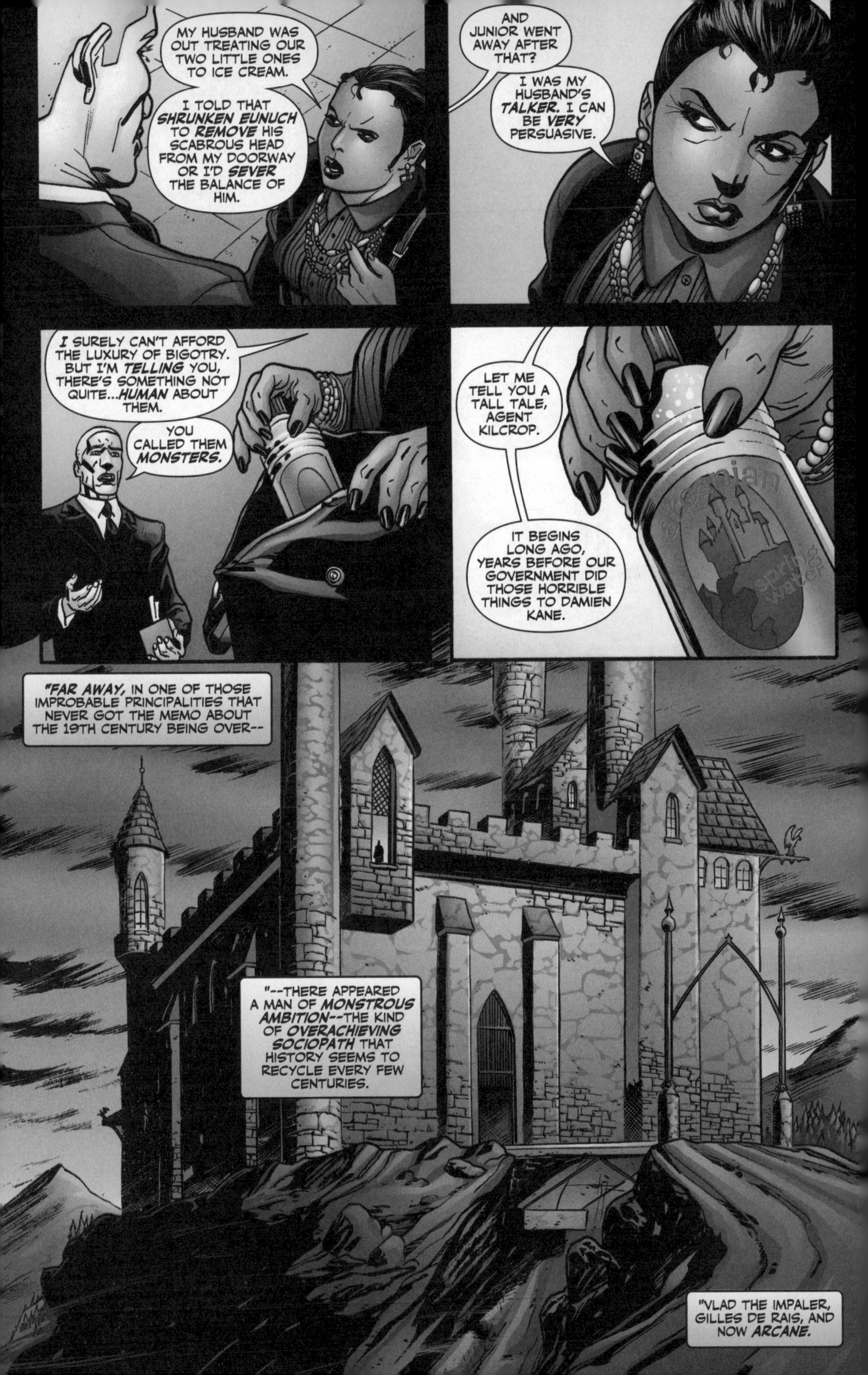
MY HUSBAND WAS OUT TREATING OUR TWO LITTLE ONES TO ICE CREAM.
I TOLD THAT SHRUNKEN EUNUCH TO REMOVE HIS SCABROUS HEAD FROM MY DOORWAY OR I'D SEVER THE BALANCE OF HIM.
AND JUNIOR WENT AWAY AFTER THAT?
I WAS MY HUSBAND'S TALKER. I CAN BE VERY PERSUASIVE.
I SURELY CAN'T AFFORD THE LUXURY OF BIGOTRY. BUT I'M TELLING YOU, THERE'S SOMETHING NOT QUITE...HUMAN ABOUT THEM.
YOU CALLED THEM MONSTERS.
LET ME TELL YOU A TALL TALE, AGENT KILCROP.
IT BEGINS LONG AGO, YEARS BEFORE OUR GOVERNMENT DID THOSE HORRIBLE THINGS TO DAMIEN KANE.
spring water
"FAR AWAY, IN ONE OF THOSE IMPROBABLE PRINCIPALITIES THAT NEVER GOT THE MEMO ABOUT THE 19TH CENTURY BEING OVER--
"--THERE APPEARED A MAN OF MONSTROUS AMBITION--THE KIND OF OVERACHIEVING SOCIOPATH THAT HISTORY SEEMS TO RECYCLE EVERY FEW CENTURIES.
"VLAD THE IMPALER, GILLES DE RAIS, AND NOW ARCANE.

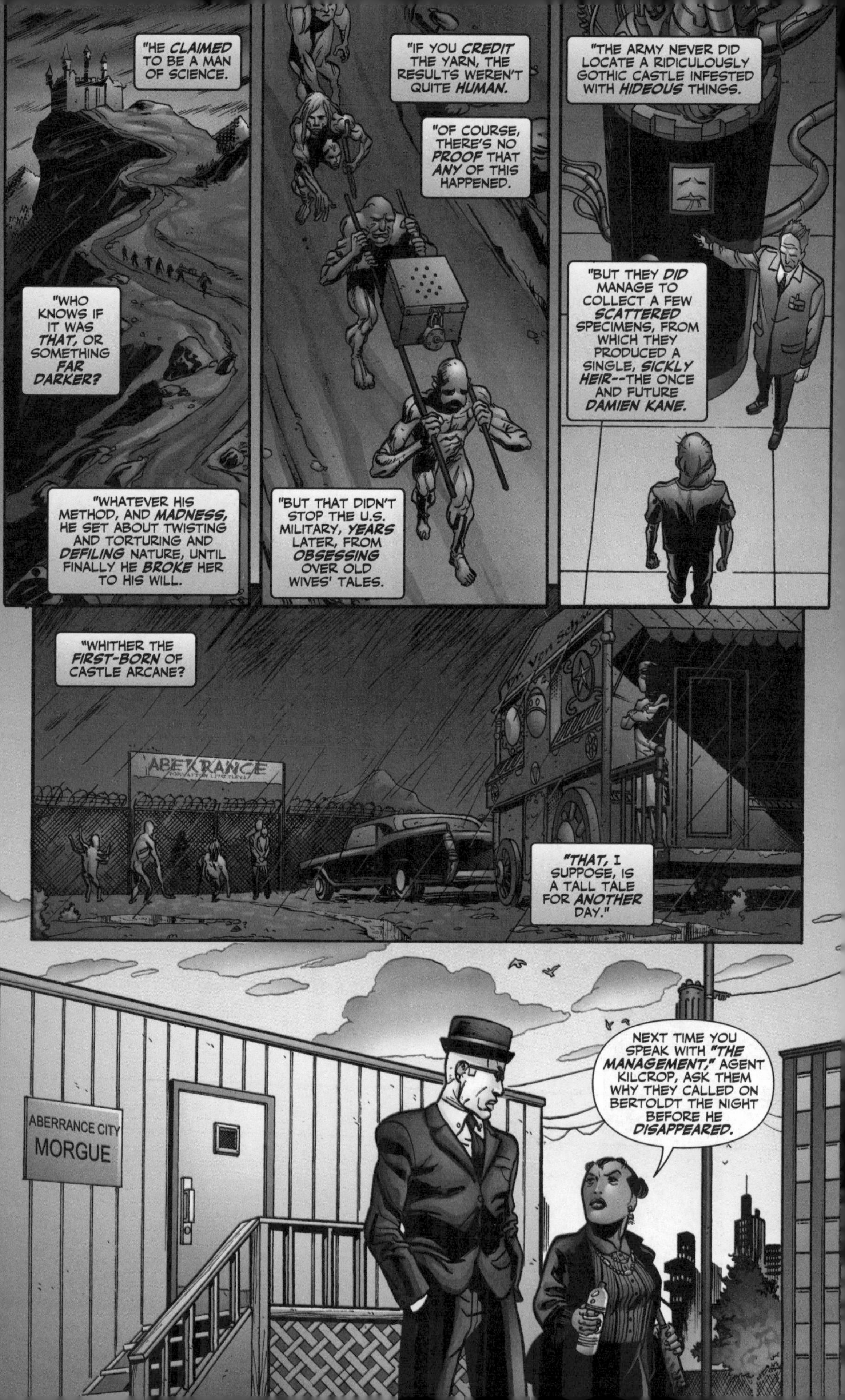
"HE CLAIMED TO BE A MAN OF SCIENCE.
"WHO KNOWS IF IT WAS THAT, OR SOMETHING FAR DARKER?
"WHATEVER HIS METHOD, AND MADNESS, HE SET ABOUT TWISTING AND TORTURING AND DEFILING NATURE, UNTIL FINALLY HE BROKE HER TO HIS WILL.
"IF YOU CREDIT THE YARN, THE RESULTS WEREN'T QUITE HUMAN.
"OF COURSE, THERE'S NO PROOF THAT ANY OF THIS HAPPENED.
"BUT THAT DIDN'T STOP THE U.S. MILITARY, YEARS LATER, FROM OBSESSING OVER OLD WIVES' TALES.
"THE ARMY NEVER DID LOCATE A RIDICULOUSLY GOTHIC CASTLE INFESTED WITH HIDEOUS THINGS.
"BUT THEY DID MANAGE TO COLLECT A FEW SCATTERED SPECIMENS, FROM WHICH THEY PRODUCED A SINGLE, SICKLY HEIR--THE ONCE AND FUTURE DAMIEN KANE.
"WHITHER THE FIRST-BORN OF CASTLE ARCANE?
ABERRANCE
"THAT, I SUPPOSE, IS A TALL TALE FOR ANOTHER DAY."
ABERRANCE CITY
MORGUE
NEXT TIME YOU SPEAK WITH "THE MANAGEMENT," AGENT KILCROP, ASK THEM WHY THEY CALLED ON BERTOLDT THE NIGHT BEFORE HE DISAPPEARED.

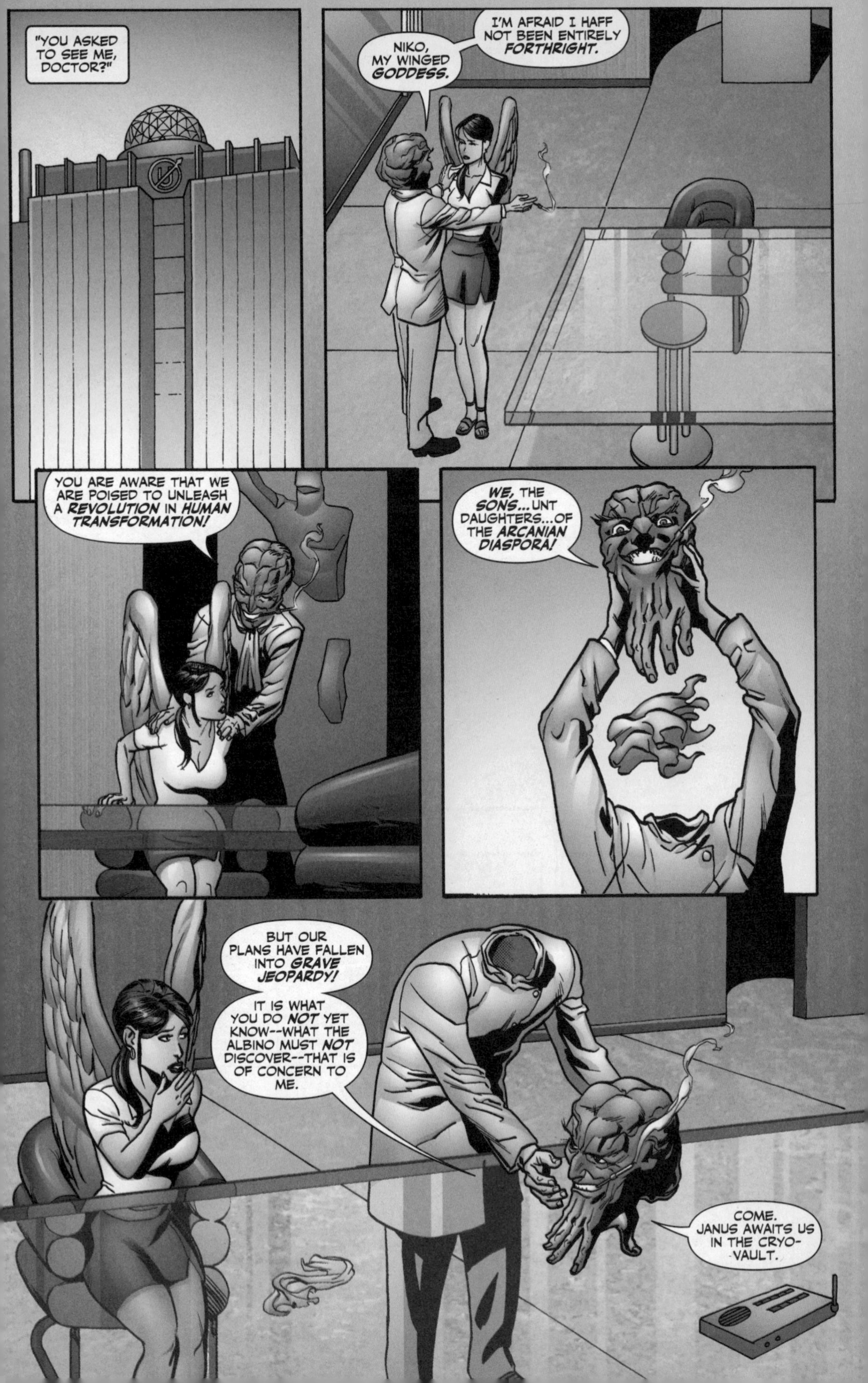
"YOU ASKED TO SEE ME, DOCTOR?"
NIKO, MY WINGED GODDESS.
I'M AFRAID I HAFF NOT BEEN ENTIRELY FORTHRIGHT.
YOU ARE AWARE THAT WE ARE POISED TO UNLEASH A REVOLUTION IN HUMAN TRANSFORMATION!
WE, THE SONS...UNT DAUGHTERS...OF THE ARCANIAN DIASPORA!
BUT OUR PLANS HAVE FALLEN INTO GRAVE JEOPARDY!
IT IS WHAT YOU DO NOT YET KNOW--WHAT THE ALBINO MUST NOT DISCOVER--THAT IS OF CONCERN TO ME.
COME. JANUS AWAITS US IN THE CRYO-VAULT.

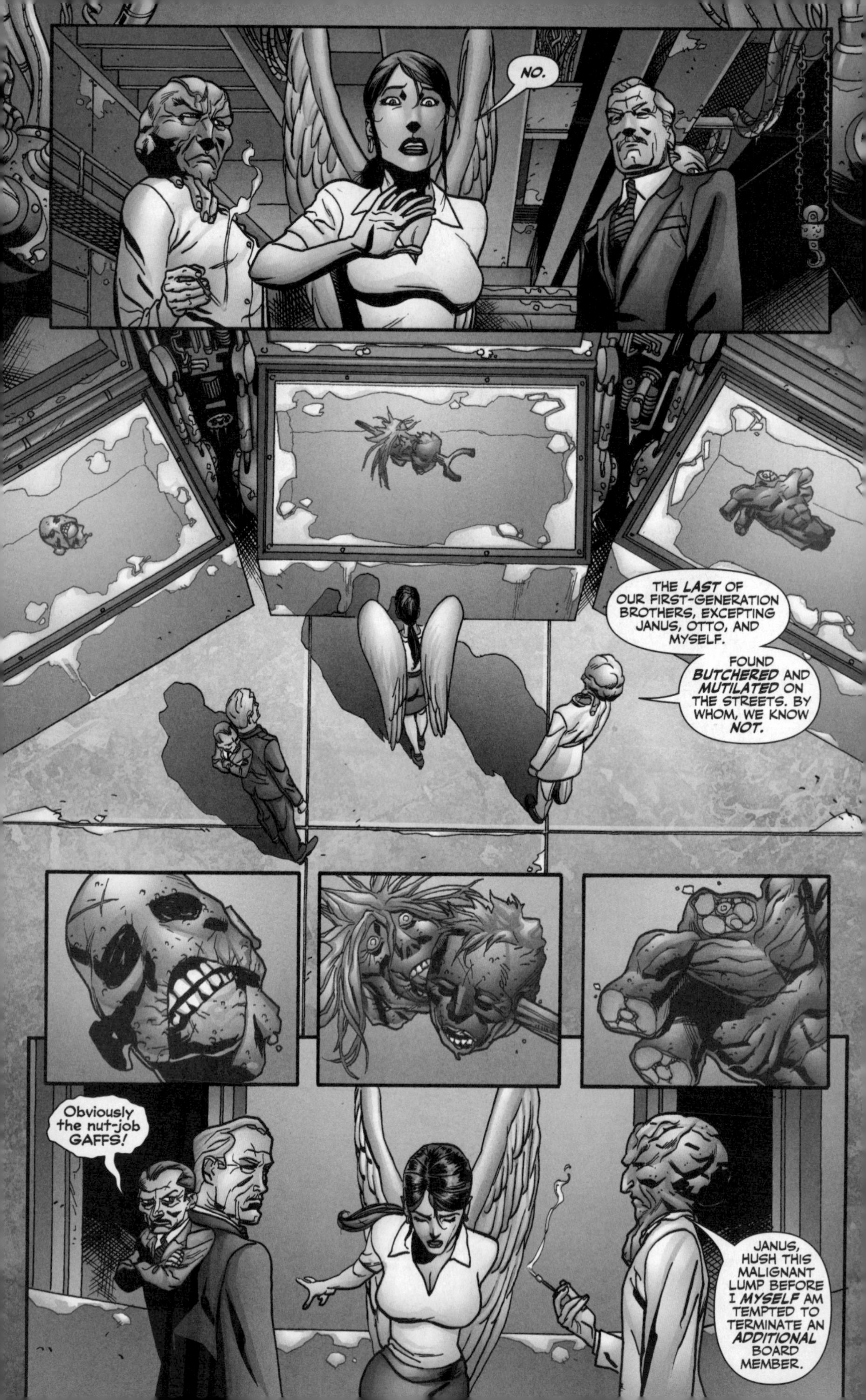
NO.
THE LAST OF OUR FIRST-GENERATION BROTHERS, EXCEPTING JANUS, OTTO, AND MYSELF.
FOUND BUTCHERED AND MUTILATED ON THE STREETS. BY WHOM, WE KNOW NOT.
Obviously the nut-job GAFFS!
JANUS, HUSH THIS MALIGNANT LUMP BEFORE I MYSELF AM TEMPTED TO TERMINATE AN ADDITIONAL BOARD MEMBER.

WHY WOULD ANYONE *DO* THIS?

THAT IS WHAT I INTEND TO *DISCOVER.*

FOR NOW, HOWEVER, IT IS IMPERATIVE THAT OUR BUSYBODY VISITOR NOT ENLARGE HIS INVESTIGATION TO INCLUDE *MULTIPLE* HOMICIDES.

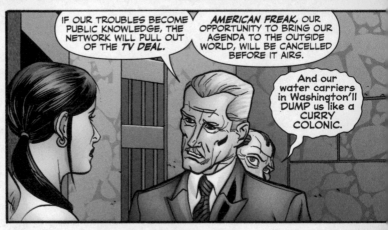

IF OUR TROUBLES BECOME PUBLIC KNOWLEDGE, THE NETWORK WILL PULL OUT OF THE *TV DEAL.*

AMERICAN FREAK, OUR OPPORTUNITY TO BRING OUR AGENDA TO THE OUTSIDE WORLD, WILL BE CANCELLED BEFORE IT AIRS.

And our water carriers in Washington'll *DUMP* us like a CURRY COLONIC.

GOVERNMENT SANCTION IS ONLY *HALF* OF THE EQUATION.

WITHOUT *PUBLIC* ACCEPTANCE OF OUR GOALS, THE HUMAN RACE WILL REMAIN *STUPIDLY* MIRED IN THIS *BIOLOGICAL DARK AGE.*

BUT IT *WON'T* BE A PROBLEM. WE'VE MADE A CALL. KILCROP WILL SHORTLY BE *RE-ASSIGNED.*

I FEEL I *KNOW* THIS MAN.

IF HE GAINS *PURCHASE,* HE WILL *NOT* LET GO.

I UNDERSTAND, DR. *CRANIUS.* I *WON'T* LET YOU DOWN.

OF THAT I AM CERTAIN, MY *WREN.*

JANUS, YOU HAVE IN CUSTODY THE ASSAILANT OF MY *MONUMENT?*

Yes, Doctor.

BRING HIM TO ME.

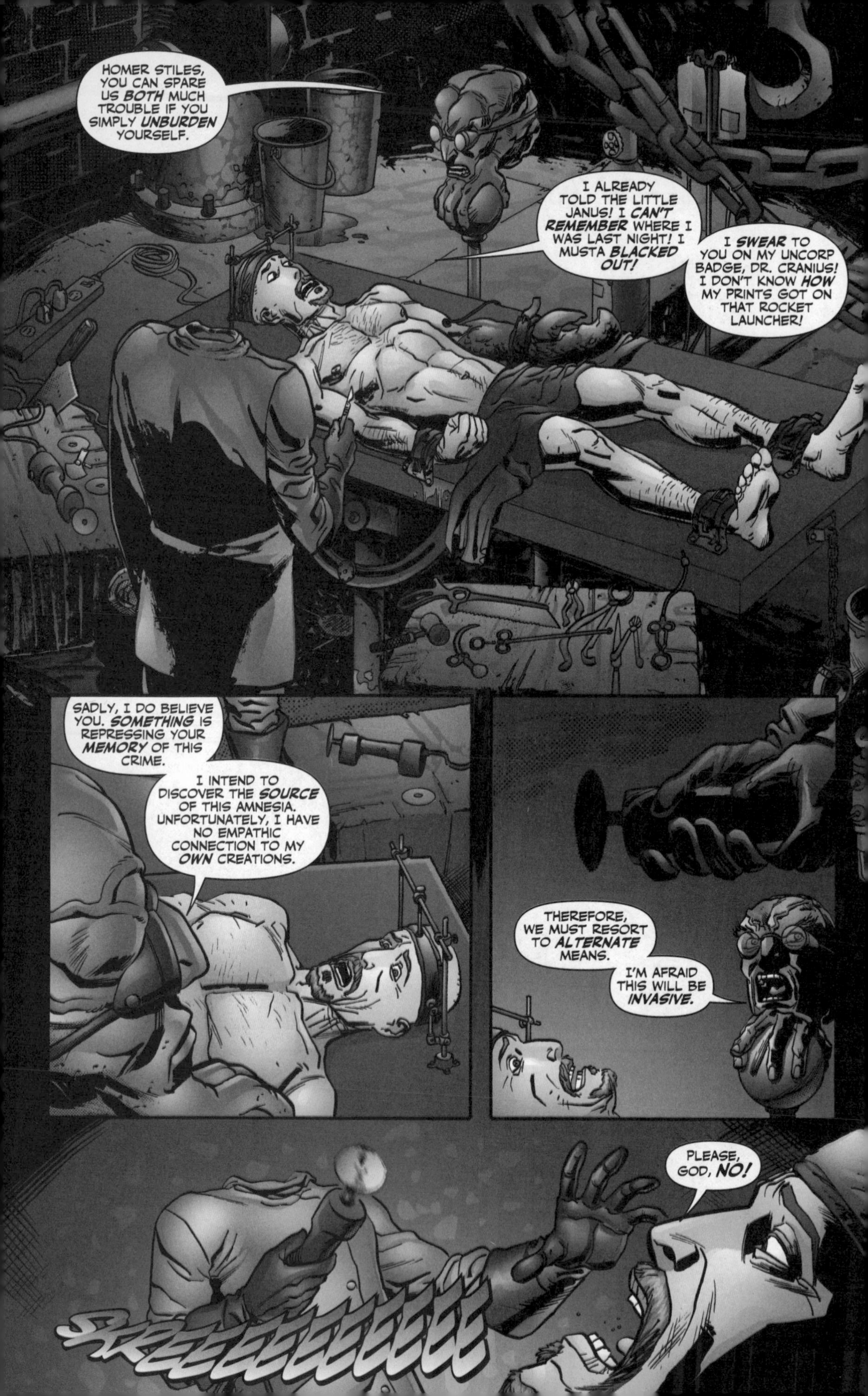
HOMER STILES, YOU CAN SPARE US BOTH MUCH TROUBLE IF YOU SIMPLY UNBURDEN YOURSELF.
I ALREADY TOLD THE LITTLE JANUS! I CAN'T REMEMBER WHERE I WAS LAST NIGHT! I MUSTA BLACKED OUT!
I SWEAR TO YOU ON MY UNCORP BADGE, DR. CRANIUS! I DON'T KNOW HOW MY PRINTS GOT ON THAT ROCKET LAUNCHER!
SADLY, I DO BELIEVE YOU. SOMETHING IS REPRESSING YOUR MEMORY OF THIS CRIME.
I INTEND TO DISCOVER THE SOURCE OF THIS AMNESIA. UNFORTUNATELY, I HAVE NO EMPATHIC CONNECTION TO MY OWN CREATIONS.
THEREFORE, WE MUST RESORT TO ALTERNATE MEANS.
I'M AFRAID THIS WILL BE INVASIVE.
PLEASE, GOD, NO!
SKREEEEEEEEEEE

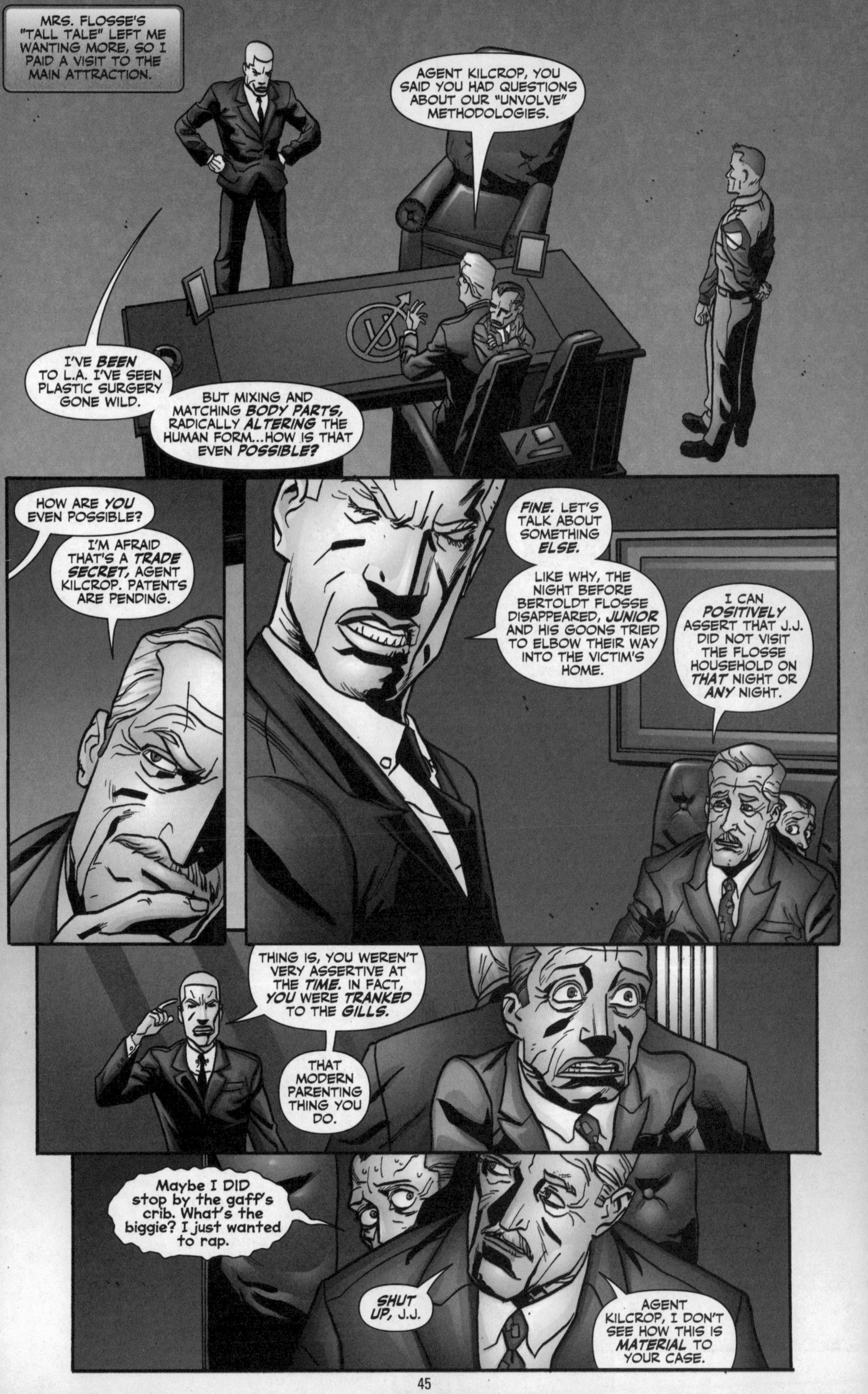
MRS. FLOSSE'S "TALL TALE" LEFT ME WANTING MORE, SO I PAID A VISIT TO THE MAIN ATTRACTION.
AGENT KILCROP, YOU SAID YOU HAD QUESTIONS ABOUT OUR "UNVOLVE" METHODOLOGIES.
I'VE BEEN TO L.A. I'VE SEEN PLASTIC SURGERY GONE WILD.
BUT MIXING AND MATCHING BODY PARTS, RADICALLY ALTERING THE HUMAN FORM...HOW IS THAT EVEN POSSIBLE?
HOW ARE YOU EVEN POSSIBLE?
I'M AFRAID THAT'S A TRADE SECRET, AGENT KILCROP. PATENTS ARE PENDING.
FINE. LET'S TALK ABOUT SOMETHING ELSE.
LIKE WHY, THE NIGHT BEFORE BERTOLDT FLOSSE DISAPPEARED, JUNIOR AND HIS GOONS TRIED TO ELBOW THEIR WAY INTO THE VICTIM'S HOME.
I CAN POSITIVELY ASSERT THAT J.J. DID NOT VISIT THE FLOSSE HOUSEHOLD ON THAT NIGHT OR ANY NIGHT.
THING IS, YOU WEREN'T VERY ASSERTIVE AT THE TIME. IN FACT, YOU WERE TRANKED TO THE GILLS.
THAT MODERN PARENTING THING YOU DO.
Maybe I DID stop by the gaff's crib. What's the biggie? I just wanted to rap.
SHUT UP, J.J.
AGENT KILCROP, I DON'T SEE HOW THIS IS MATERIAL TO YOUR CASE.

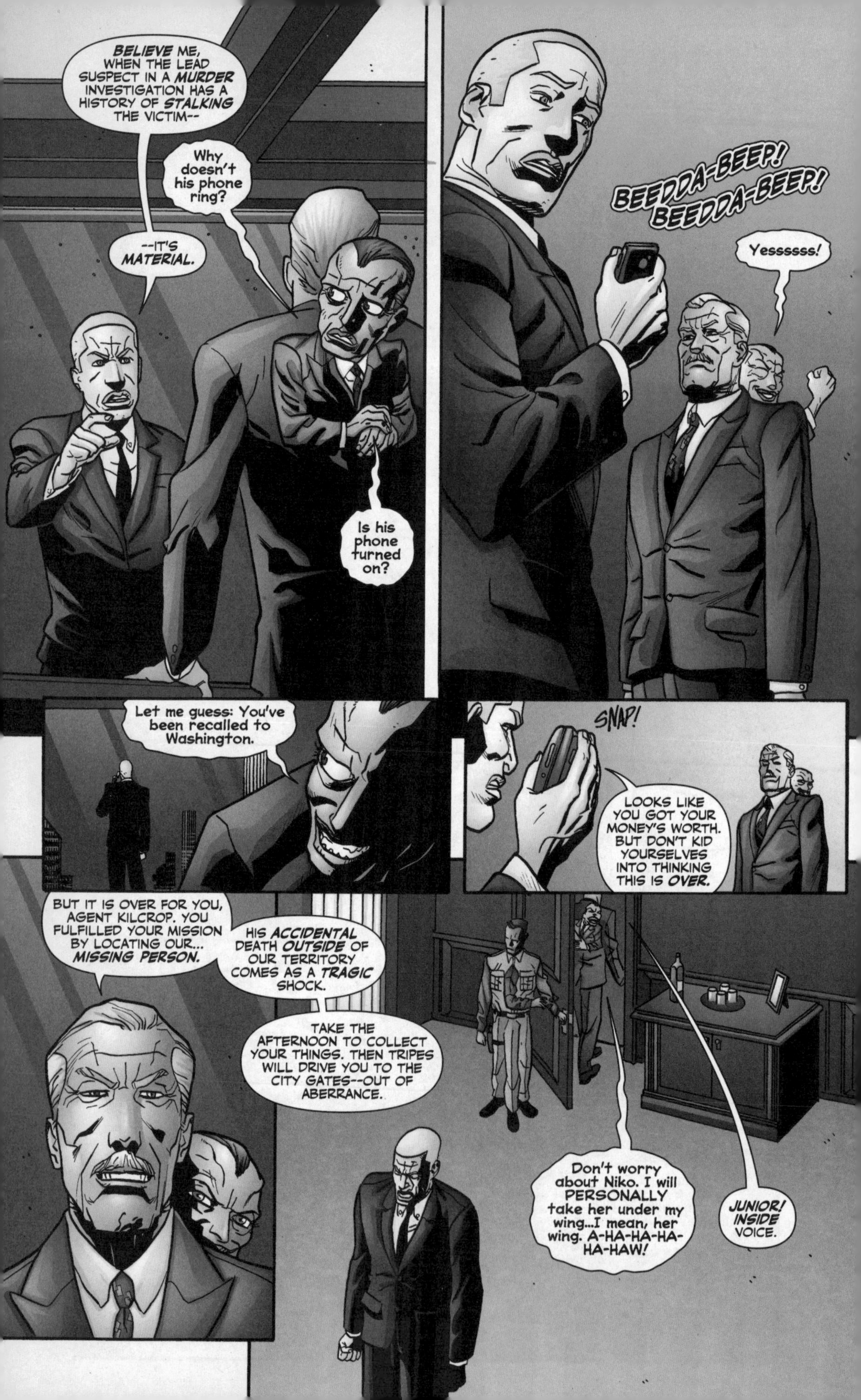
BELIEVE ME, WHEN THE LEAD SUSPECT IN A MURDER INVESTIGATION HAS A HISTORY OF STALKING THE VICTIM--
Why doesn't his phone ring?
--IT'S MATERIAL.
Is his phone turned on?
BEEDDA-BEEP! BEEDDA-BEEP!
Yessssss!
Let me guess: You've been recalled to Washington.
SNAP!
LOOKS LIKE YOU GOT YOUR MONEY'S WORTH. BUT DON'T KID YOURSELVES INTO THINKING THIS IS OVER.
BUT IT IS OVER FOR YOU, AGENT KILCROP. YOU FULFILLED YOUR MISSION BY LOCATING OUR... MISSING PERSON.
HIS ACCIDENTAL DEATH OUTSIDE OF OUR TERRITORY COMES AS A TRAGIC SHOCK.
TAKE THE AFTERNOON TO COLLECT YOUR THINGS. THEN TRIPES WILL DRIVE YOU TO THE CITY GATES--OUT OF ABERRANCE.
Don't worry about Niko. I will PERSONALLY take her under my wing...I mean, her wing. A-HA-HA-HA-HA-HAW!
JUNIOR! INSIDE VOICE.

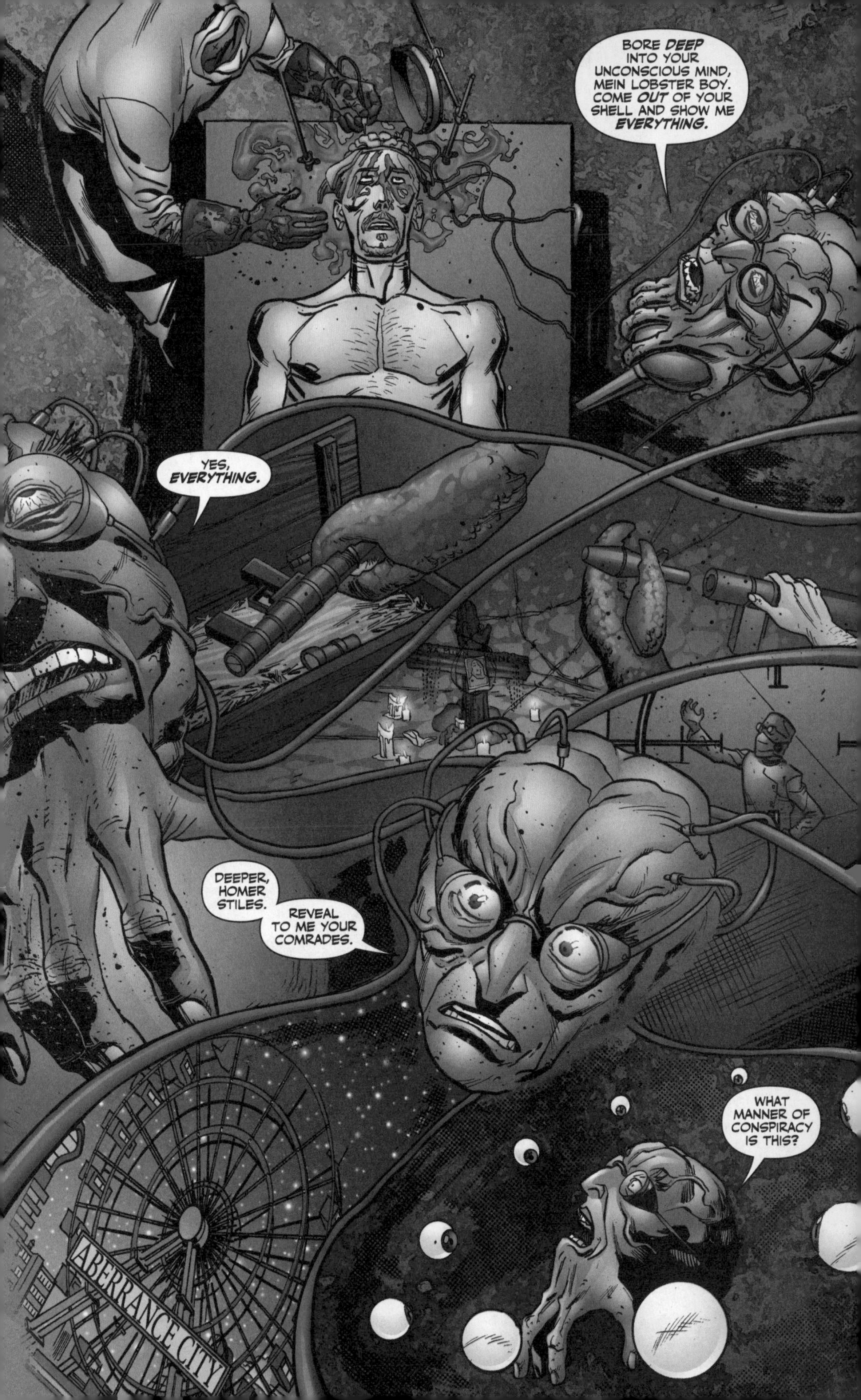
BORE DEEP INTO YOUR UNCONSCIOUS MIND, MEIN LOBSTER BOY. COME OUT OF YOUR SHELL AND SHOW ME EVERYTHING.
YES, EVERYTHING.
DEEPER, HOMER STILES.
REVEAL TO ME YOUR COMRADES.
WHAT MANNER OF CONSPIRACY IS THIS?
ABERRANCE CITY

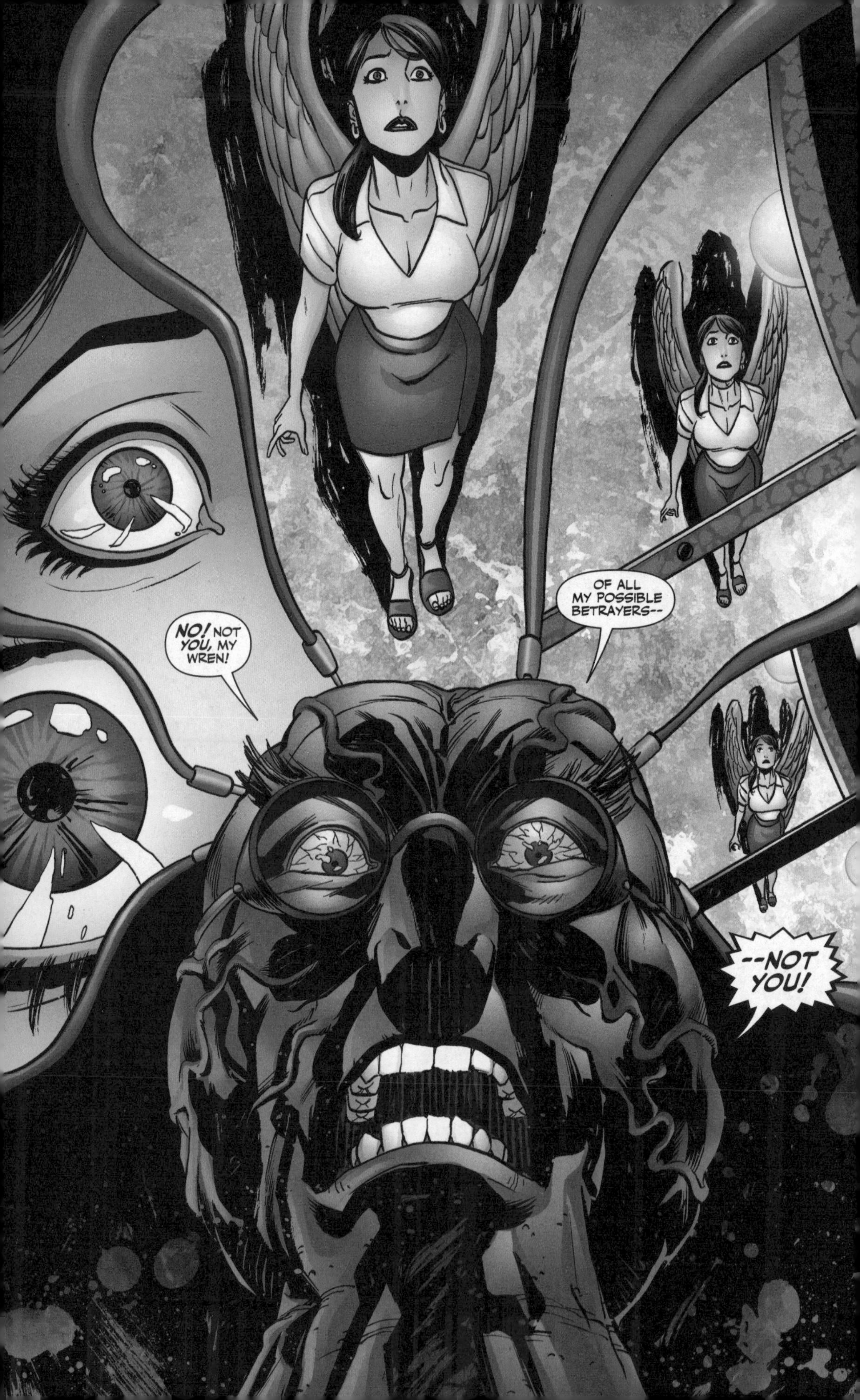
NO! NOT YOU, MY WREN!
OF ALL MY POSSIBLE BETRAYERS--
--NOT YOU!

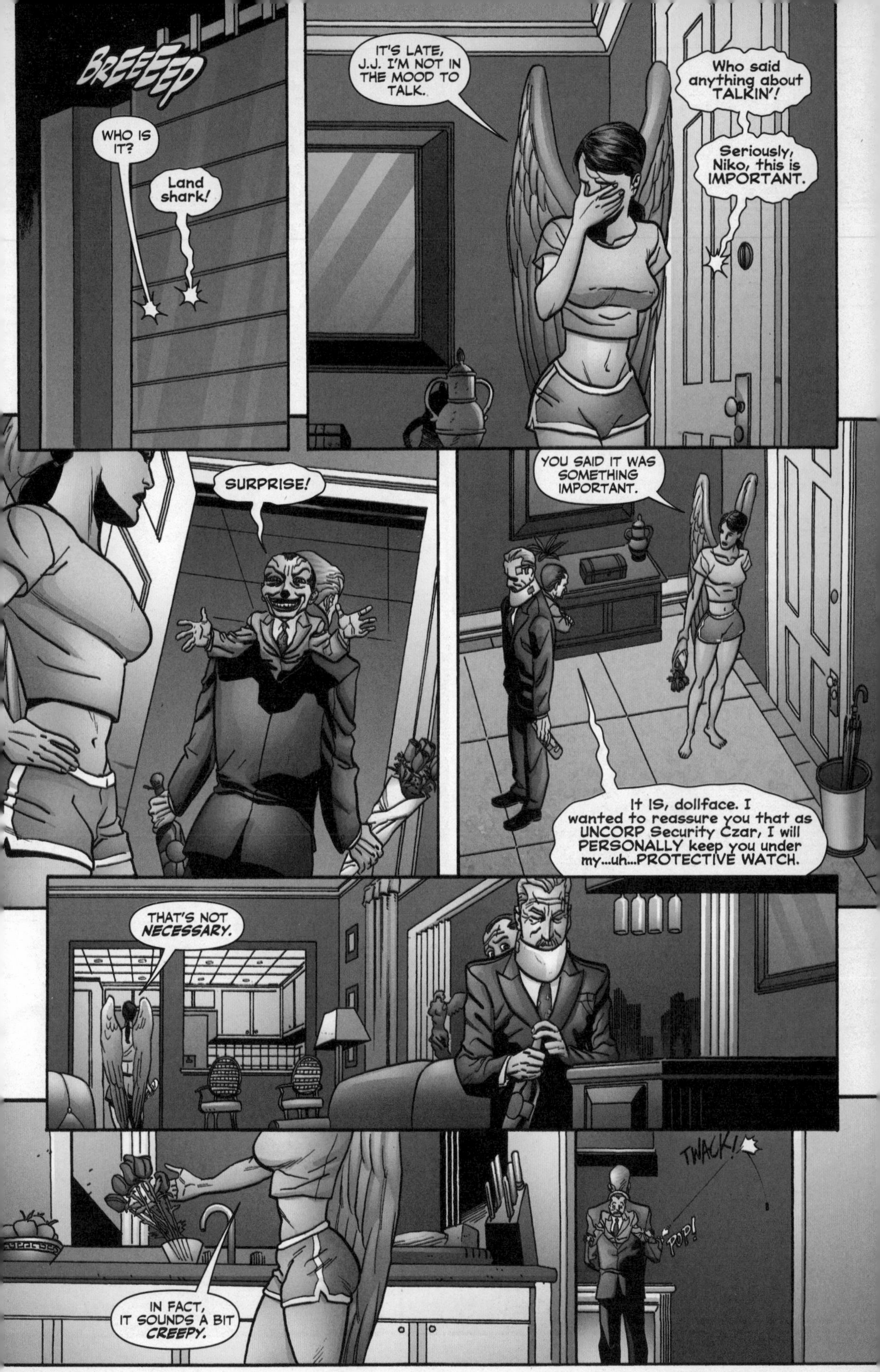
BREEEEP
WHO IS IT?
Land shark!
IT'S LATE, J.J. I'M NOT IN THE MOOD TO TALK.
Who said anything about TALKIN'!
Seriously, Niko, this is IMPORTANT.
SURPRISE!
YOU SAID IT WAS SOMETHING IMPORTANT.
It IS, dollface. I wanted to reassure you that as UNCORP Security Czar, I will PERSONALLY keep you under my...uh...PROTECTIVE WATCH.
THAT'S NOT NECESSARY.
IN FACT, IT SOUNDS A BIT CREEPY.
TWACK!
POP!

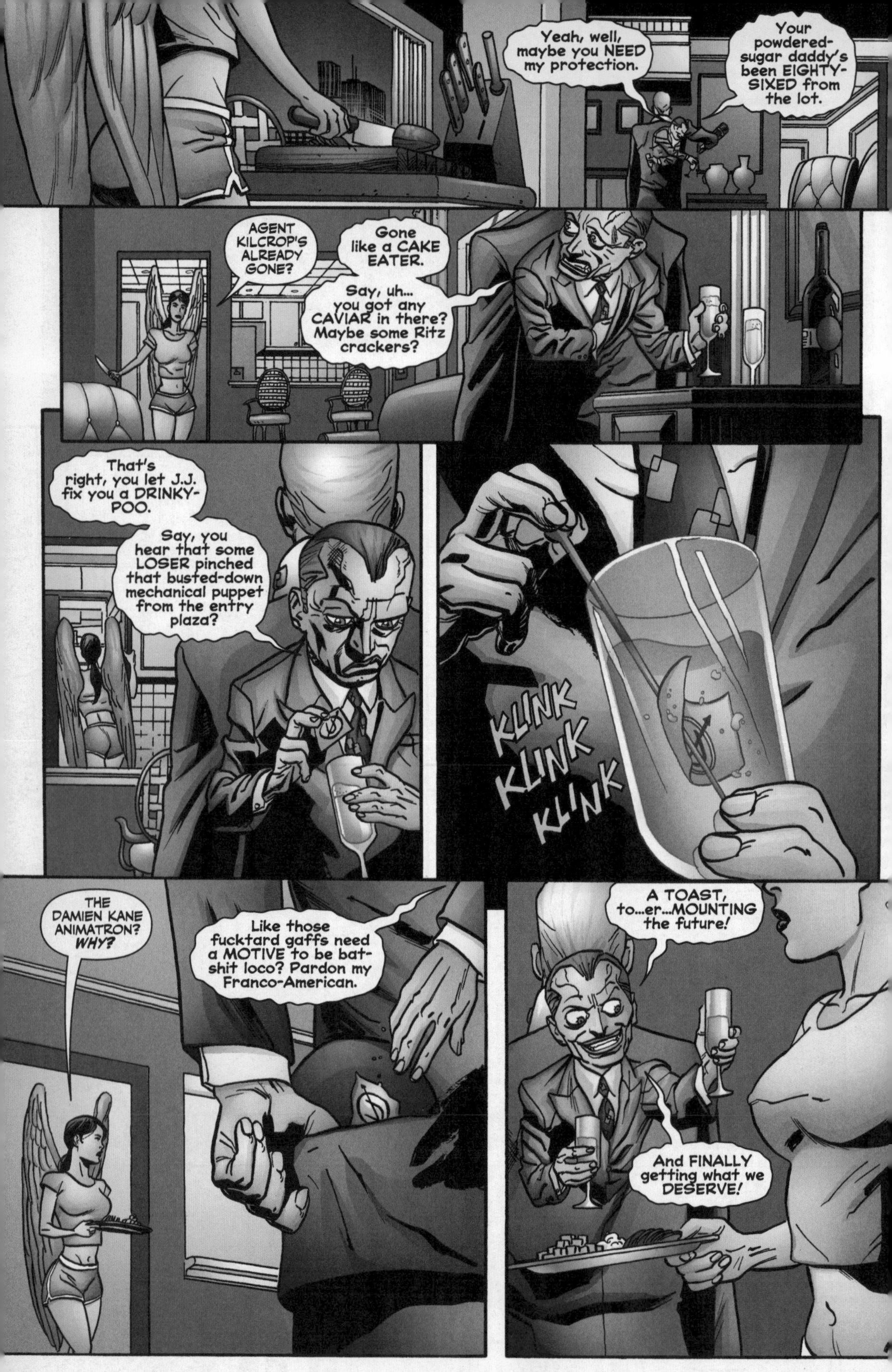
Yeah, well, maybe you NEED my protection.
Your powdered-sugar daddy's been EIGHTY-SIXED from the lot.
AGENT KILCROP'S ALREADY GONE?
Gone like a CAKE EATER.
Say, uh... you got any CAVIAR in there? Maybe some Ritz crackers?
That's right, you let J.J. fix you a DRINKY-POO.
Say, you hear that some LOSER pinched that busted-down mechanical puppet from the entry plaza?
KLINK KLINK KLINK
THE DAMIEN KANE ANIMATRON? WHY?
Like those fucktard gaffs need a MOTIVE to be bat-shit loco? Pardon my Franco-American.
A TOAST, to...er...MOUNTING the future!
And FINALLY getting what we DESERVE!

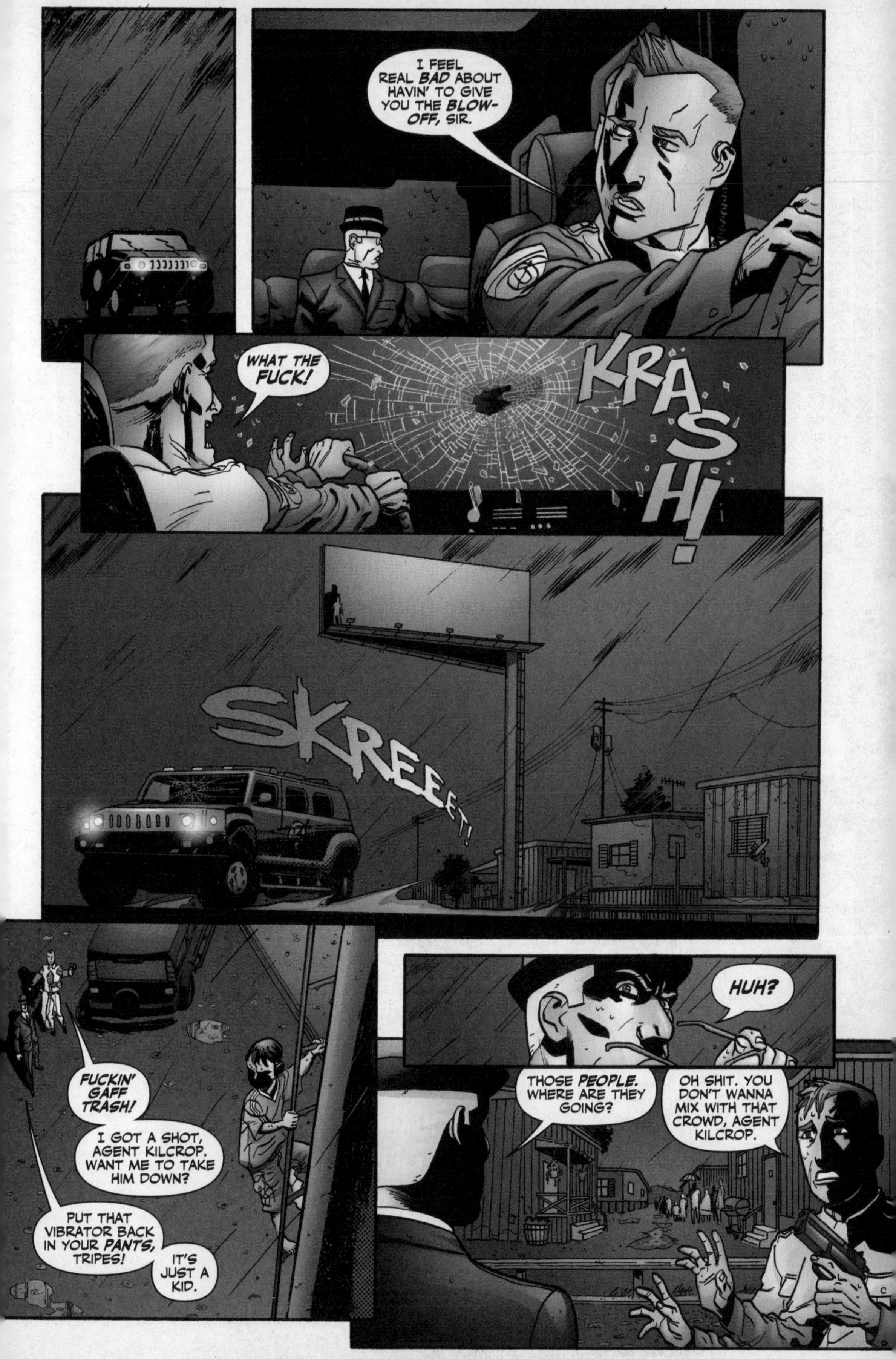

I FEEL REAL BAD ABOUT HAVIN' TO GIVE YOU THE BLOW-OFF, SIR.
WHAT THE FUCK!
KRASH!
SKREEEET!
HUH?
FUCKIN' GAFF TRASH!
I GOT A SHOT, AGENT KILCROP. WANT ME TO TAKE HIM DOWN?
PUT THAT VIBRATOR BACK IN YOUR PANTS, TRIPES!
IT'S JUST A KID.
THOSE PEOPLE. WHERE ARE THEY GOING?
OH SHIT. YOU DON'T WANNA MIX WITH THAT CROWD, AGENT KILCROP.

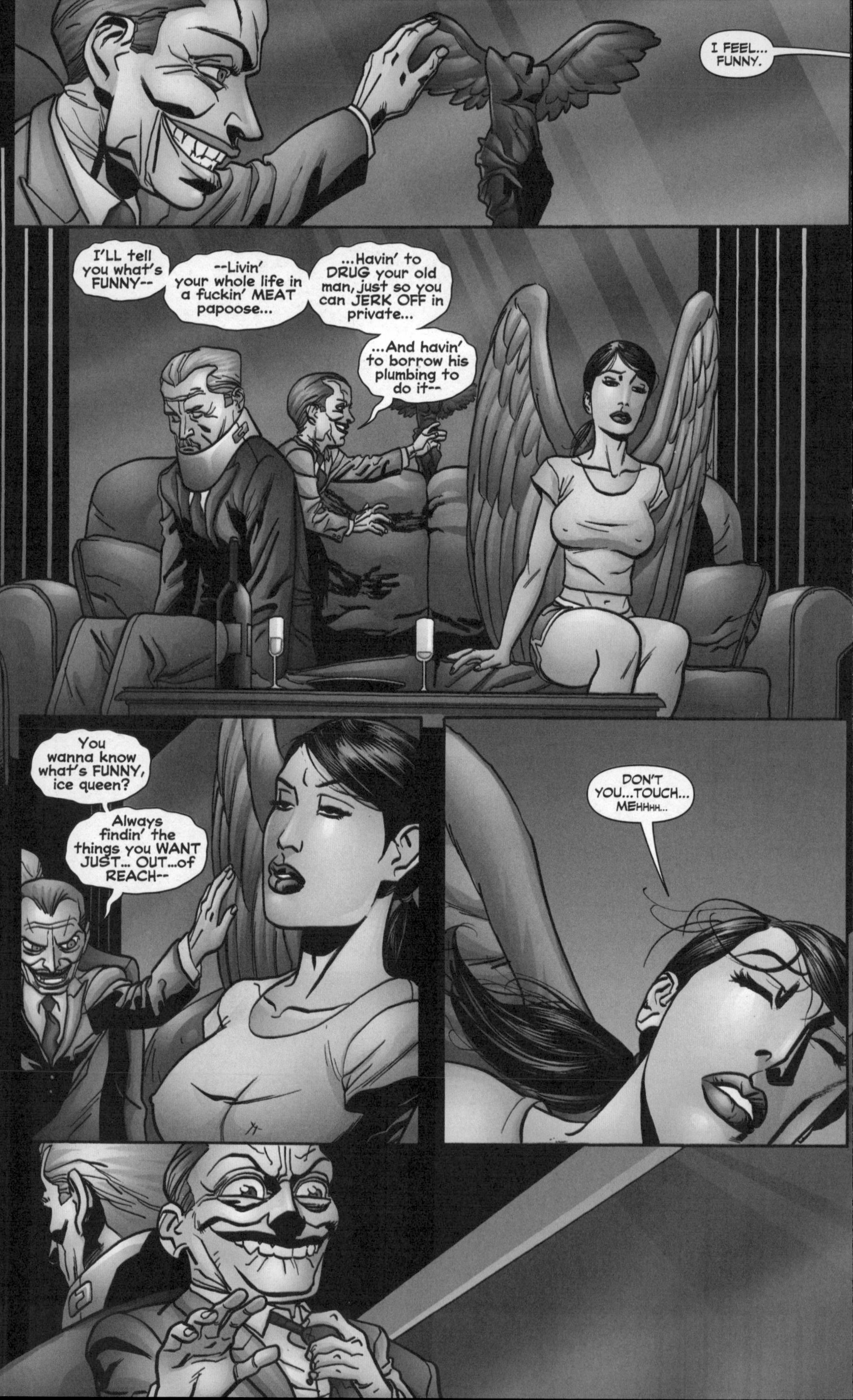
I FEEL... FUNNY.
I'LL tell you what's FUNNY--
--Livin' your whole life in a fuckin' MEAT papoose...
...Havin' to DRUG your old man, just so you can JERK OFF in private...
...And havin' to borrow his plumbing to do it--
You wanna know what's FUNNY, ice queen?
Always findin' the things you WANT JUST... OUT...of REACH--
DON'T YOU...TOUCH... MEHHHH...

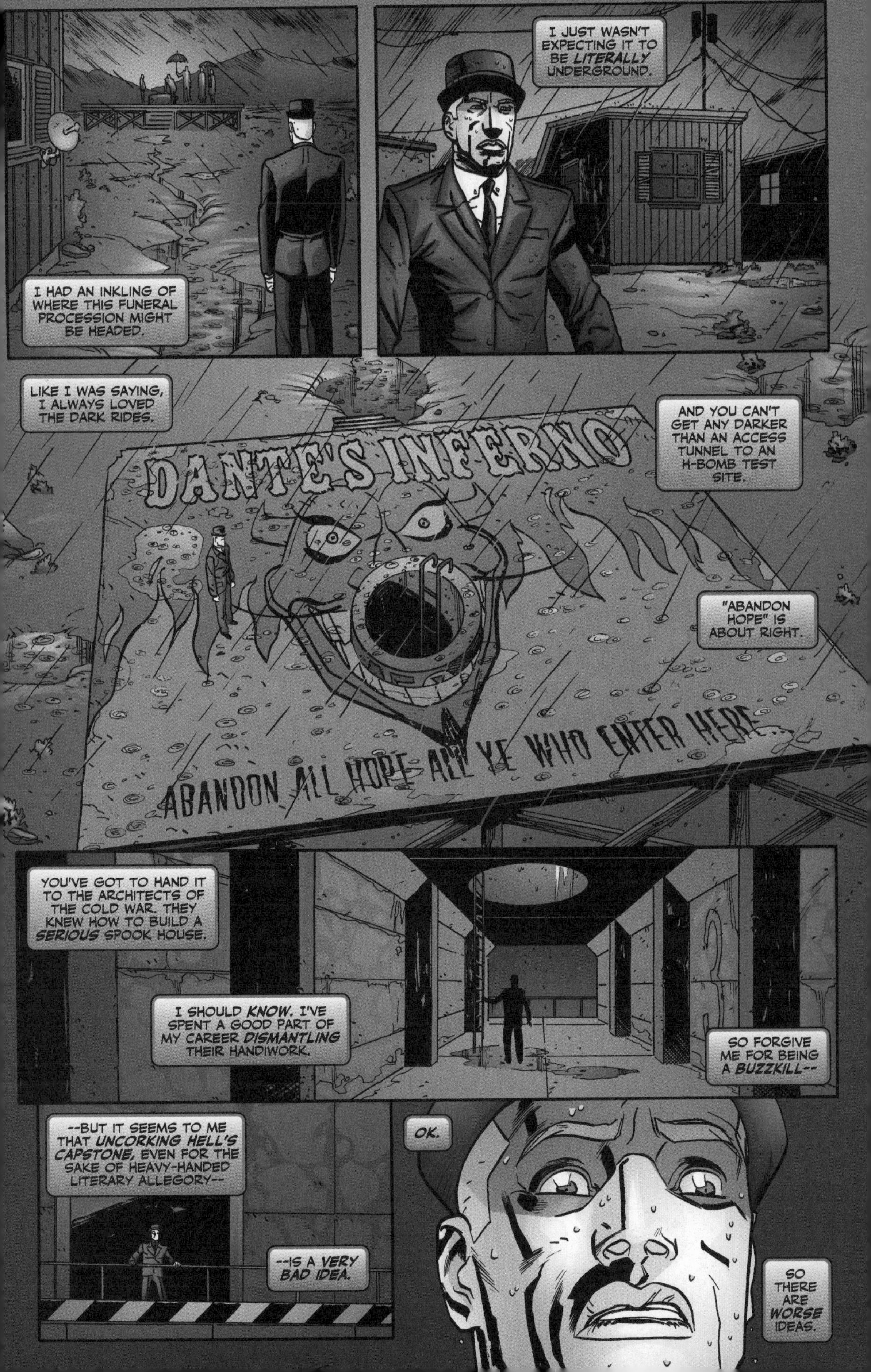
I HAD AN INKLING OF WHERE THIS FUNERAL PROCESSION MIGHT BE HEADED.
I JUST WASN'T EXPECTING IT TO BE *LITERALLY* UNDERGROUND.
LIKE I WAS SAYING, I ALWAYS LOVED THE DARK RIDES.
DANTE'S INFERNO
AND YOU CAN'T GET ANY DARKER THAN AN ACCESS TUNNEL TO AN H-BOMB TEST SITE.
"ABANDON HOPE" IS ABOUT RIGHT.
ABANDON ALL HOPE ALL YE WHO ENTER HERE
YOU'VE GOT TO HAND IT TO THE ARCHITECTS OF THE COLD WAR. THEY KNEW HOW TO BUILD A *SERIOUS* SPOOK HOUSE.
I SHOULD *KNOW*. I'VE SPENT A GOOD PART OF MY CAREER *DISMANTLING* THEIR HANDIWORK.
SO FORGIVE ME FOR BEING A *BUZZKILL*--
--BUT IT SEEMS TO ME THAT *UNCORKING HELL'S CAPSTONE*, EVEN FOR THE SAKE OF HEAVY-HANDED LITERARY ALLEGORY--
--IS A *VERY BAD IDEA.*
OK.
SO THERE ARE *WORSE* IDEAS.

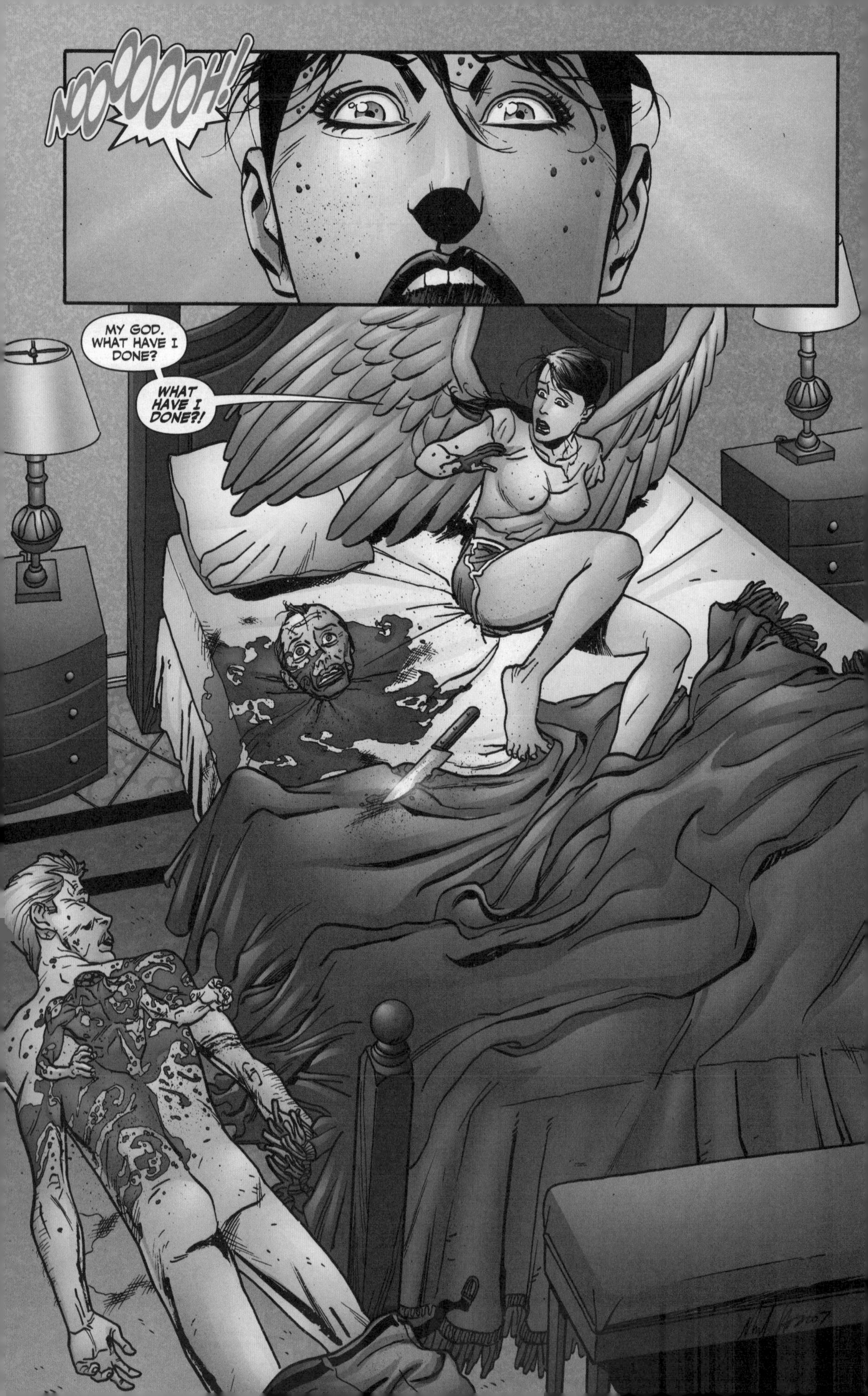
NOOOOOOH!!
MY GOD. WHAT HAVE I DONE?
WHAT HAVE I DONE?!

"We ALL WANT JUSTICE. BUT WHEN IT NEVER COMES, ONE BEGINS TO LOOK ELSEWHERE FOR HOPE."

CHAPTER THREE

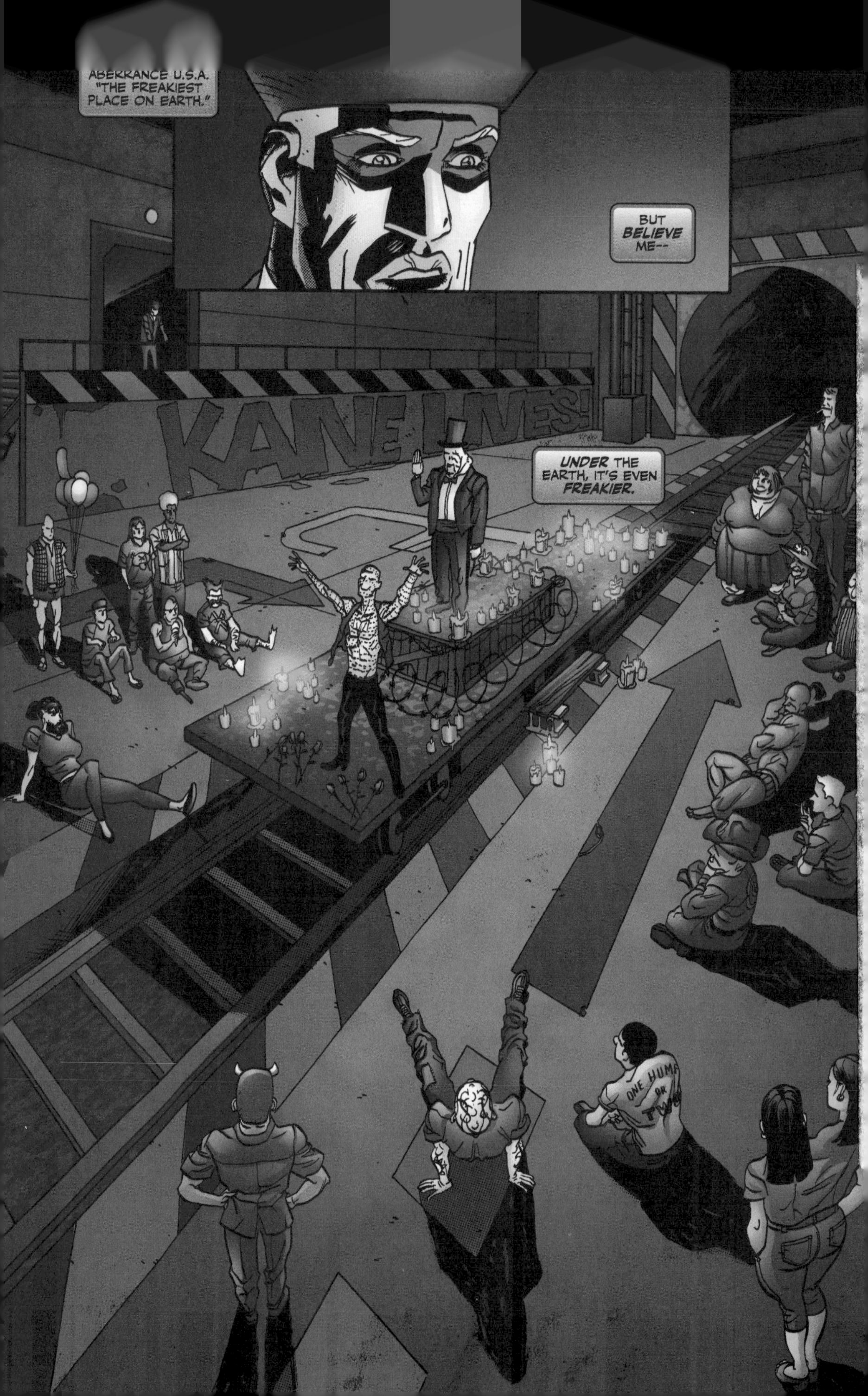
ABERRANCE U.S.A. "THE FREAKIEST PLACE ON EARTH."
BUT *BELIEVE* ME--
KANE LIVES!
UNDER THE EARTH, IT'S EVEN *FREAKIER.*

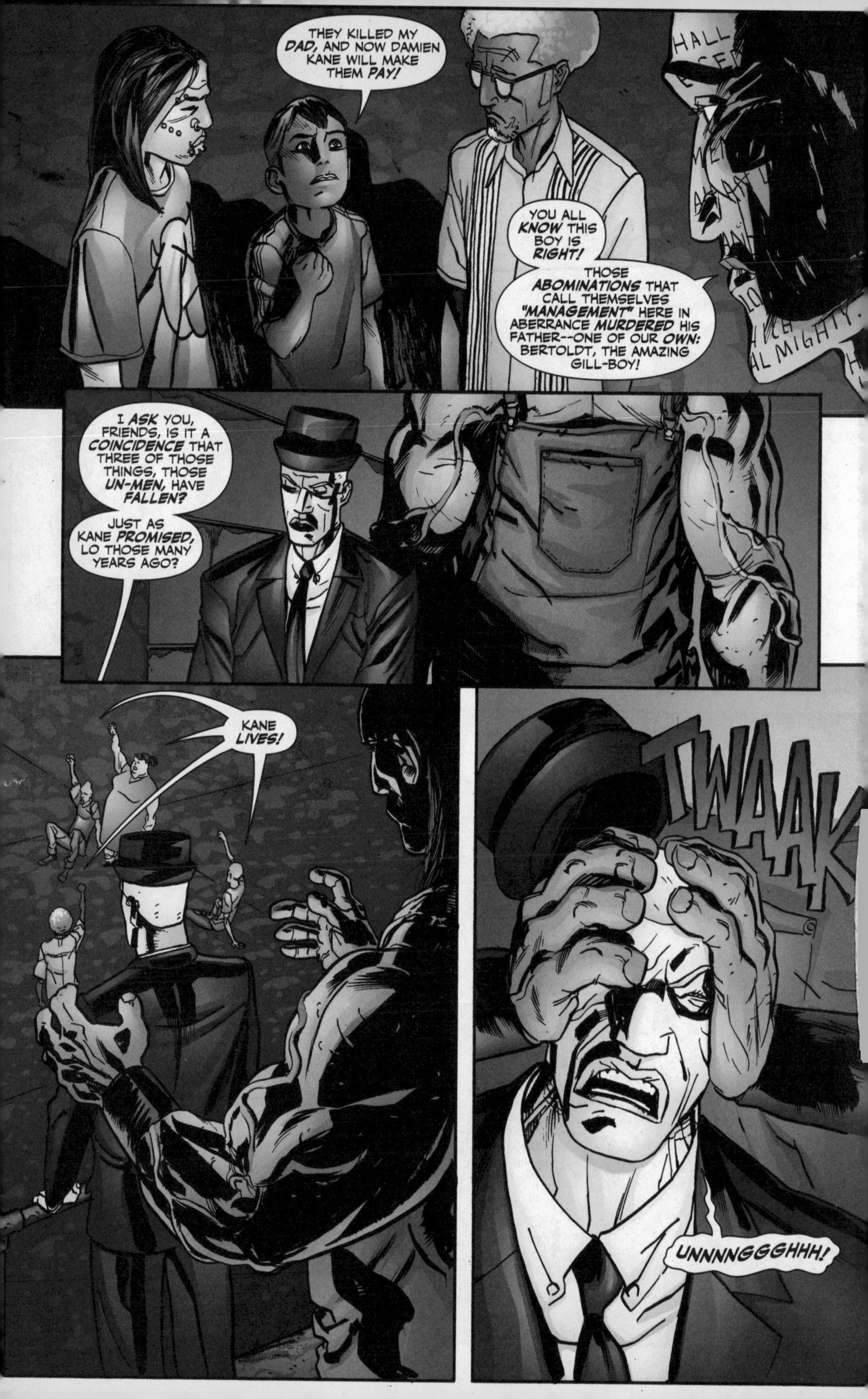
THEY KILLED MY DAD, AND NOW DAMIEN KANE WILL MAKE THEM PAY!
YOU ALL KNOW THIS BOY IS RIGHT!
THOSE ABOMINATIONS THAT CALL THEMSELVES "MANAGEMENT" HERE IN ABERRANCE MURDERED HIS FATHER--ONE OF OUR OWN: BERTOLDT, THE AMAZING GILL-BOY!
I ASK YOU, FRIENDS, IS IT A COINCIDENCE THAT THREE OF THOSE THINGS, THOSE UN-MEN, HAVE FALLEN?
JUST AS KANE PROMISED, LO THOSE MANY YEARS AGO?
KANE LIVES!
TWAAK
UNNNGGGHHH!

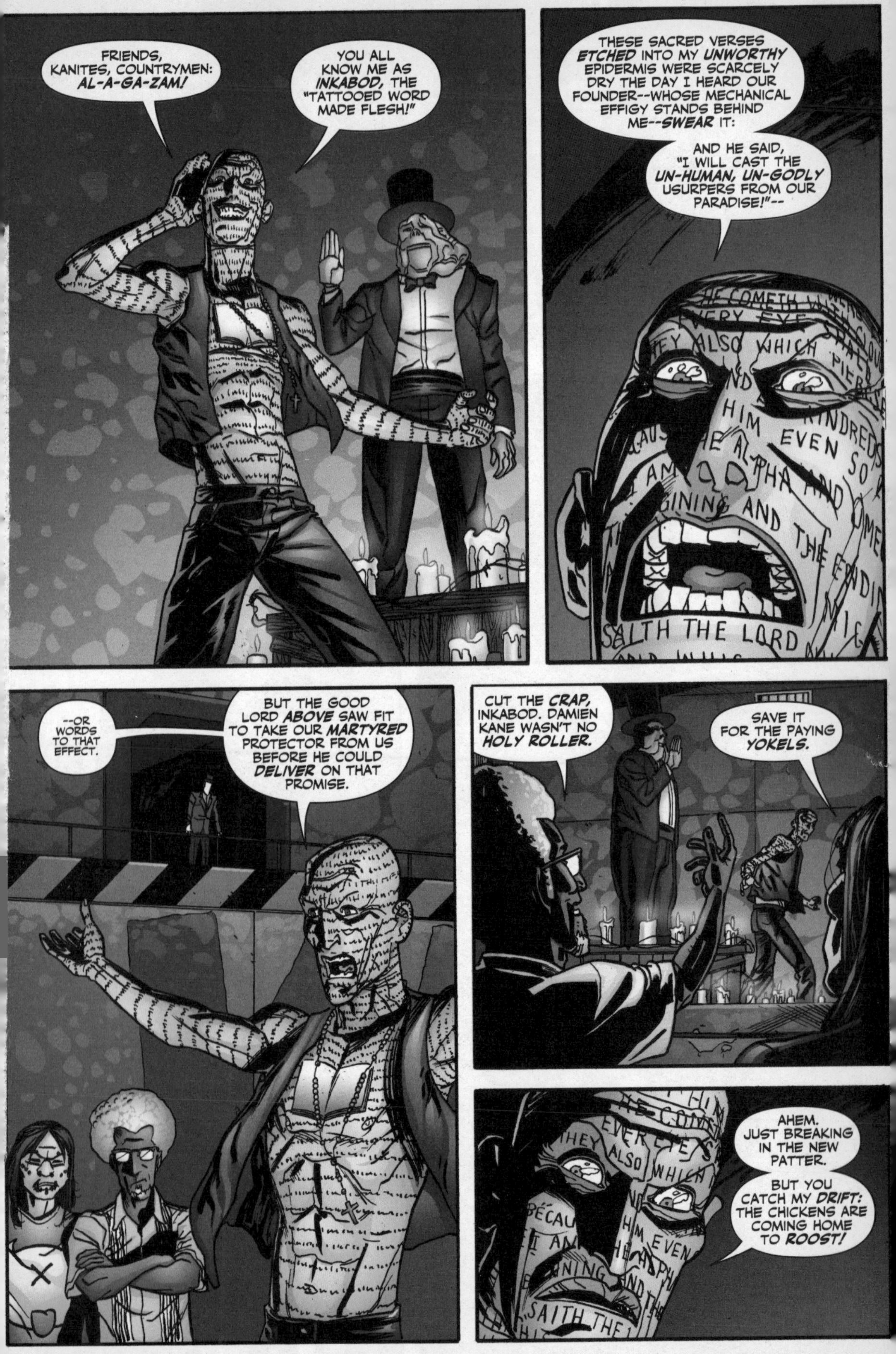
FRIENDS, KANITES, COUNTRYMEN: AL-A-GA-ZAM!
YOU ALL KNOW ME AS INKABOD, THE "TATTOOED WORD MADE FLESH!"
THESE SACRED VERSES ETCHED INTO MY UNWORTHY EPIDERMIS WERE SCARCELY DRY THE DAY I HEARD OUR FOUNDER--WHOSE MECHANICAL EFFIGY STANDS BEHIND ME--SWEAR IT:
AND HE SAID, "I WILL CAST THE UN-HUMAN, UN-GODLY USURPERS FROM OUR PARADISE!"--
--OR WORDS TO THAT EFFECT.
BUT THE GOOD LORD ABOVE SAW FIT TO TAKE OUR MARTYRED PROTECTOR FROM US BEFORE HE COULD DELIVER ON THAT PROMISE.
CUT THE CRAP, INKABOD. DAMIEN KANE WASN'T NO HOLY ROLLER.
SAVE IT FOR THE PAYING YOKELS.
AHEM. JUST BREAKING IN THE NEW PATTER.
BUT YOU CATCH MY DRIFT: THE CHICKENS ARE COMING HOME TO ROOST!

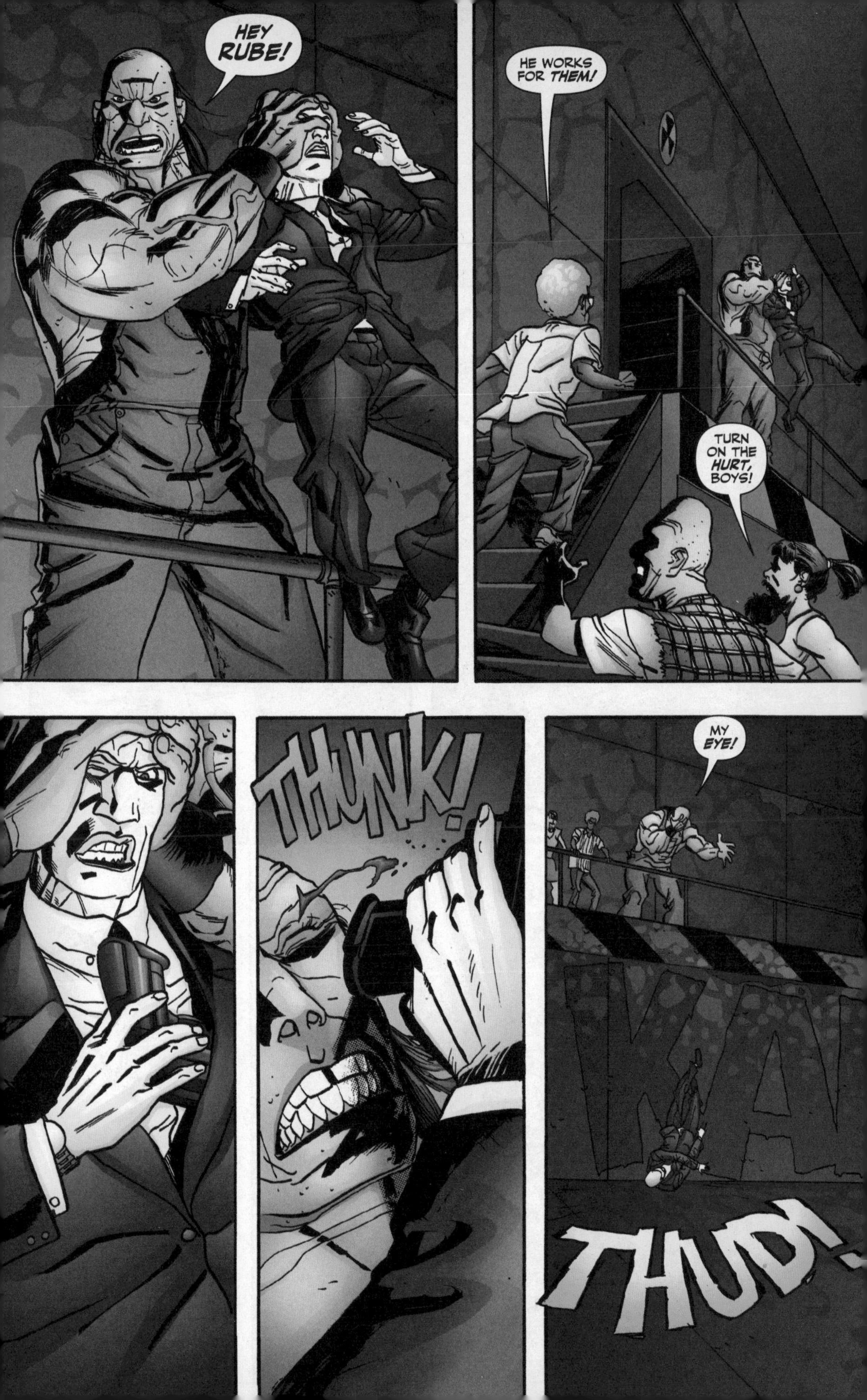
HEY RUBE!
HE WORKS FOR THEM!
TURN ON THE HURT, BOYS!
THUNK!
MY EYE!
THUD!

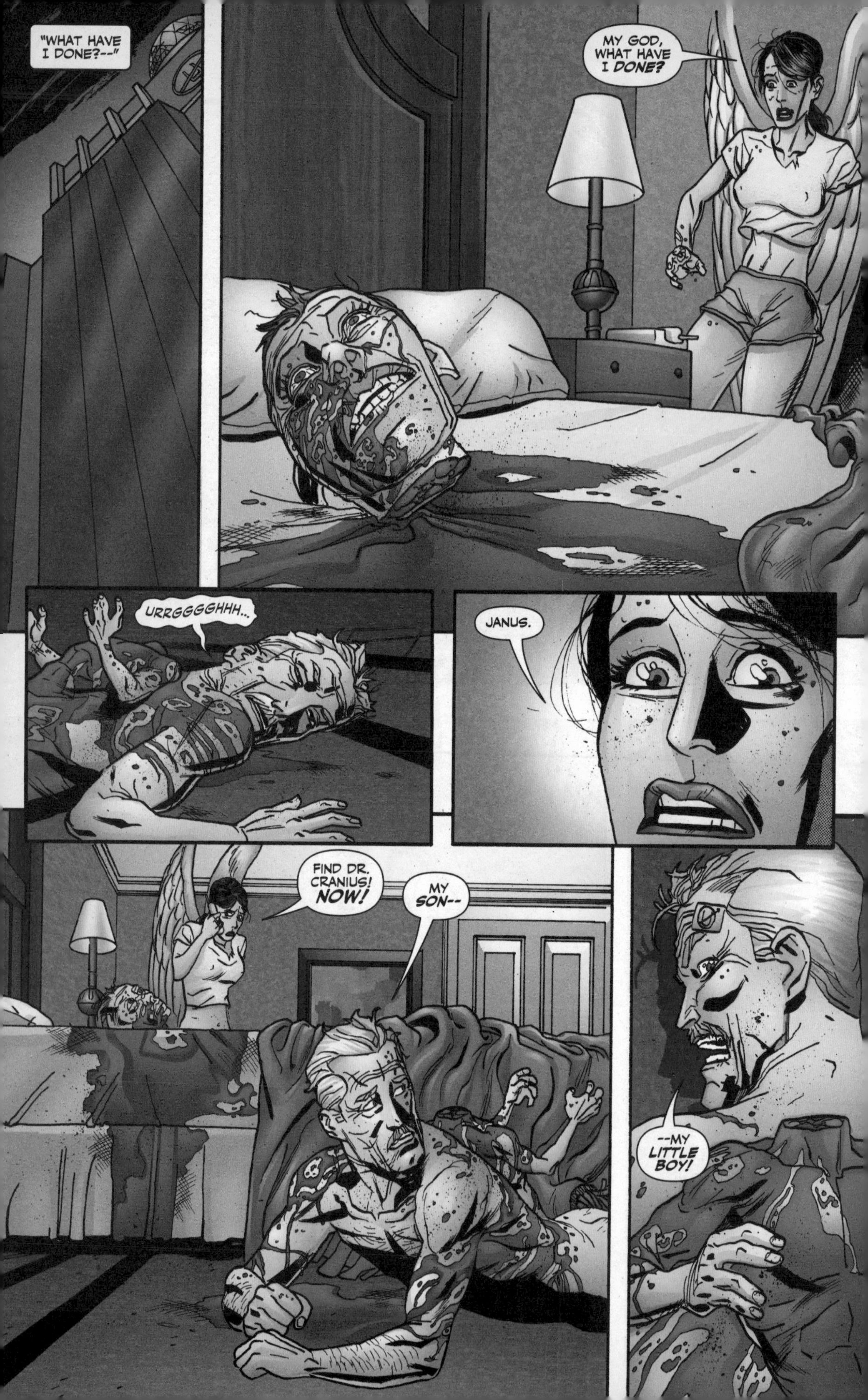
"WHAT HAVE I DONE?--"
MY GOD, WHAT HAVE I DONE?
URRGGGGHHH...
JANUS.
FIND DR. CRANIUS! NOW!
MY SON--
--MY LITTLE BOY!

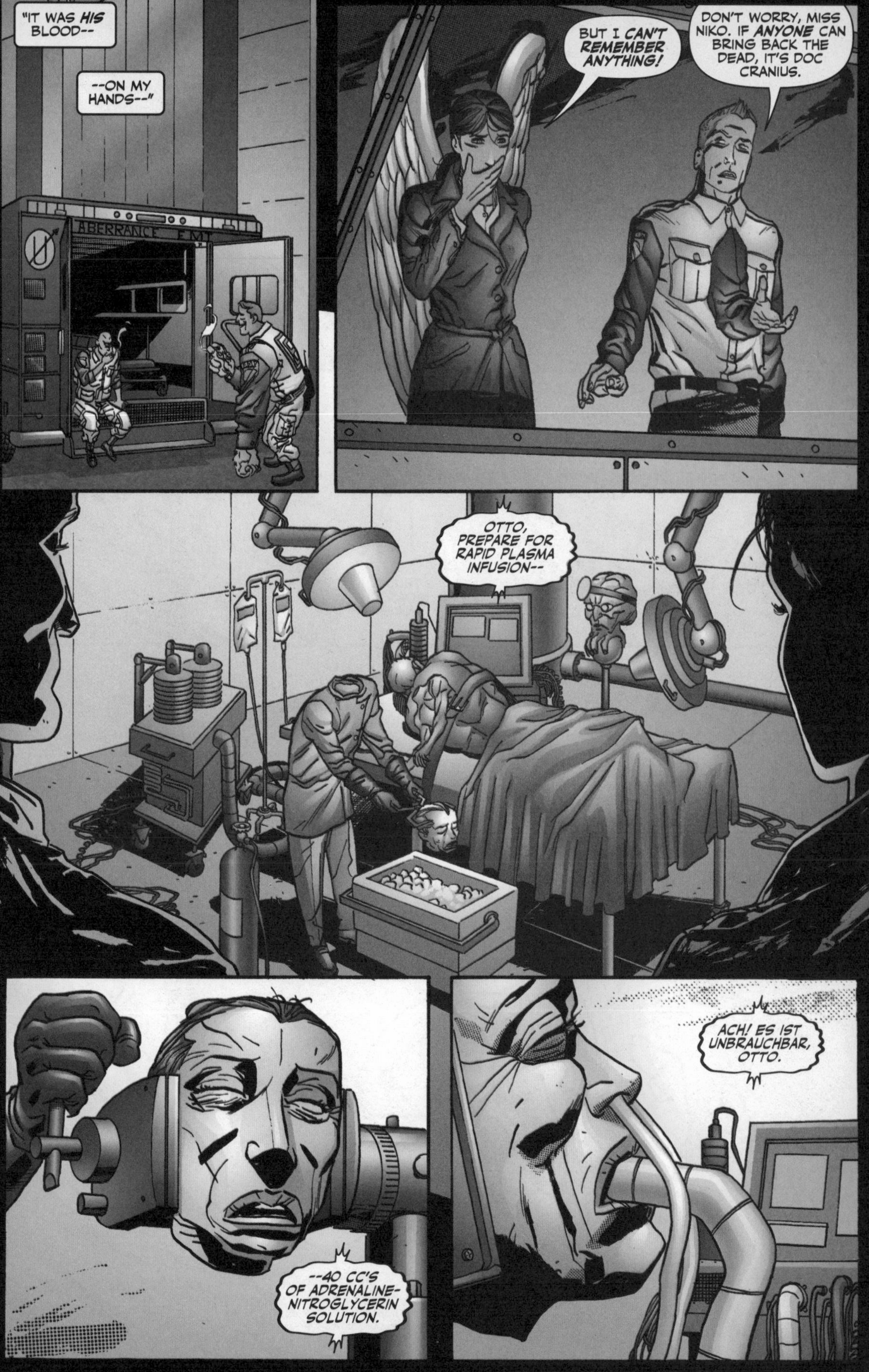

"IT WAS HIS BLOOD--
--ON MY HANDS--"
ABERRANCE EMT
BUT I CAN'T REMEMBER ANYTHING!
DON'T WORRY, MISS NIKO. IF ANYONE CAN BRING BACK THE DEAD, IT'S DOC CRANIUS.
OTTO, PREPARE FOR RAPID PLASMA INFUSION--
--40 CC'S OF ADRENALINE-NITROGLYCERIN SOLUTION.
ACH! ES IST UNBRAUCHBAR, OTTO.

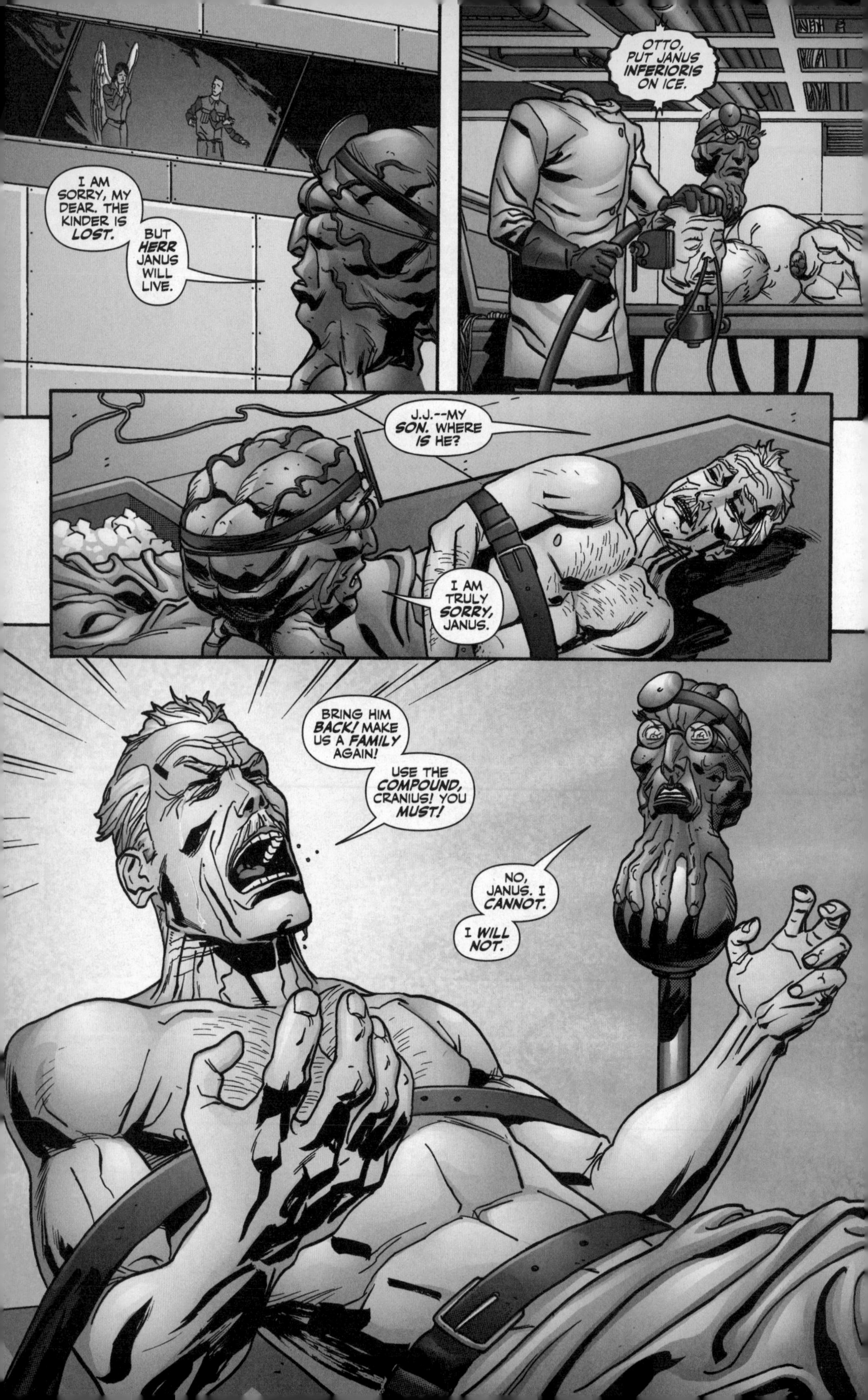
OTTO, PUT JANUS INFERIORIS ON ICE.
I AM SORRY, MY DEAR. THE KINDER IS LOST.
BUT HERR JANUS WILL LIVE.
J.J.--MY SON. WHERE IS HE?
I AM TRULY SORRY, JANUS.
BRING HIM BACK! MAKE US A FAMILY AGAIN!
USE THE COMPOUND, CRANIUS! YOU MUST!
NO, JANUS. I CANNOT.
I WILL NOT.

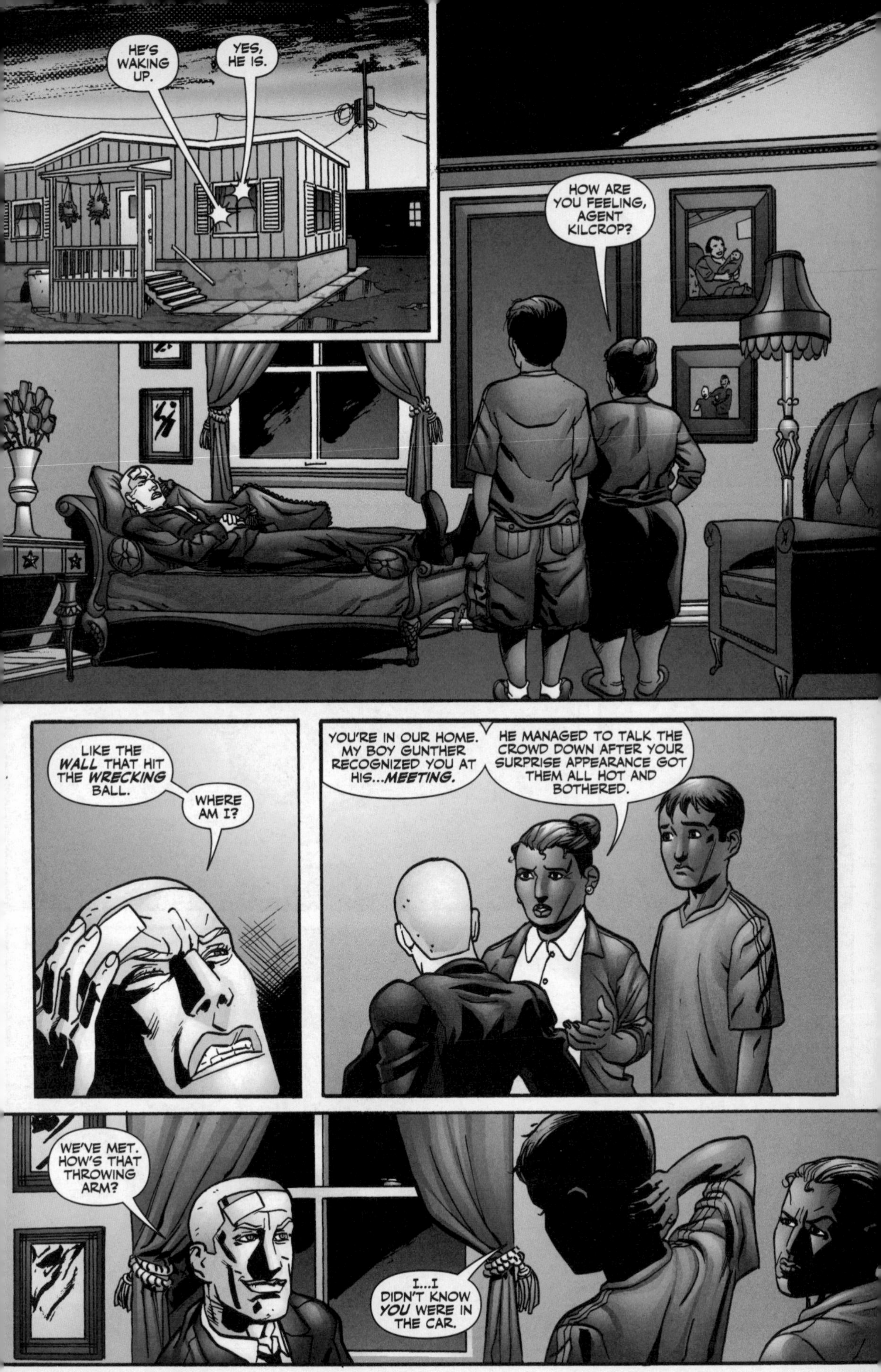

HE'S WAKING UP.
YES, HE IS.
HOW ARE YOU FEELING, AGENT KILCROP?
LIKE THE WALL THAT HIT THE WRECKING BALL.
WHERE AM I?
YOU'RE IN OUR HOME. MY BOY GUNTHER RECOGNIZED YOU AT HIS...MEETING.
HE MANAGED TO TALK THE CROWD DOWN AFTER YOUR SURPRISE APPEARANCE GOT THEM ALL HOT AND BOTHERED.
WE'VE MET. HOW'S THAT THROWING ARM?
I...I DIDN'T KNOW YOU WERE IN THE CAR.

I'M SORRY ABOUT YOUR FATHER, GUNTHER.

BUT I *PROMISE* YOU: I WILL FIND THE MEN WHO MUR--THE MEN *RESPONSIBLE*.

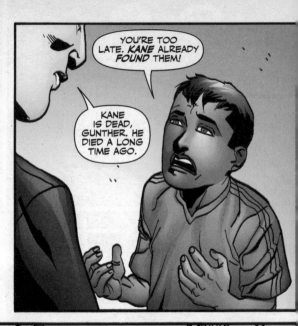

YOU'RE TOO LATE. *KANE* ALREADY *FOUND* THEM!

KANE IS DEAD, GUNTHER. HE DIED A LONG TIME AGO.

GET YOURSELF TO BED, BOY. AND MIND YOU DON'T WAKE YOUR BROTHER.

HIS FATHER'S DEATH CAME AS SUCH A SHOCK. I DON'T APPROVE, BUT I UNDERSTAND *WHY* GUNTHER'S DRAWN TO THEM...THE *KANITES*.

WE *ALL* WANT JUSTICE. BUT WHEN IT NEVER COMES, ONE BEGINS TO LOOK *ELSEWHERE* FOR HOPE--

THE FIREBRAND WITH THE TATTOOS SAID THREE UN-MEN HAD "FALLEN."

FALLEN? YES, I SUPPOSE SO. CAN'T VERY WELL CALL SOMETHING *DEAD* IF IT WASN'T ALIVE TO *BEGIN* WITH.

AND LAST NIGHT, *ANOTHER* ONE TOOK THE PLUNGE: THE WEE JANUS.

YOUR FLIGHTLESS ANGEL HAS TURNED HERSELF IN.

NIKO?

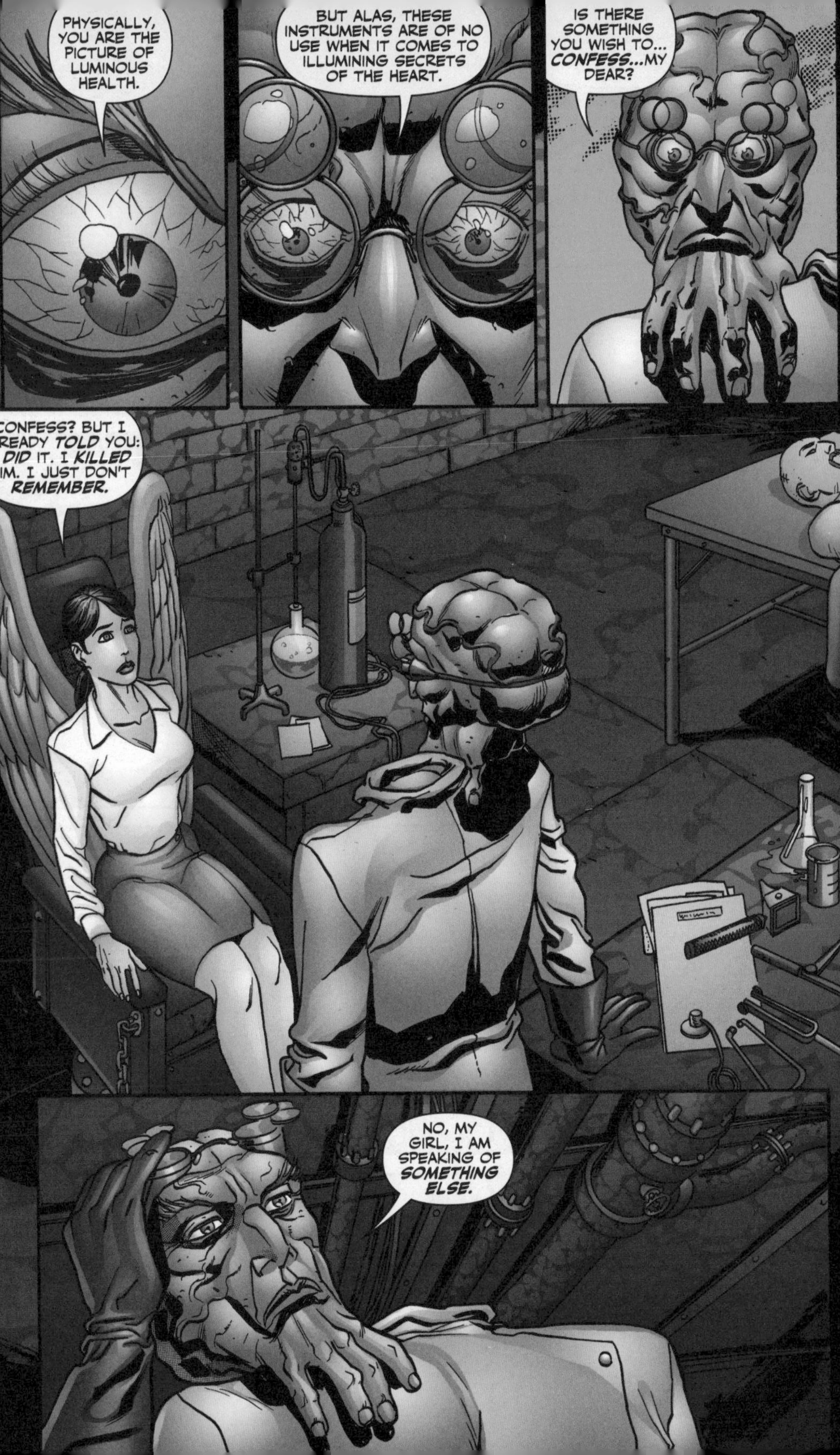
PHYSICALLY, YOU ARE THE PICTURE OF LUMINOUS HEALTH.
BUT ALAS, THESE INSTRUMENTS ARE OF NO USE WHEN IT COMES TO ILLUMINING SECRETS OF THE HEART.
IS THERE SOMETHING YOU WISH TO... CONFESS...MY DEAR?
CONFESS? BUT I ALREADY TOLD YOU: I DID IT. I KILLED HIM. I JUST DON'T REMEMBER.
NO, MY GIRL, I AM SPEAKING OF SOMETHING ELSE.

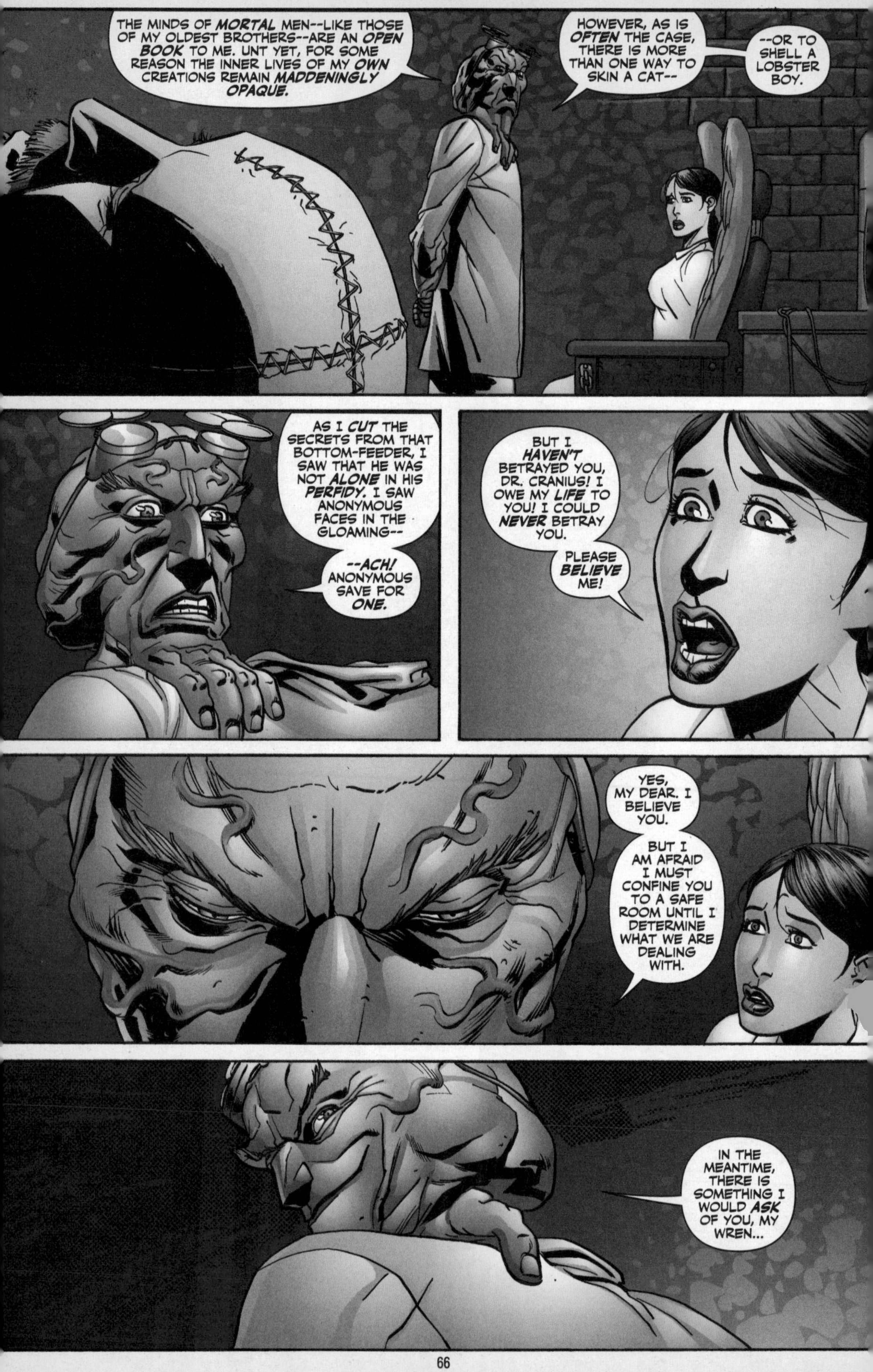
THE MINDS OF MORTAL MEN--LIKE THOSE OF MY OLDEST BROTHERS--ARE AN OPEN BOOK TO ME. UNT YET, FOR SOME REASON THE INNER LIVES OF MY OWN CREATIONS REMAIN MADDENINGLY OPAQUE.
HOWEVER, AS IS OFTEN THE CASE, THERE IS MORE THAN ONE WAY TO SKIN A CAT--
--OR TO SHELL A LOBSTER BOY.
AS I CUT THE SECRETS FROM THAT BOTTOM-FEEDER, I SAW THAT HE WAS NOT ALONE IN HIS PERFIDY. I SAW ANONYMOUS FACES IN THE GLOAMING--
--ACH! ANONYMOUS SAVE FOR ONE.
BUT I HAVEN'T BETRAYED YOU, DR. CRANIUS! I OWE MY LIFE TO YOU! I COULD NEVER BETRAY YOU.
PLEASE BELIEVE ME!
YES, MY DEAR. I BELIEVE YOU.
BUT I AM AFRAID I MUST CONFINE YOU TO A SAFE ROOM UNTIL I DETERMINE WHAT WE ARE DEALING WITH.
IN THE MEANTIME, THERE IS SOMETHING I WOULD ASK OF YOU, MY WREN...

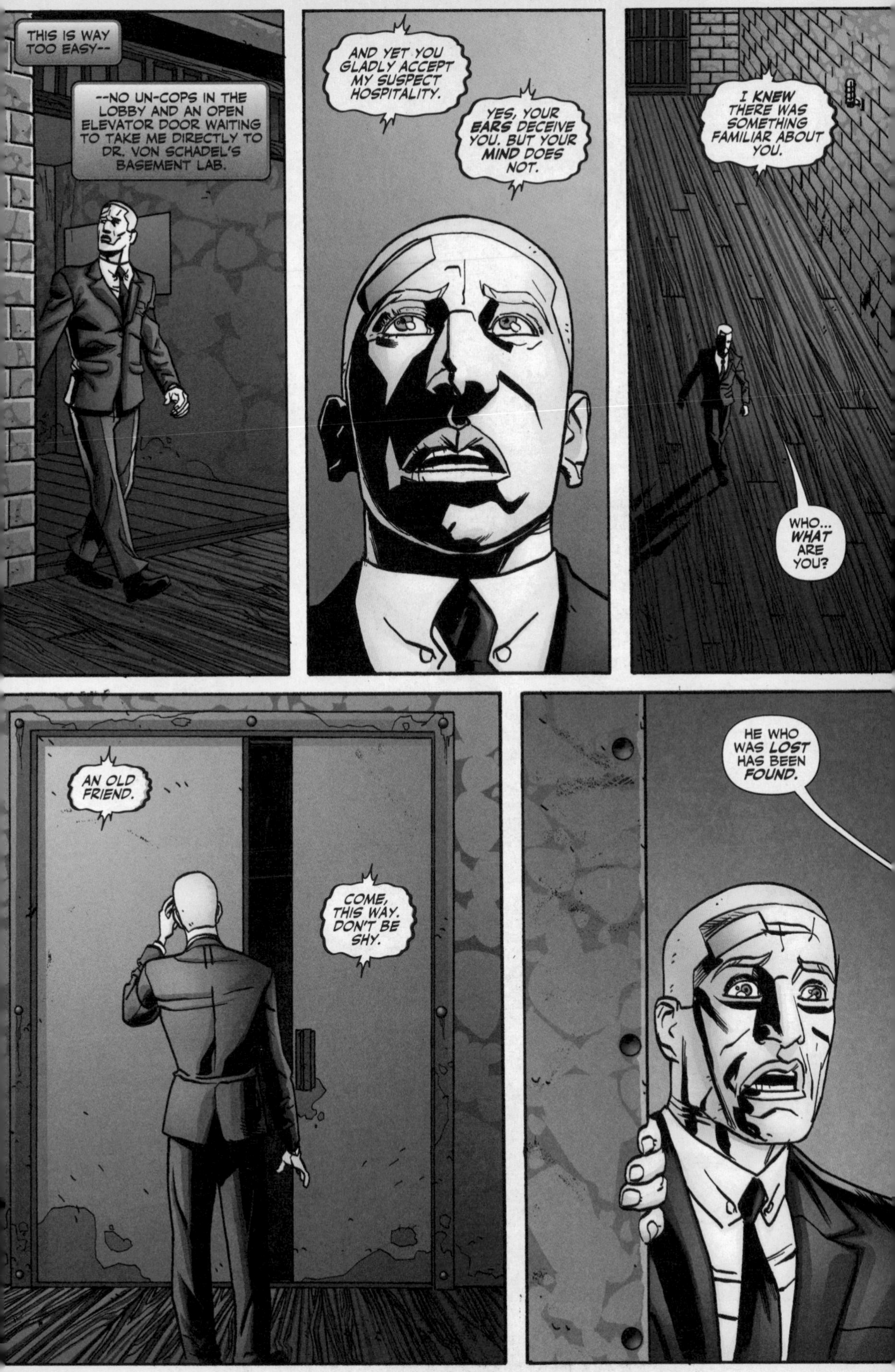
THIS IS WAY TOO EASY--
--NO UN-COPS IN THE LOBBY AND AN OPEN ELEVATOR DOOR WAITING TO TAKE ME DIRECTLY TO DR. VON SCHADEL'S BASEMENT LAB.
AND YET YOU GLADLY ACCEPT MY SUSPECT HOSPITALITY.
YES, YOUR EARS DECEIVE YOU. BUT YOUR MIND DOES NOT.
I KNEW THERE WAS SOMETHING FAMILIAR ABOUT YOU.
WHO... WHAT ARE YOU?
AN OLD FRIEND.
COME, THIS WAY. DON'T BE SHY.
HE WHO WAS LOST HAS BEEN FOUND.

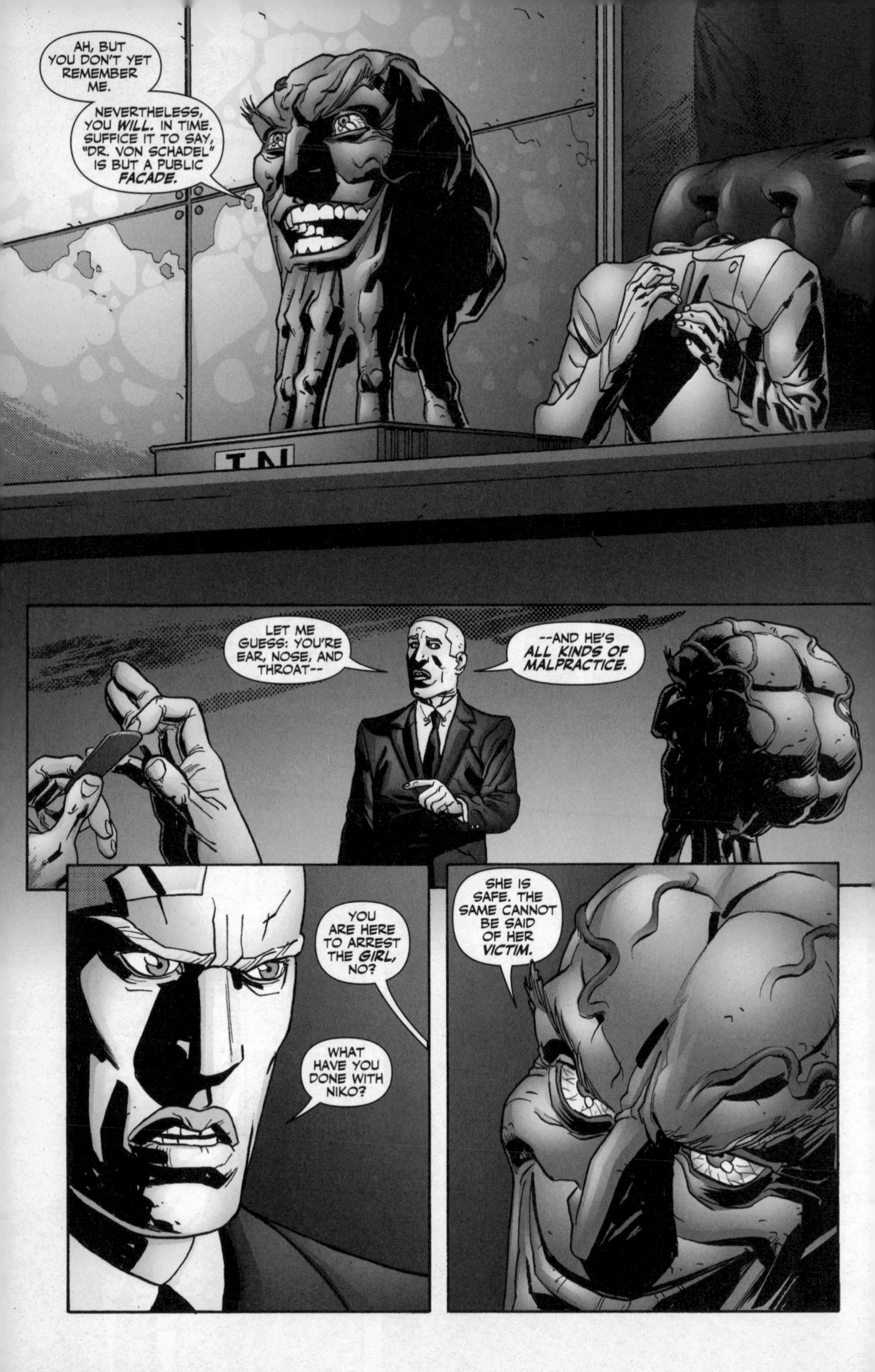
AH, BUT YOU DON'T YET REMEMBER ME.
NEVERTHELESS, YOU *WILL.* IN TIME. SUFFICE IT TO SAY, "DR. VON SCHADEL" IS BUT A PUBLIC *FACADE.*
LET ME GUESS: YOU'RE EAR, NOSE, AND THROAT--
--AND HE'S *ALL KINDS OF MALPRACTICE.*
YOU ARE HERE TO ARREST THE *GIRL,* NO?
WHAT HAVE YOU DONE WITH NIKO?
SHE IS SAFE. THE SAME CANNOT BE SAID OF HER *VICTIM.*

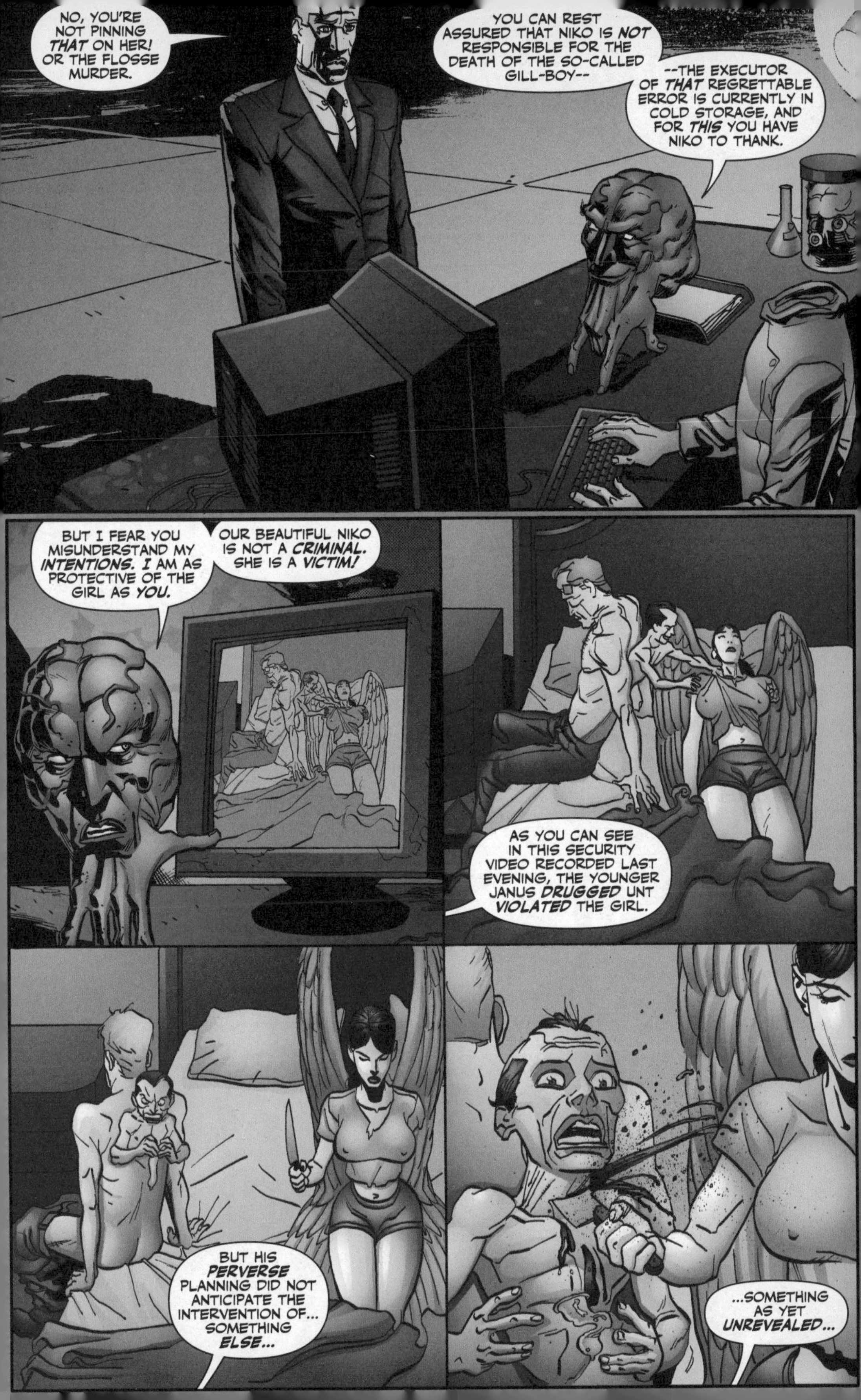
NO, YOU'RE NOT PINNING *THAT* ON HER! OR THE FLOSSE MURDER.
YOU CAN REST ASSURED THAT NIKO IS *NOT* RESPONSIBLE FOR THE DEATH OF THE SO-CALLED GILL-BOY--
--THE EXECUTOR OF *THAT* REGRETTABLE ERROR IS CURRENTLY IN COLD STORAGE, AND FOR *THIS* YOU HAVE NIKO TO THANK.
BUT I FEAR YOU MISUNDERSTAND MY *INTENTIONS. I* AM AS PROTECTIVE OF THE GIRL AS *YOU.*
OUR BEAUTIFUL NIKO IS NOT A *CRIMINAL.* SHE IS A *VICTIM!*
AS YOU CAN SEE IN THIS SECURITY VIDEO RECORDED LAST EVENING, THE YOUNGER JANUS *DRUGGED* UNT *VIOLATED* THE GIRL.
BUT HIS *PERVERSE* PLANNING DID NOT ANTICIPATE THE INTERVENTION OF... SOMETHING *ELSE...*
...SOMETHING AS YET *UNREVEALED...*

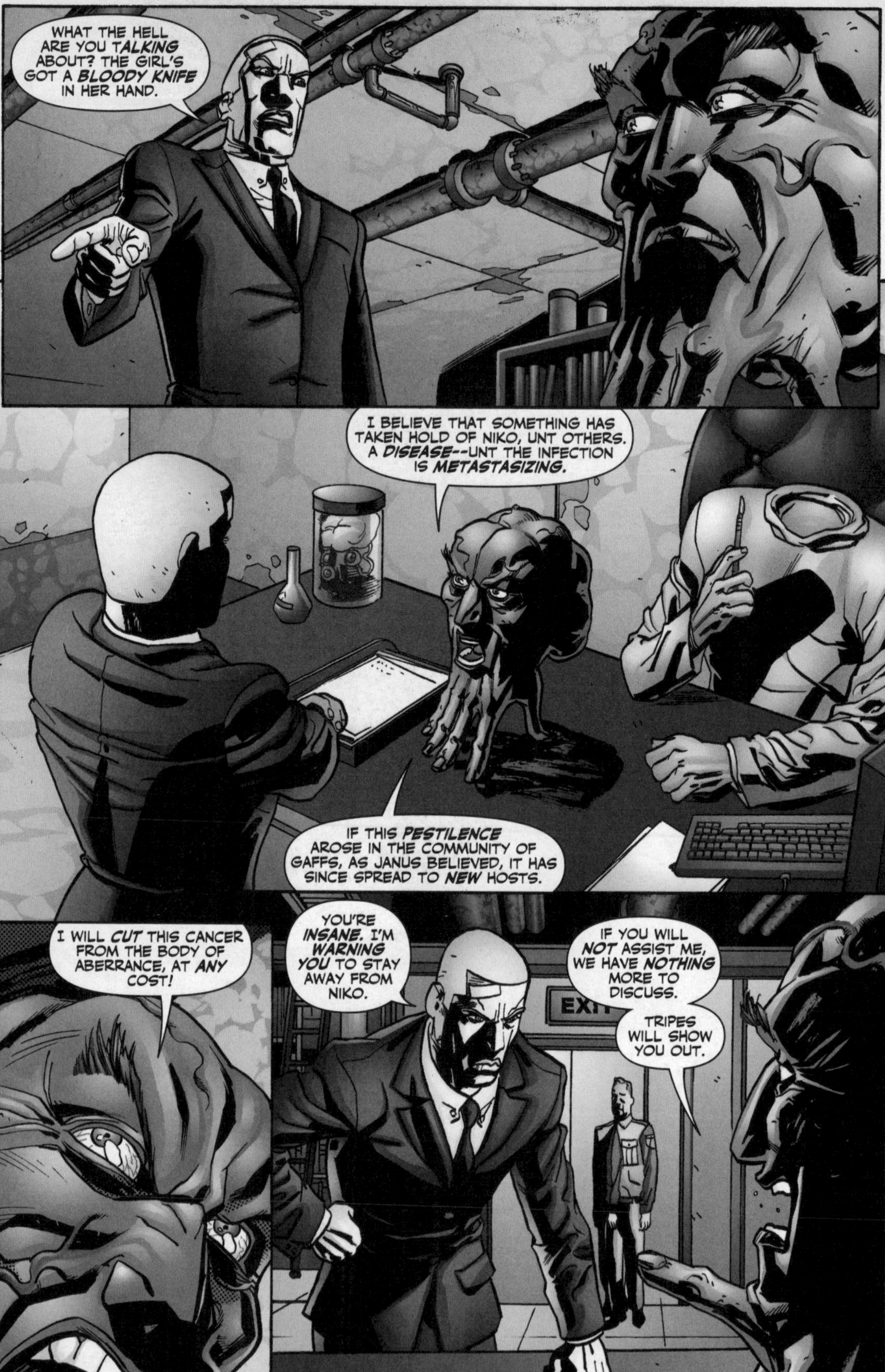
WHAT THE HELL ARE YOU TALKING ABOUT? THE GIRL'S GOT A BLOODY KNIFE IN HER HAND.
I BELIEVE THAT SOMETHING HAS TAKEN HOLD OF NIKO, UNT OTHERS. A DISEASE--UNT THE INFECTION IS METASTASIZING.
IF THIS PESTILENCE AROSE IN THE COMMUNITY OF GAFFS, AS JANUS BELIEVED, IT HAS SINCE SPREAD TO NEW HOSTS.
I WILL CUT THIS CANCER FROM THE BODY OF ABERRANCE, AT ANY COST!
YOU'RE INSANE. I'M WARNING YOU TO STAY AWAY FROM NIKO.
IF YOU WILL NOT ASSIST ME, WE HAVE NOTHING MORE TO DISCUSS.
TRIPES WILL SHOW YOU OUT.
EXIT

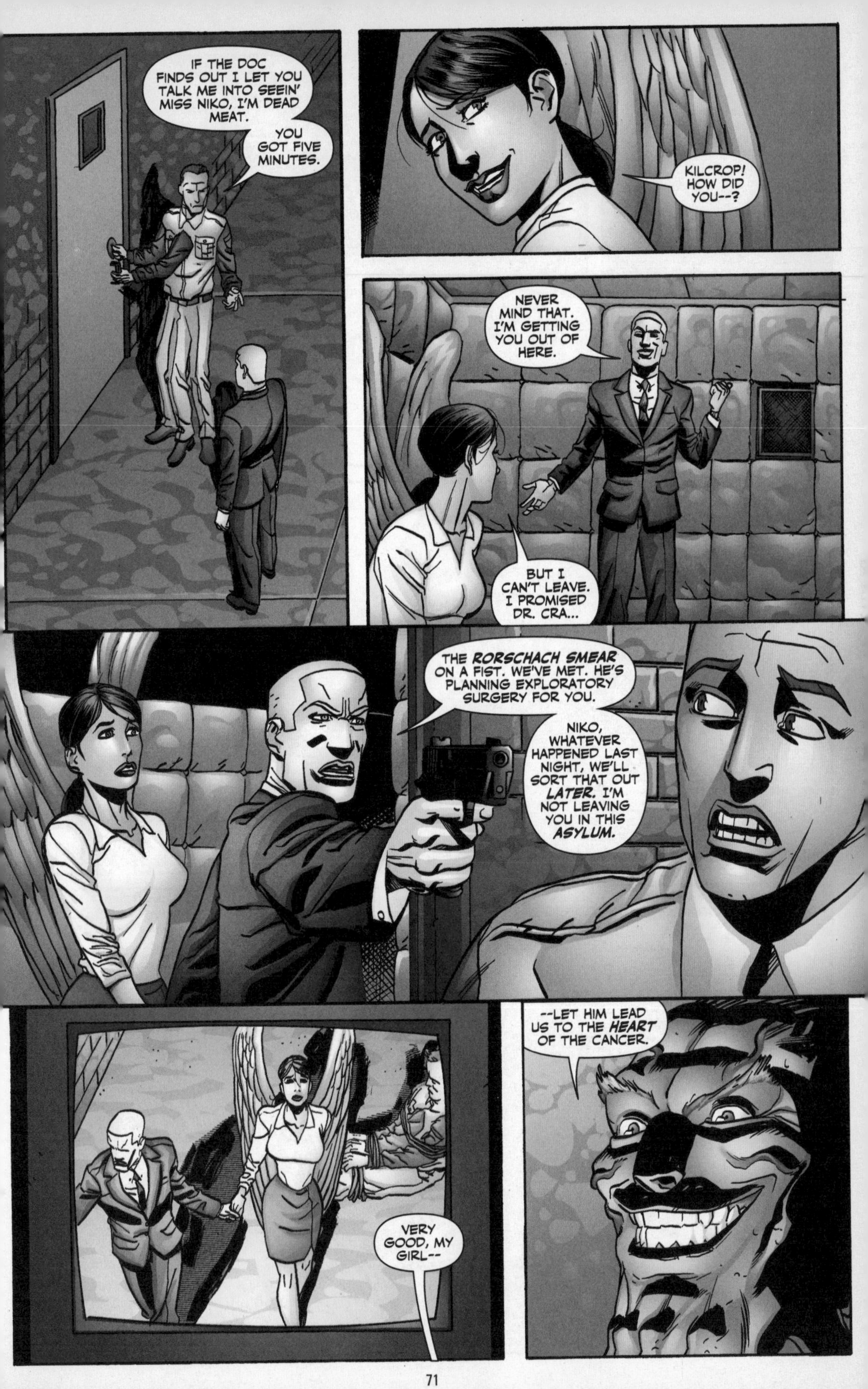
IF THE DOC FINDS OUT I LET YOU TALK ME INTO SEEIN' MISS NIKO, I'M DEAD MEAT.
YOU GOT FIVE MINUTES.
KILCROP! HOW DID YOU--?
NEVER MIND THAT. I'M GETTING YOU OUT OF HERE.
BUT I CAN'T LEAVE. I PROMISED DR. CRA...
THE RORSCHACH SMEAR ON A FIST. WE'VE MET. HE'S PLANNING EXPLORATORY SURGERY FOR YOU.
NIKO, WHATEVER HAPPENED LAST NIGHT, WE'LL SORT THAT OUT LATER. I'M NOT LEAVING YOU IN THIS ASYLUM.
VERY GOOD, MY GIRL--
--LET HIM LEAD US TO THE HEART OF THE CANCER.

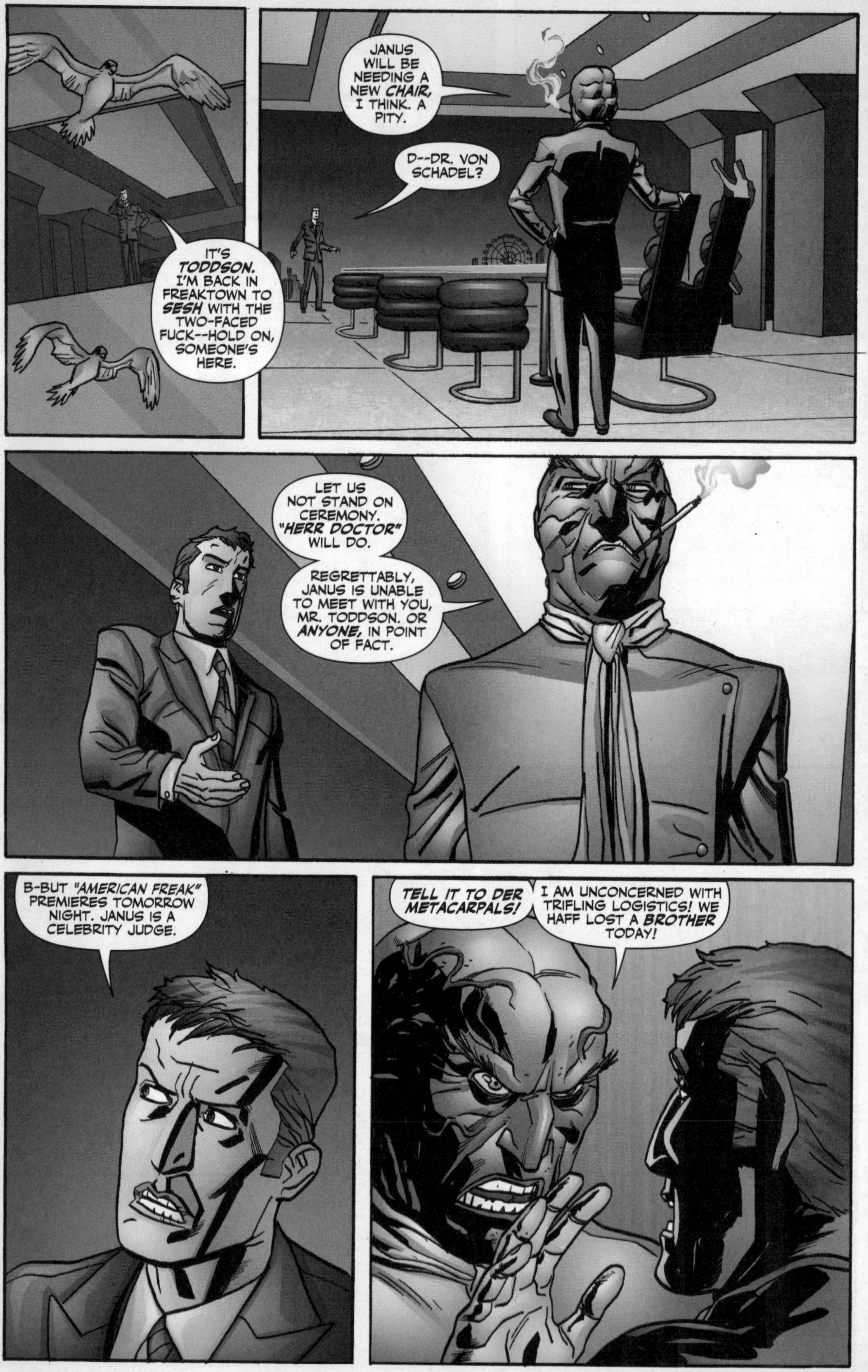
IT'S TODDSON. I'M BACK IN FREAKTOWN TO SESH WITH THE TWO-FACED FUCK--HOLD ON, SOMEONE'S HERE.
JANUS WILL BE NEEDING A NEW CHAIR, I THINK. A PITY.
D--DR. VON SCHADEL?
LET US NOT STAND ON CEREMONY. "HERR DOCTOR" WILL DO.
REGRETTABLY, JANUS IS UNABLE TO MEET WITH YOU, MR. TODDSON. OR ANYONE, IN POINT OF FACT.
B-BUT "AMERICAN FREAK" PREMIERES TOMORROW NIGHT. JANUS IS A CELEBRITY JUDGE.
I AM UNCONCERNED WITH TRIFLING LOGISTICS! WE HAFF LOST A BROTHER TODAY!
TELL IT TO DER METACARPALS!

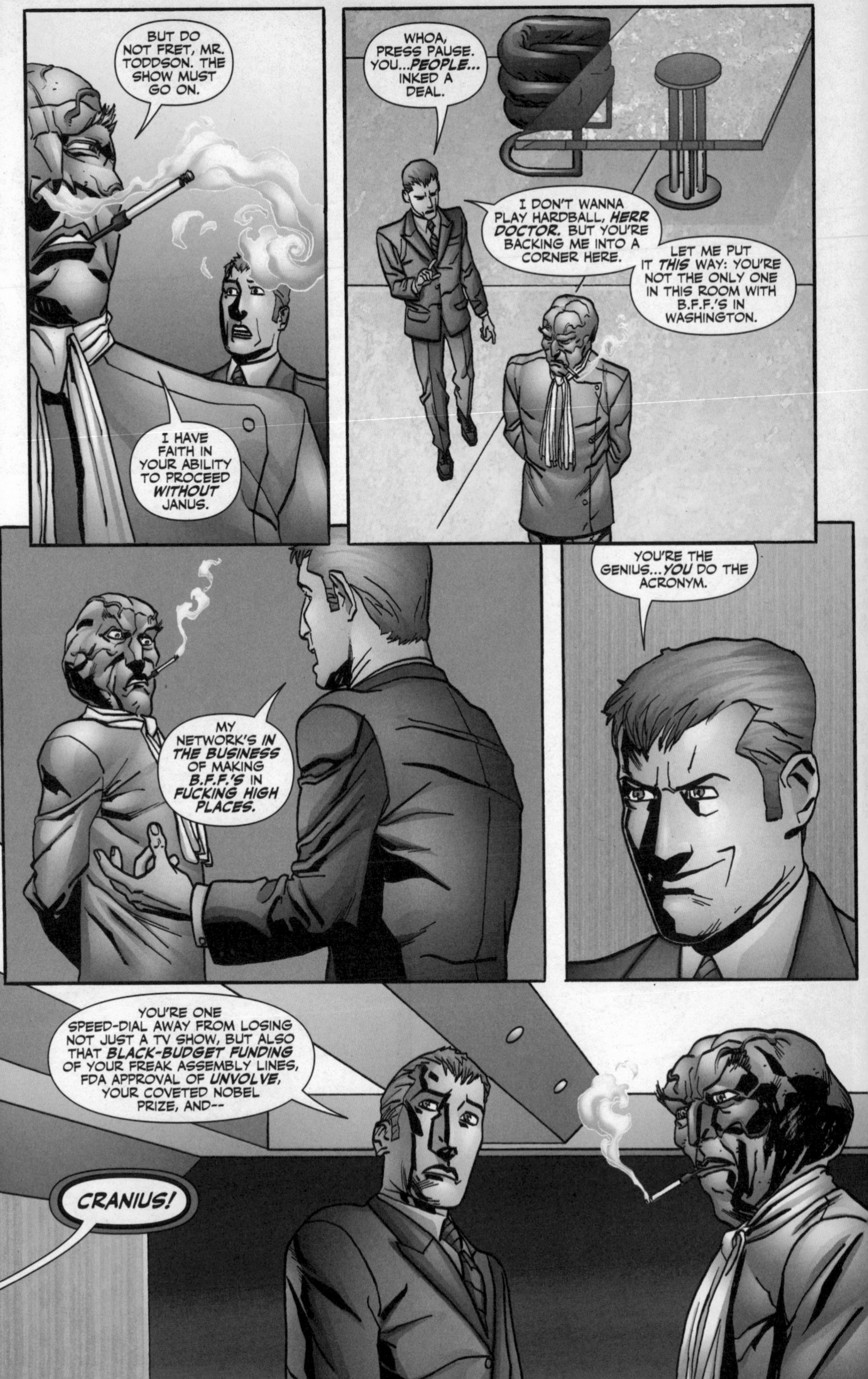
BUT DO NOT FRET, MR. TODDSON. THE SHOW MUST GO ON.
I HAVE FAITH IN YOUR ABILITY TO PROCEED *WITHOUT* JANUS.
WHOA, PRESS PAUSE. YOU...*PEOPLE...* INKED A DEAL.
I DON'T WANNA PLAY HARDBALL, *HERR DOCTOR.* BUT YOU'RE BACKING ME INTO A CORNER HERE.
LET ME PUT IT *THIS* WAY: YOU'RE NOT THE ONLY ONE IN THIS ROOM WITH B.F.F.'S IN WASHINGTON.
MY NETWORK'S *IN THE BUSINESS* OF MAKING *B.F.F.'S* IN *FUCKING HIGH PLACES.*
YOU'RE THE GENIUS...*YOU* DO THE ACRONYM.
YOU'RE ONE SPEED-DIAL AWAY FROM LOSING NOT JUST A TV SHOW, BUT ALSO THAT *BLACK-BUDGET FUNDING* OF YOUR FREAK ASSEMBLY LINES, FDA APPROVAL OF *UNVOLVE,* YOUR COVETED NOBEL PRIZE, AND--
CRANIUS!

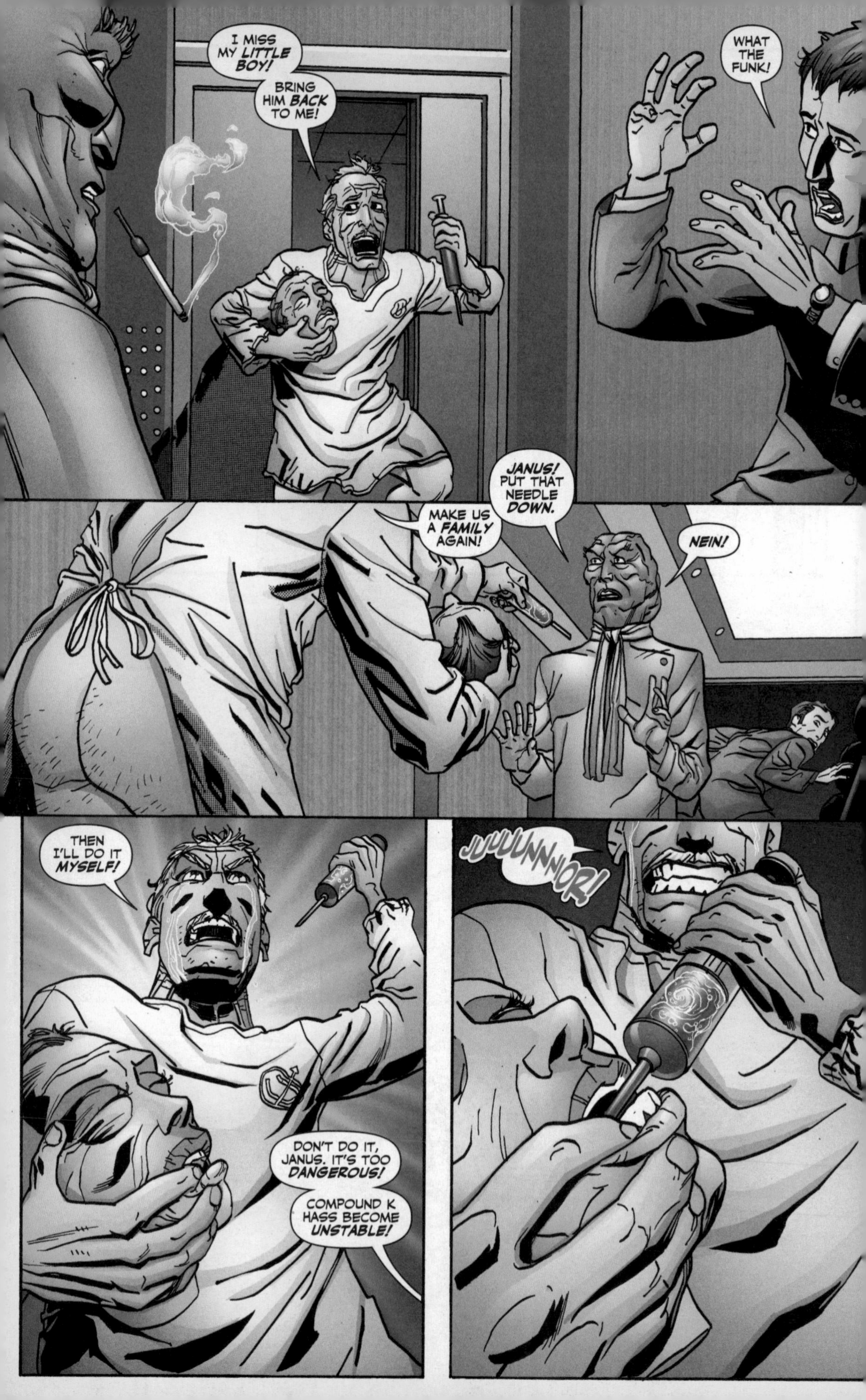
I MISS MY LITTLE BOY!
BRING HIM BACK TO ME!
WHAT THE FUNK!
MAKE US A FAMILY AGAIN!
JANUS! PUT THAT NEEDLE DOWN.
NEIN!
THEN I'LL DO IT MYSELF!
DON'T DO IT, JANUS. IT'S TOO DANGEROUS!
COMPOUND K HASS BECOME UNSTABLE!
JUUUUNNNIOR!

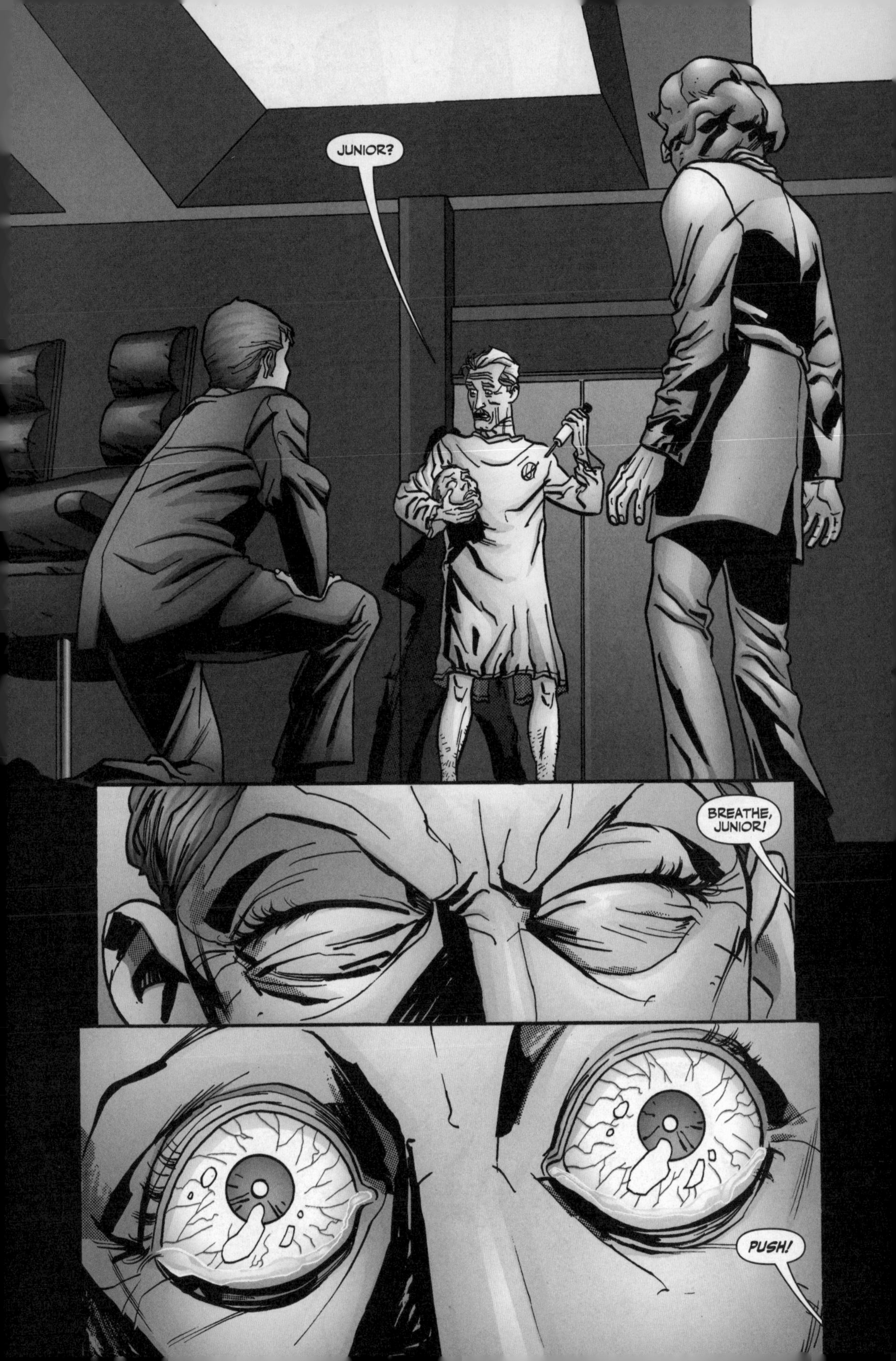
JUNIOR?
BREATHE, JUNIOR!
PUSH!

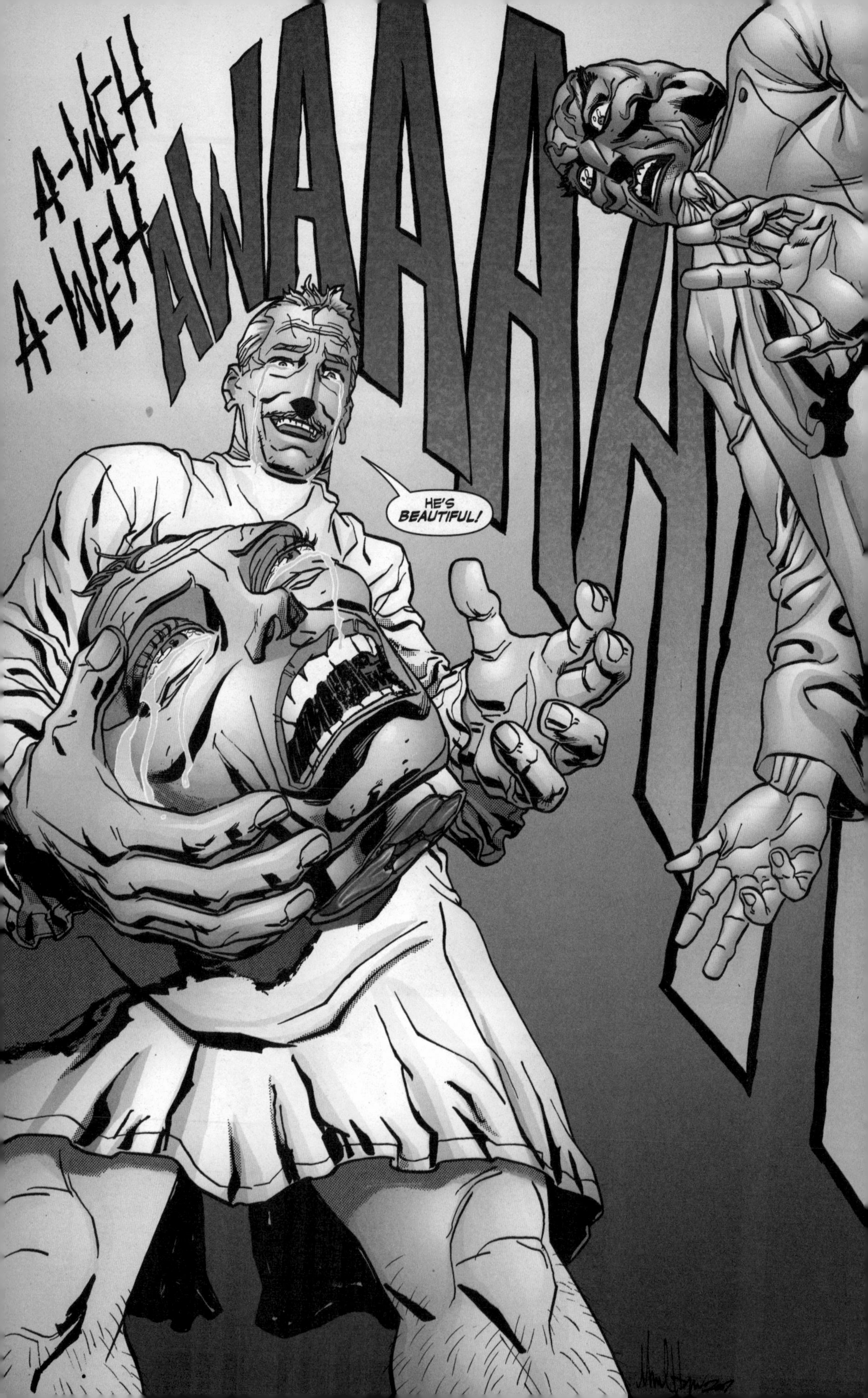
A-WEH A-WEH
AWAAAHHH
HE'S BEAUTIFUL!

"If I had my priorities straight,
I'd be a thousand miles from Aberrance by now."

CHAPTER FOUR

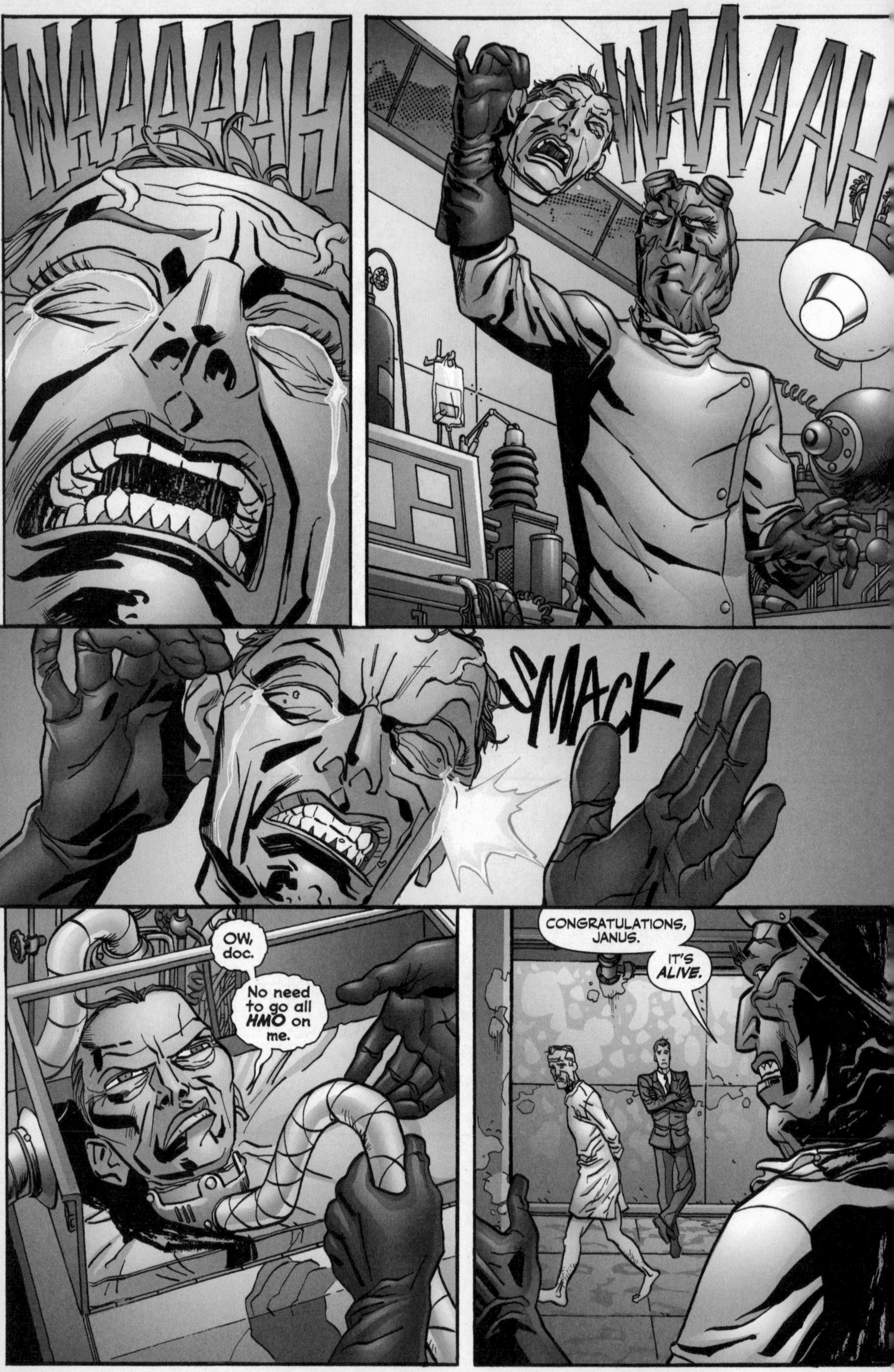
WAAAAAH
WAAAAAH
SMACK
OW, doc.
No need to go all HMO on me.
CONGRATULATIONS, JANUS.
IT'S ALIVE.

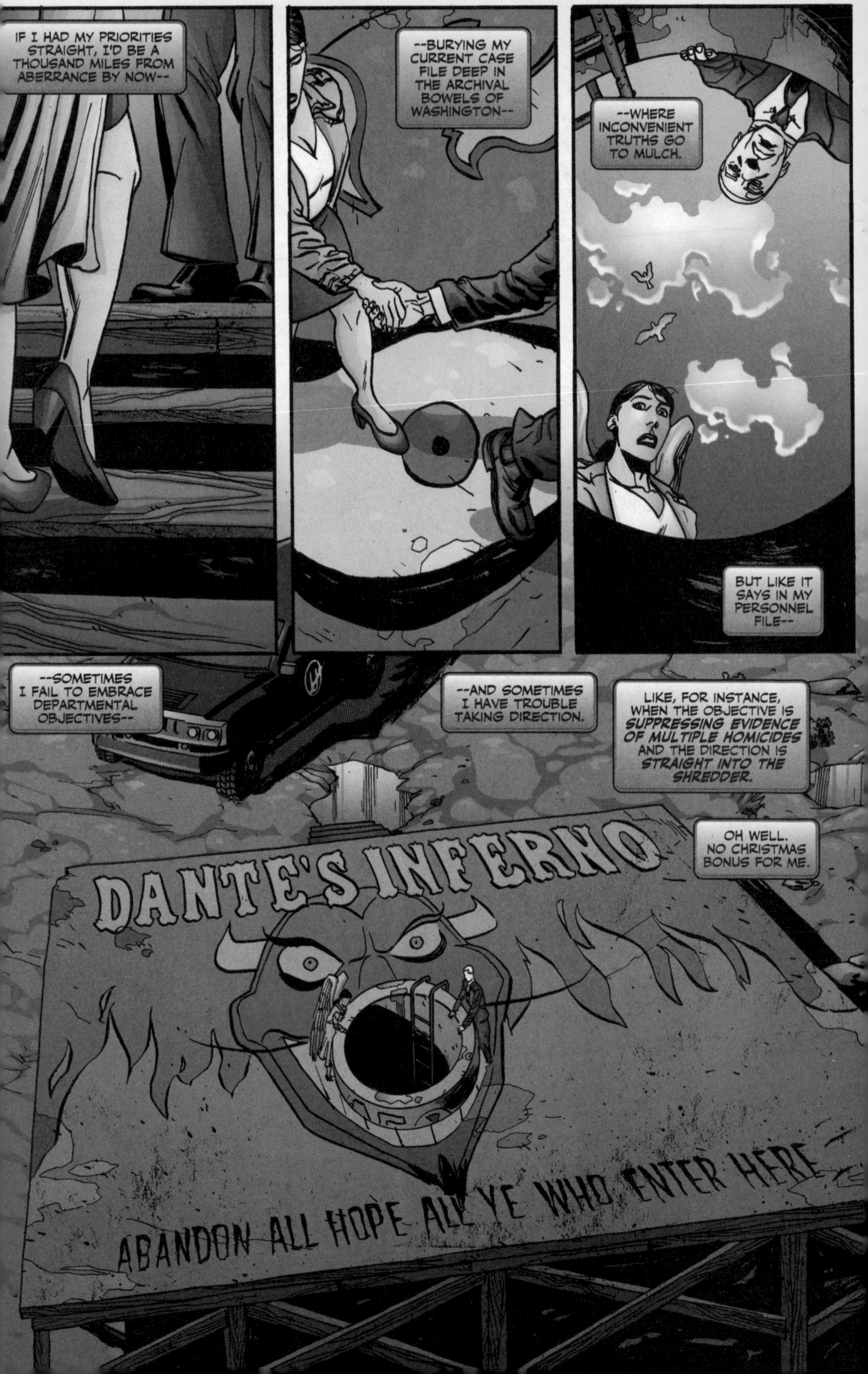
IF I HAD MY PRIORITIES STRAIGHT, I'D BE A THOUSAND MILES FROM ABERRANCE BY NOW--
--BURYING MY CURRENT CASE FILE DEEP IN THE ARCHIVAL BOWELS OF WASHINGTON--
--WHERE INCONVENIENT TRUTHS GO TO MULCH.
BUT LIKE IT SAYS IN MY PERSONNEL FILE--
--SOMETIMES I FAIL TO EMBRACE DEPARTMENTAL OBJECTIVES--
--AND SOMETIMES I HAVE TROUBLE TAKING DIRECTION.
LIKE, FOR INSTANCE, WHEN THE OBJECTIVE IS *SUPPRESSING EVIDENCE OF MULTIPLE HOMICIDES* AND THE DIRECTION IS *STRAIGHT INTO THE SHREDDER.*
OH WELL. NO CHRISTMAS BONUS FOR ME.
DANTE'S INFERNO
ABANDON ALL HOPE ALL YE WHO ENTER HERE

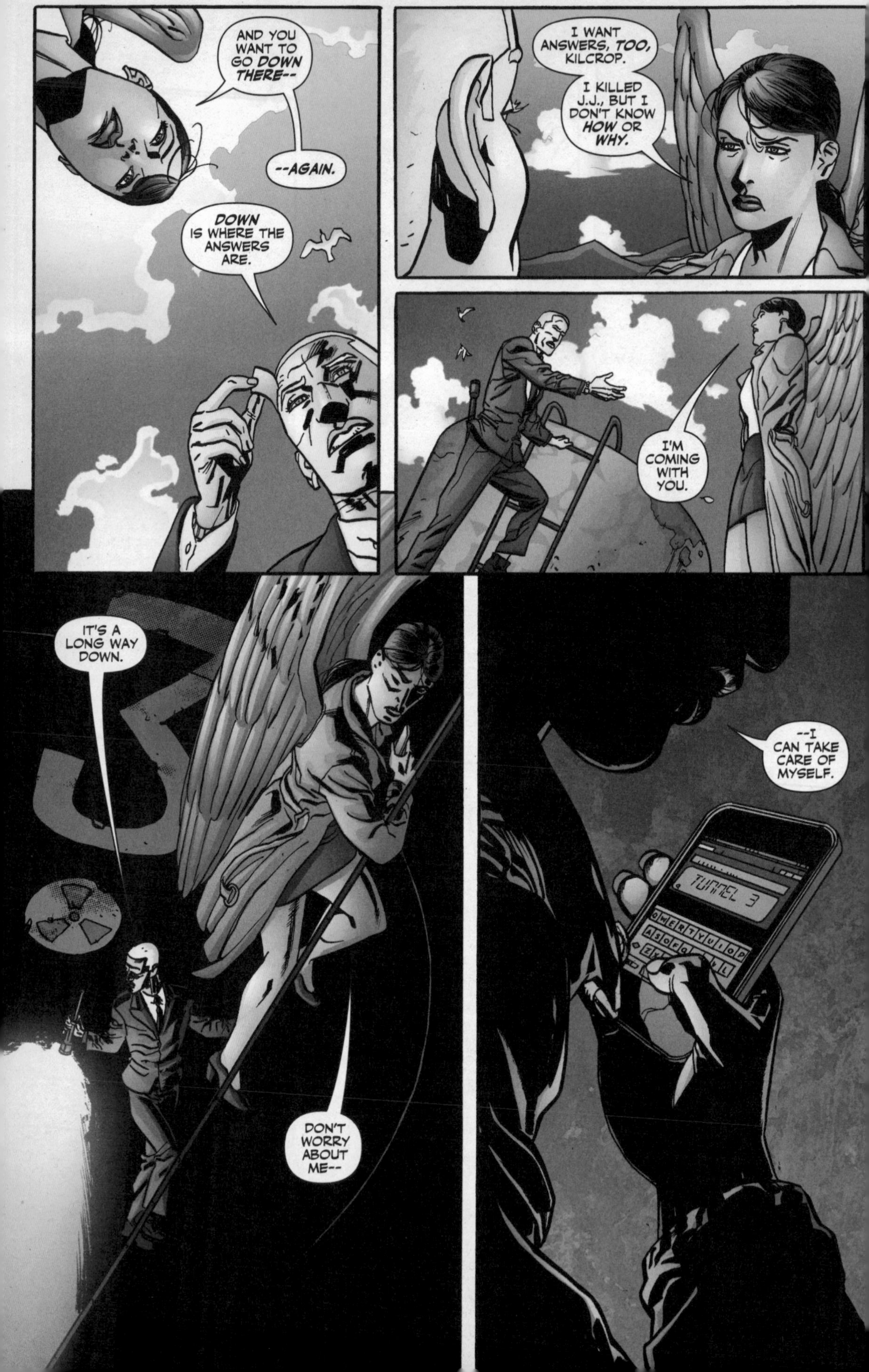
AND YOU WANT TO GO DOWN THERE--
--AGAIN.
DOWN IS WHERE THE ANSWERS ARE.
I WANT ANSWERS, TOO, KILCROP.
I KILLED J.J., BUT I DON'T KNOW HOW OR WHY.
I'M COMING WITH YOU.
IT'S A LONG WAY DOWN.
DON'T WORRY ABOUT ME--
--I CAN TAKE CARE OF MYSELF.
TUNNEL 3

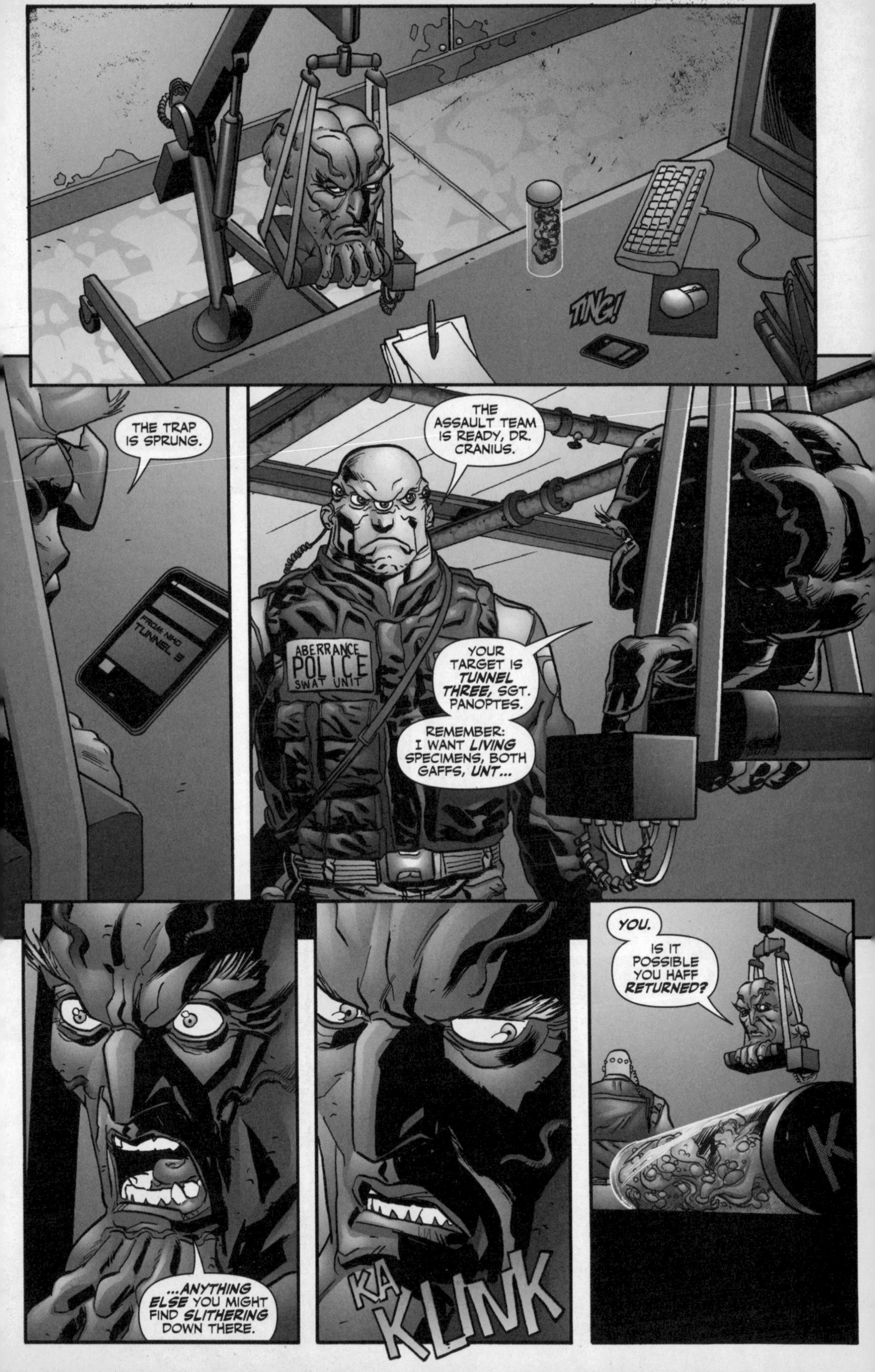
TING!
THE TRAP IS SPRUNG.
FROM NIKO
TUNNEL 3
THE ASSAULT TEAM IS READY, DR. CRANIUS.
ABERRANCE POLICE SWAT UNIT
YOUR TARGET IS TUNNEL THREE, SGT. PANOPTES.
REMEMBER: I WANT LIVING SPECIMENS, BOTH GAFFS, UNT...
...ANYTHING ELSE YOU MIGHT FIND SLITHERING DOWN THERE.
KA KLINK
YOU.
IS IT POSSIBLE YOU HAFF RETURNED?
K

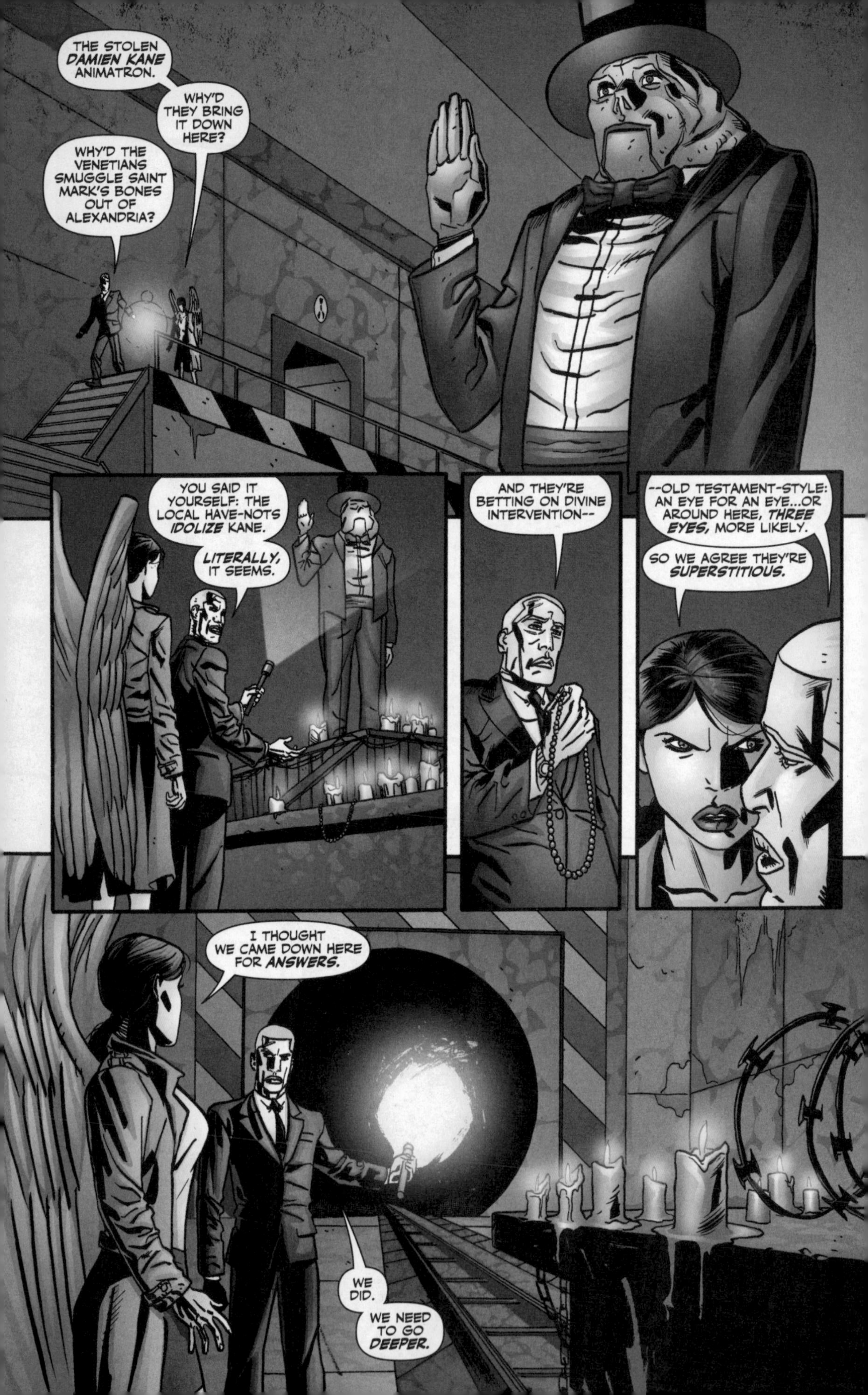
THE STOLEN DAMIEN KANE ANIMATRON.
WHY'D THEY BRING IT DOWN HERE?
WHY'D THE VENETIANS SMUGGLE SAINT MARK'S BONES OUT OF ALEXANDRIA?
YOU SAID IT YOURSELF: THE LOCAL HAVE-NOTS IDOLIZE KANE.
LITERALLY, IT SEEMS.
AND THEY'RE BETTING ON DIVINE INTERVENTION--
--OLD TESTAMENT-STYLE: AN EYE FOR AN EYE...OR AROUND HERE, THREE EYES, MORE LIKELY.
SO WE AGREE THEY'RE SUPERSTITIOUS.
I THOUGHT WE CAME DOWN HERE FOR ANSWERS.
WE DID.
WE NEED TO GO DEEPER.

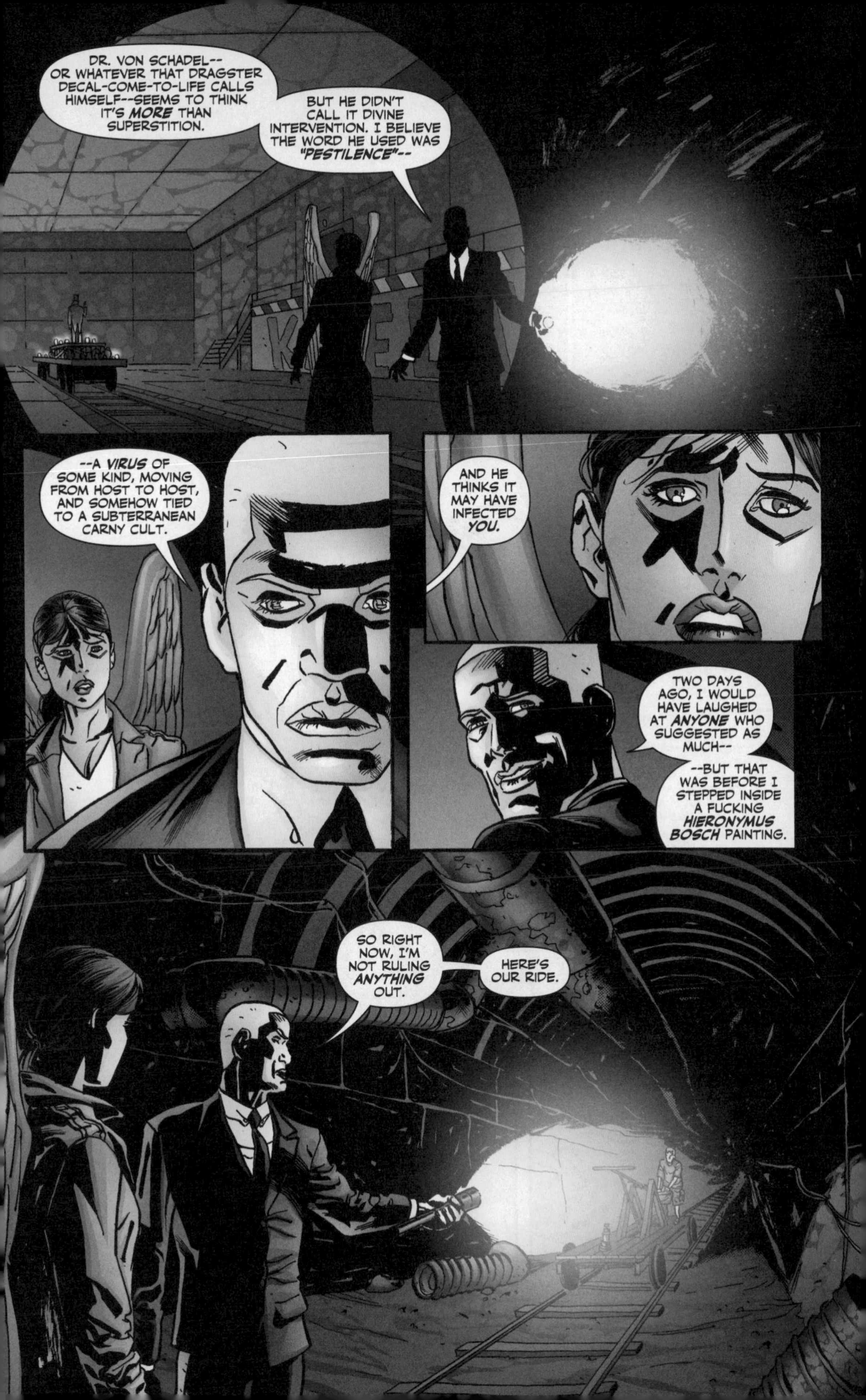
DR. VON SCHADEL-- OR WHATEVER THAT DRAGSTER DECAL-COME-TO-LIFE CALLS HIMSELF--SEEMS TO THINK IT'S *MORE* THAN SUPERSTITION.
BUT HE DIDN'T CALL IT DIVINE INTERVENTION. I BELIEVE THE WORD HE USED WAS *"PESTILENCE"*--
--A *VIRUS* OF SOME KIND, MOVING FROM HOST TO HOST, AND SOMEHOW TIED TO A SUBTERRANEAN CARNY CULT.
AND HE THINKS IT MAY HAVE INFECTED *YOU.*
TWO DAYS AGO, I WOULD HAVE LAUGHED AT *ANYONE* WHO SUGGESTED AS MUCH--
--BUT THAT WAS BEFORE I STEPPED INSIDE A FUCKING *HIERONYMUS BOSCH* PAINTING.
SO RIGHT NOW, I'M NOT RULING *ANYTHING* OUT.
HERE'S OUR RIDE.

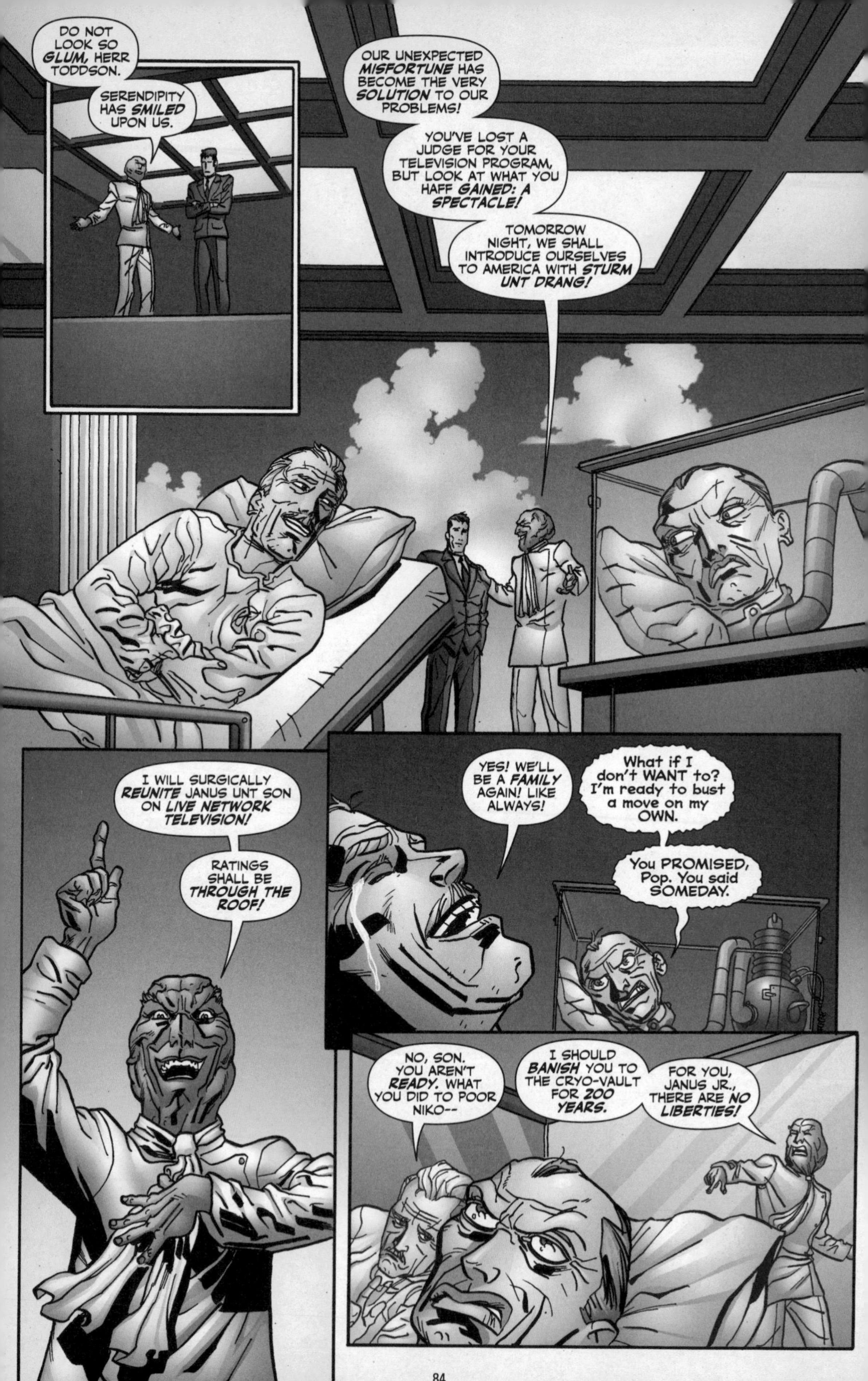
DO NOT LOOK SO GLUM, HERR TODDSON.
SERENDIPITY HAS SMILED UPON US.
OUR UNEXPECTED MISFORTUNE HAS BECOME THE VERY SOLUTION TO OUR PROBLEMS!
YOU'VE LOST A JUDGE FOR YOUR TELEVISION PROGRAM, BUT LOOK AT WHAT YOU HAFF GAINED: A SPECTACLE!
TOMORROW NIGHT, WE SHALL INTRODUCE OURSELVES TO AMERICA WITH STURM UNT DRANG!
I WILL SURGICALLY REUNITE JANUS UNT SON ON LIVE NETWORK TELEVISION!
RATINGS SHALL BE THROUGH THE ROOF!
YES! WE'LL BE A FAMILY AGAIN! LIKE ALWAYS!
What if I don't WANT to? I'm ready to bust a move on my OWN.
You PROMISED, Pop. You said SOMEDAY.
NO, SON. YOU AREN'T READY. WHAT YOU DID TO POOR NIKO--
I SHOULD BANISH YOU TO THE CRYO-VAULT FOR 200 YEARS.
FOR YOU, JANUS JR., THERE ARE NO LIBERTIES!

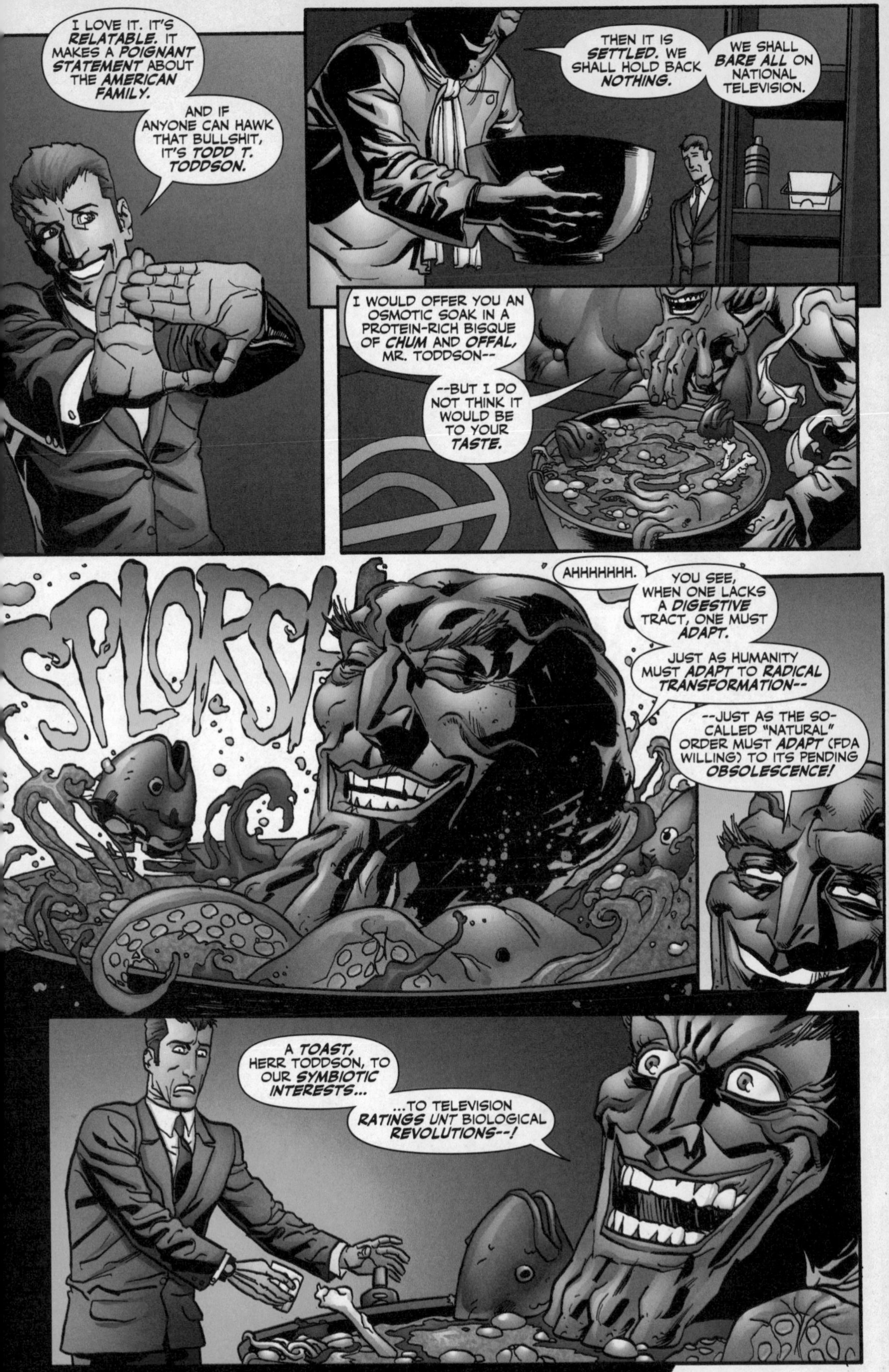

I LOVE IT. IT'S RELATABLE. IT MAKES A POIGNANT STATEMENT ABOUT THE AMERICAN FAMILY.
AND IF ANYONE CAN HAWK THAT BULLSHIT, IT'S TODD T. TODDSON.
THEN IT IS SETTLED. WE SHALL HOLD BACK NOTHING.
WE SHALL BARE ALL ON NATIONAL TELEVISION.
I WOULD OFFER YOU AN OSMOTIC SOAK IN A PROTEIN-RICH BISQUE OF CHUM AND OFFAL, MR. TODDSON--
--BUT I DO NOT THINK IT WOULD BE TO YOUR TASTE.
SPLORSH
AHHHHHHH.
YOU SEE, WHEN ONE LACKS A DIGESTIVE TRACT, ONE MUST ADAPT.
JUST AS HUMANITY MUST ADAPT TO RADICAL TRANSFORMATION--
--JUST AS THE SO-CALLED "NATURAL" ORDER MUST ADAPT (FDA WILLING) TO ITS PENDING OBSOLESCENCE!
A TOAST, HERR TODDSON, TO OUR SYMBIOTIC INTERESTS...
...TO TELEVISION RATINGS UNT BIOLOGICAL REVOLUTIONS--!

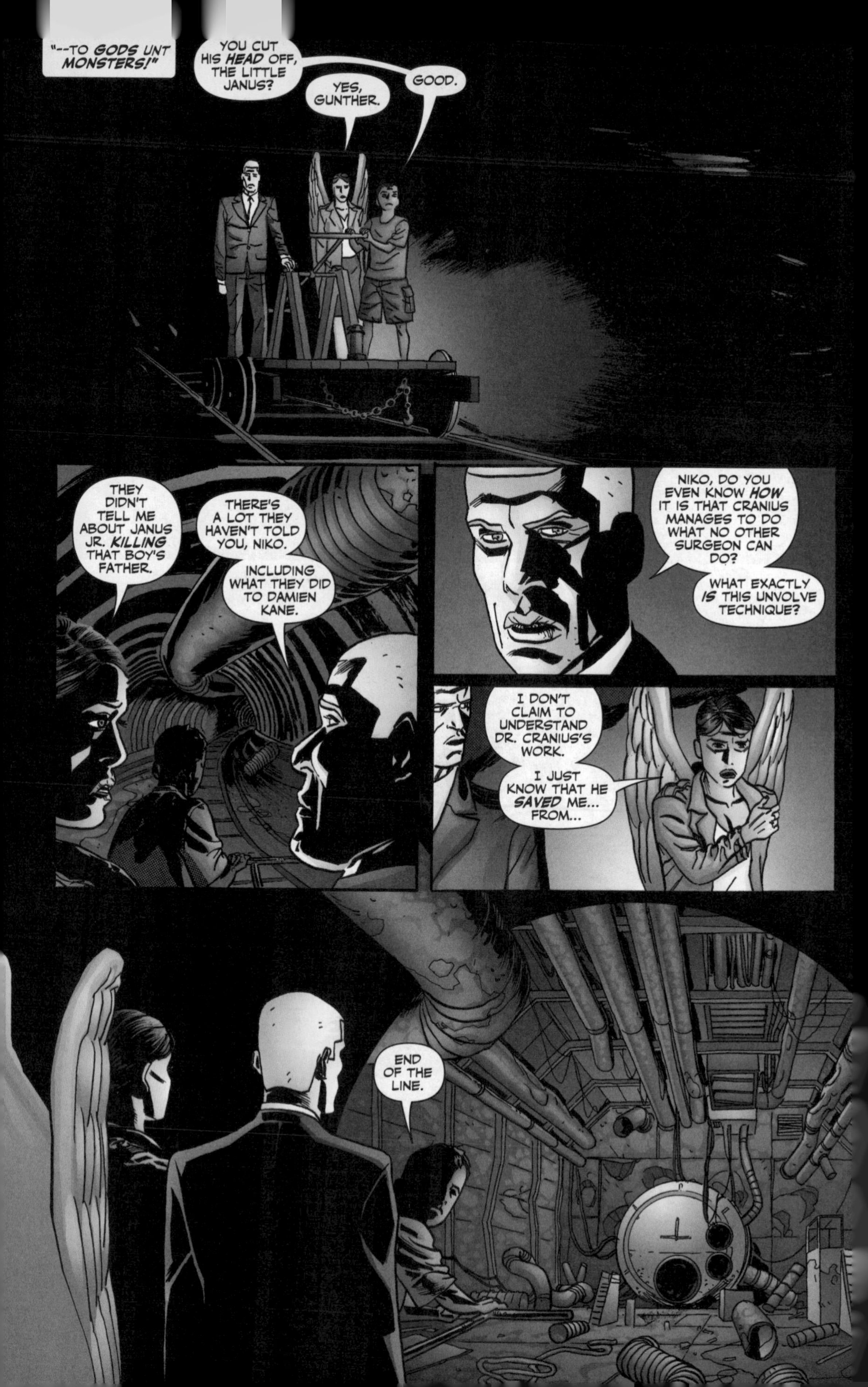
"--TO GODS UNT MONSTERS!"
YOU CUT HIS HEAD OFF, THE LITTLE JANUS?
YES, GUNTHER.
GOOD.
THEY DIDN'T TELL ME ABOUT JANUS JR. KILLING THAT BOY'S FATHER.
THERE'S A LOT THEY HAVEN'T TOLD YOU, NIKO.
INCLUDING WHAT THEY DID TO DAMIEN KANE.
NIKO, DO YOU EVEN KNOW HOW IT IS THAT CRANIUS MANAGES TO DO WHAT NO OTHER SURGEON CAN DO?
WHAT EXACTLY IS THIS UNVOLVE TECHNIQUE?
I DON'T CLAIM TO UNDERSTAND DR. CRANIUS'S WORK.
I JUST KNOW THAT HE SAVED ME... FROM...
END OF THE LINE.

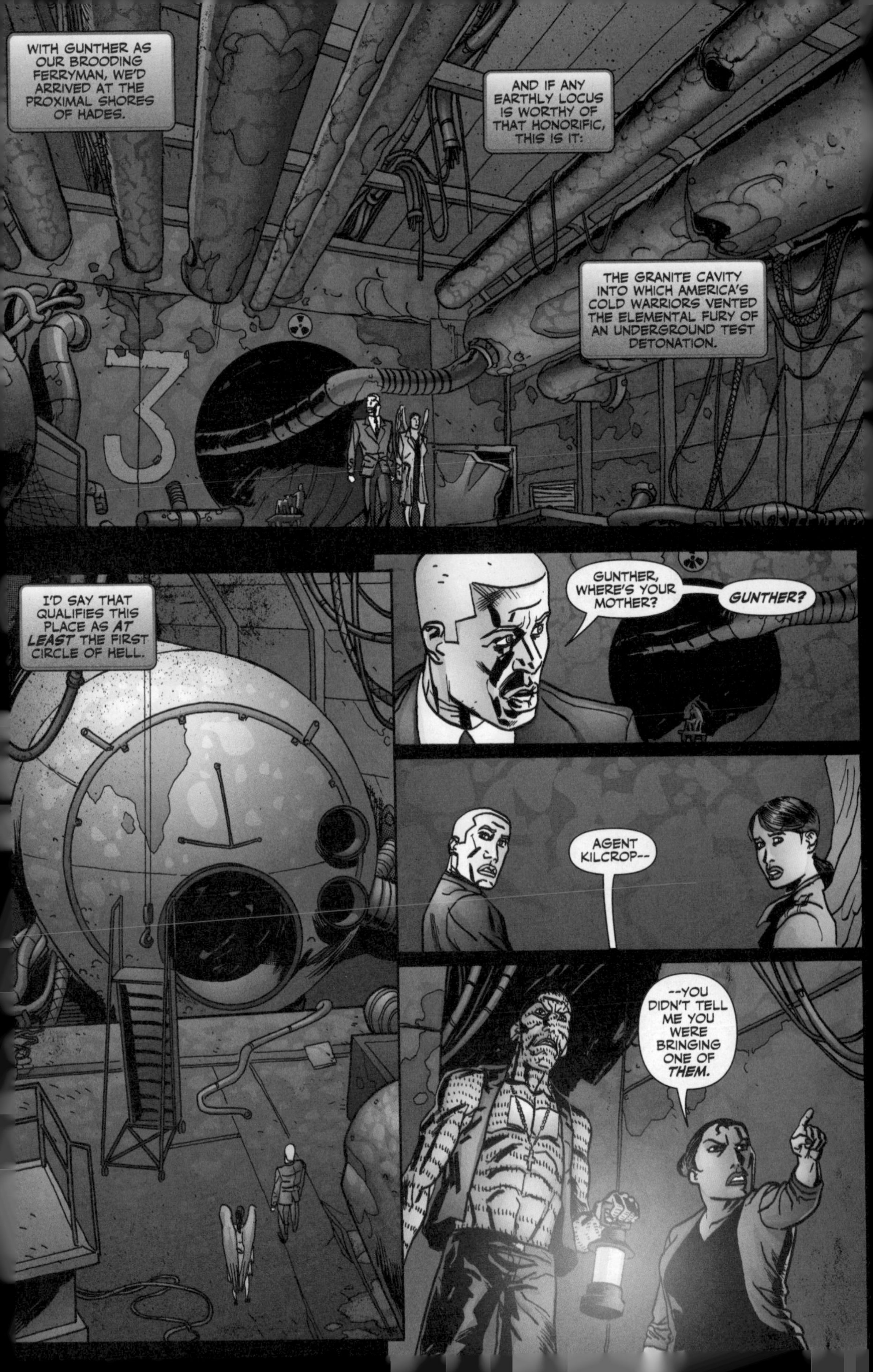
WITH GUNTHER AS OUR BROODING FERRYMAN, WE'D ARRIVED AT THE PROXIMAL SHORES OF HADES.
AND IF ANY EARTHLY LOCUS IS WORTHY OF THAT HONORIFIC, THIS IS IT:
THE GRANITE CAVITY INTO WHICH AMERICA'S COLD WARRIORS VENTED THE ELEMENTAL FURY OF AN UNDERGROUND TEST DETONATION.
3
I'D SAY THAT QUALIFIES THIS PLACE AS *AT LEAST* THE FIRST CIRCLE OF HELL.
GUNTHER, WHERE'S YOUR MOTHER?
GUNTHER?
AGENT KILCROP--
--YOU DIDN'T TELL ME YOU WERE BRINGING ONE OF *THEM.*

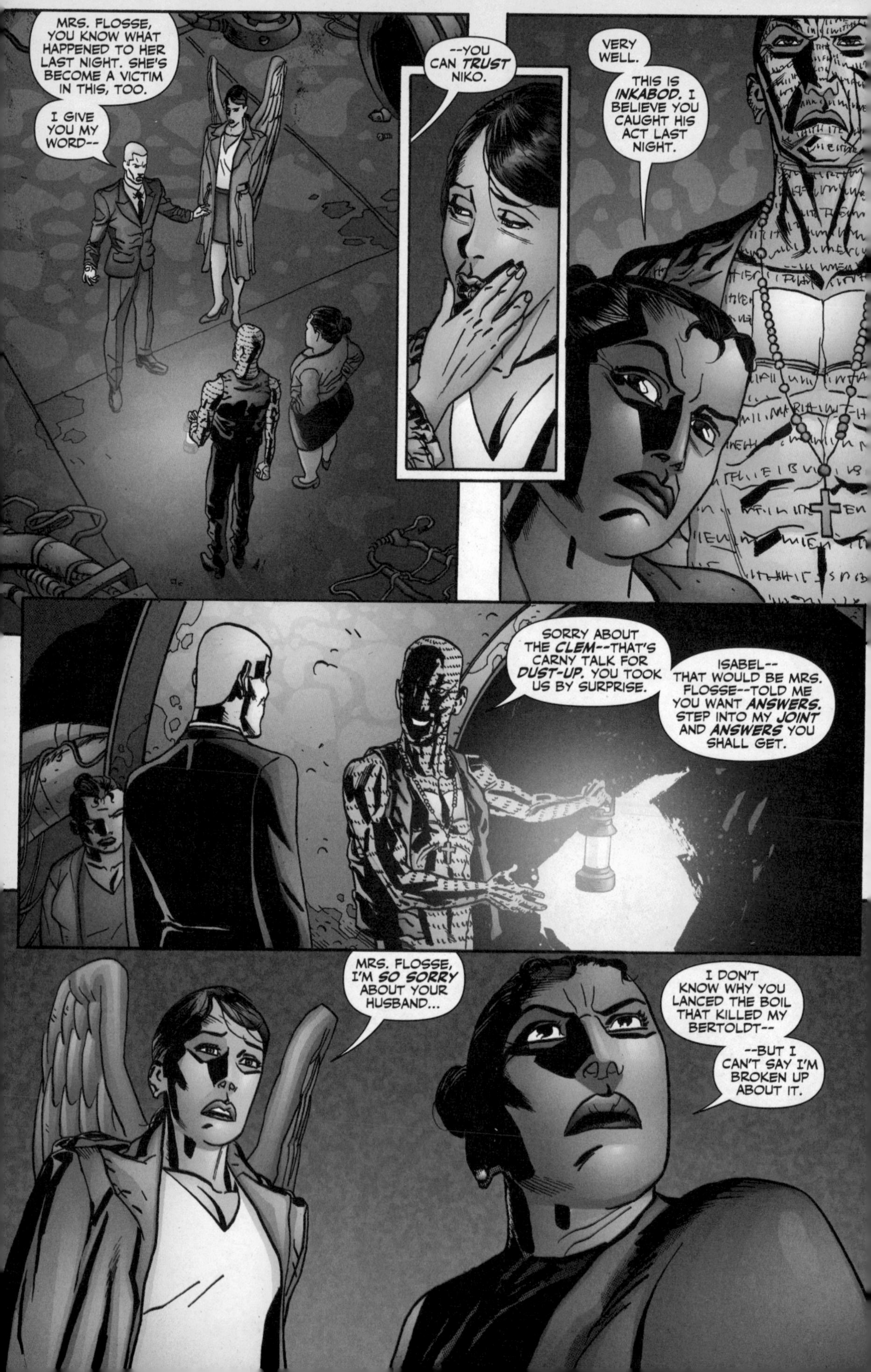
MRS. FLOSSE, YOU KNOW WHAT HAPPENED TO HER LAST NIGHT. SHE'S BECOME A VICTIM IN THIS, TOO.
I GIVE YOU MY WORD--
--YOU CAN TRUST NIKO.
VERY WELL.
THIS IS INKABOD. I BELIEVE YOU CAUGHT HIS ACT LAST NIGHT.
SORRY ABOUT THE CLEM--THAT'S CARNY TALK FOR DUST-UP. YOU TOOK US BY SURPRISE.
ISABEL--THAT WOULD BE MRS. FLOSSE--TOLD ME YOU WANT ANSWERS. STEP INTO MY JOINT AND ANSWERS YOU SHALL GET.
MRS. FLOSSE, I'M SO SORRY ABOUT YOUR HUSBAND...
I DON'T KNOW WHY YOU LANCED THE BOIL THAT KILLED MY BERTOLDT--
--BUT I CAN'T SAY I'M BROKEN UP ABOUT IT.

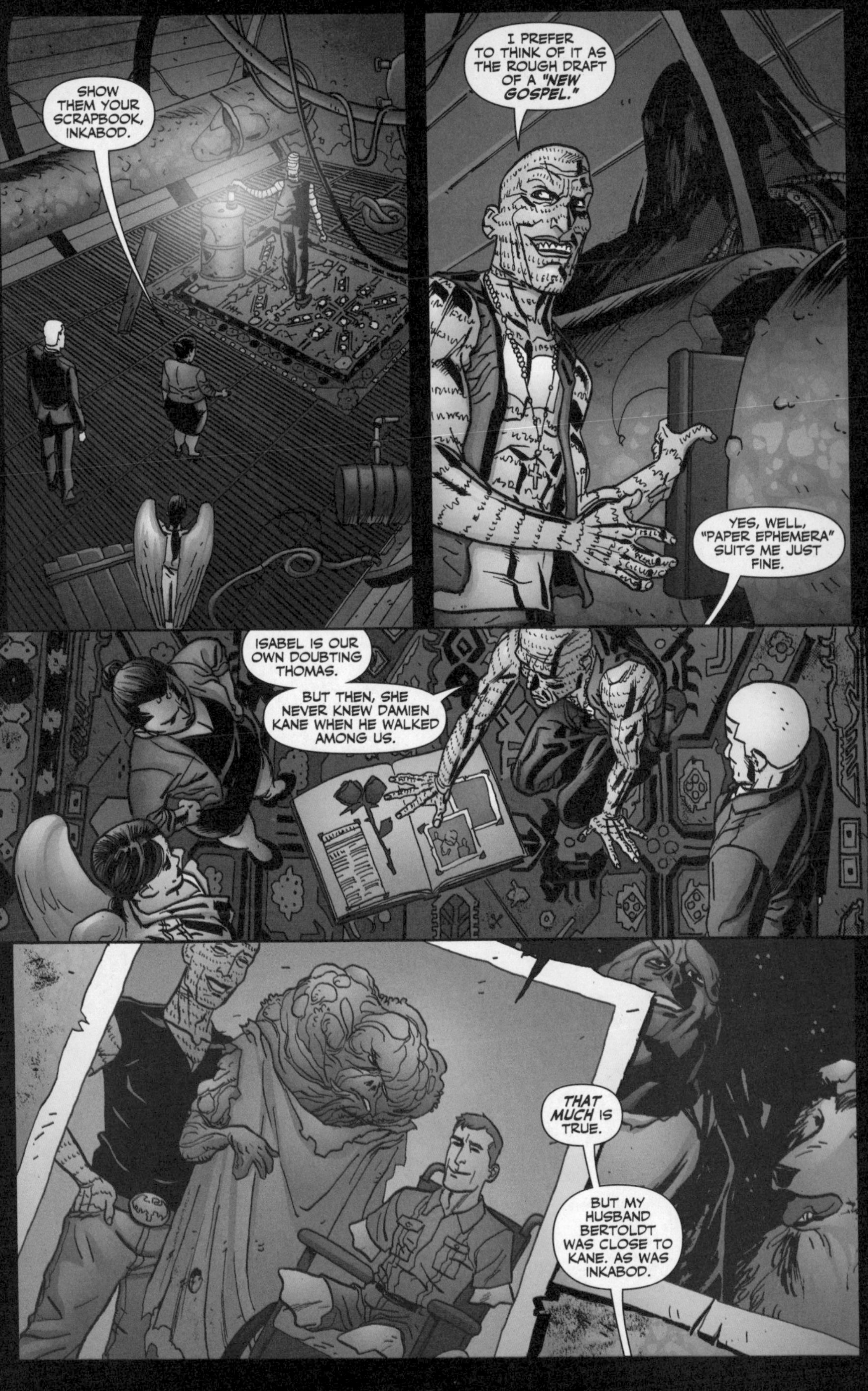
SHOW THEM YOUR SCRAPBOOK, INKABOD.
I PREFER TO THINK OF IT AS THE ROUGH DRAFT OF A "NEW GOSPEL."
YES, WELL, "PAPER EPHEMERA" SUITS ME JUST FINE.
ISABEL IS OUR OWN DOUBTING THOMAS.
BUT THEN, SHE NEVER KNEW DAMIEN KANE WHEN HE WALKED AMONG US.
THAT MUCH IS TRUE.
BUT MY HUSBAND BERTOLDT WAS CLOSE TO KANE. AS WAS INKABOD.

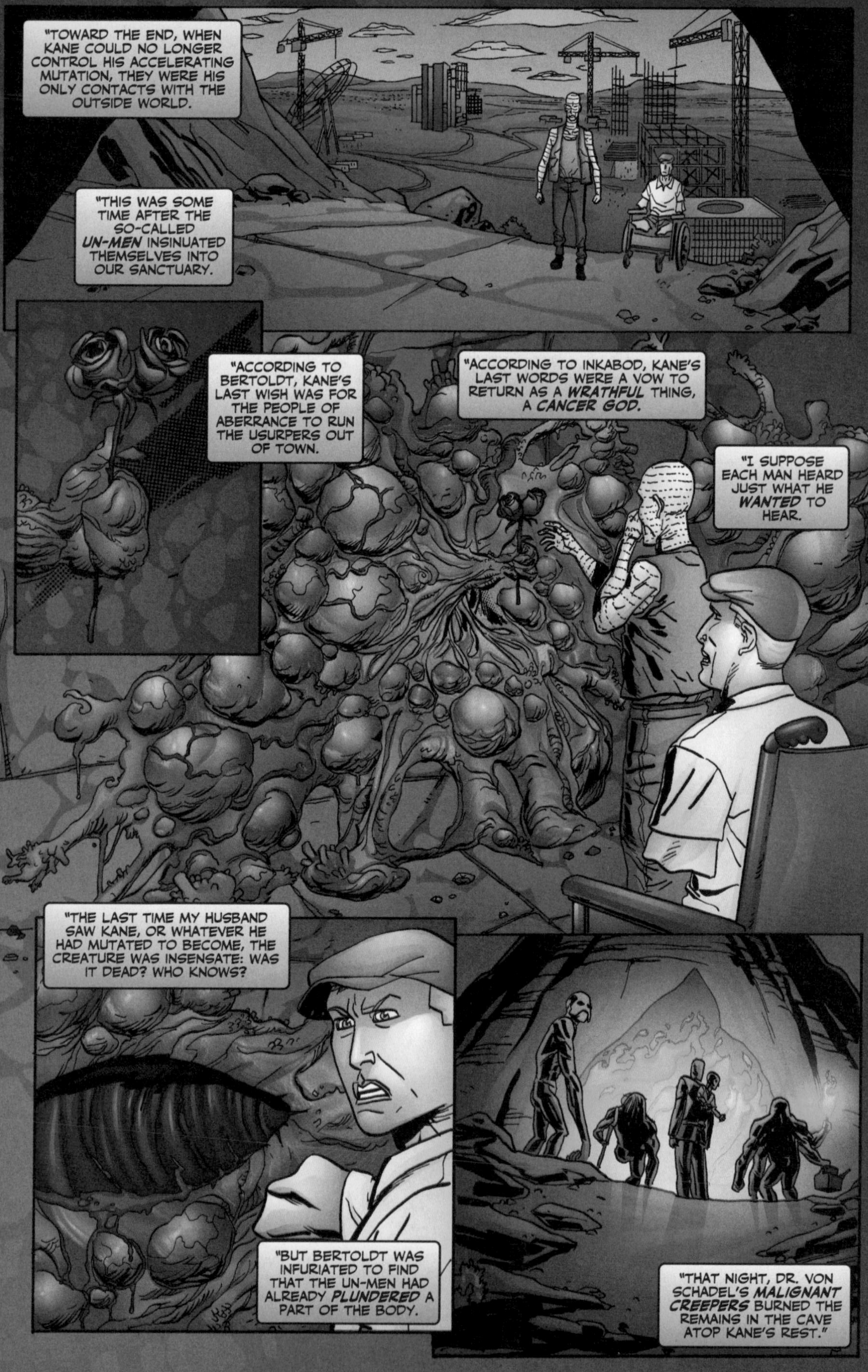
"TOWARD THE END, WHEN KANE COULD NO LONGER CONTROL HIS ACCELERATING MUTATION, THEY WERE HIS ONLY CONTACTS WITH THE OUTSIDE WORLD.
"THIS WAS SOME TIME AFTER THE SO-CALLED UN-MEN INSINUATED THEMSELVES INTO OUR SANCTUARY.
"ACCORDING TO BERTOLDT, KANE'S LAST WISH WAS FOR THE PEOPLE OF ABERRANCE TO RUN THE USURPERS OUT OF TOWN.
"ACCORDING TO INKABOD, KANE'S LAST WORDS WERE A VOW TO RETURN AS A WRATHFUL THING, A CANCER GOD.
"I SUPPOSE EACH MAN HEARD JUST WHAT HE WANTED TO HEAR.
"THE LAST TIME MY HUSBAND SAW KANE, OR WHATEVER HE HAD MUTATED TO BECOME, THE CREATURE WAS INSENSATE: WAS IT DEAD? WHO KNOWS?
"BUT BERTOLDT WAS INFURIATED TO FIND THAT THE UN-MEN HAD ALREADY PLUNDERED A PART OF THE BODY.
"THAT NIGHT, DR. VON SCHADEL'S MALIGNANT CREEPERS BURNED THE REMAINS IN THE CAVE ATOP KANE'S REST."

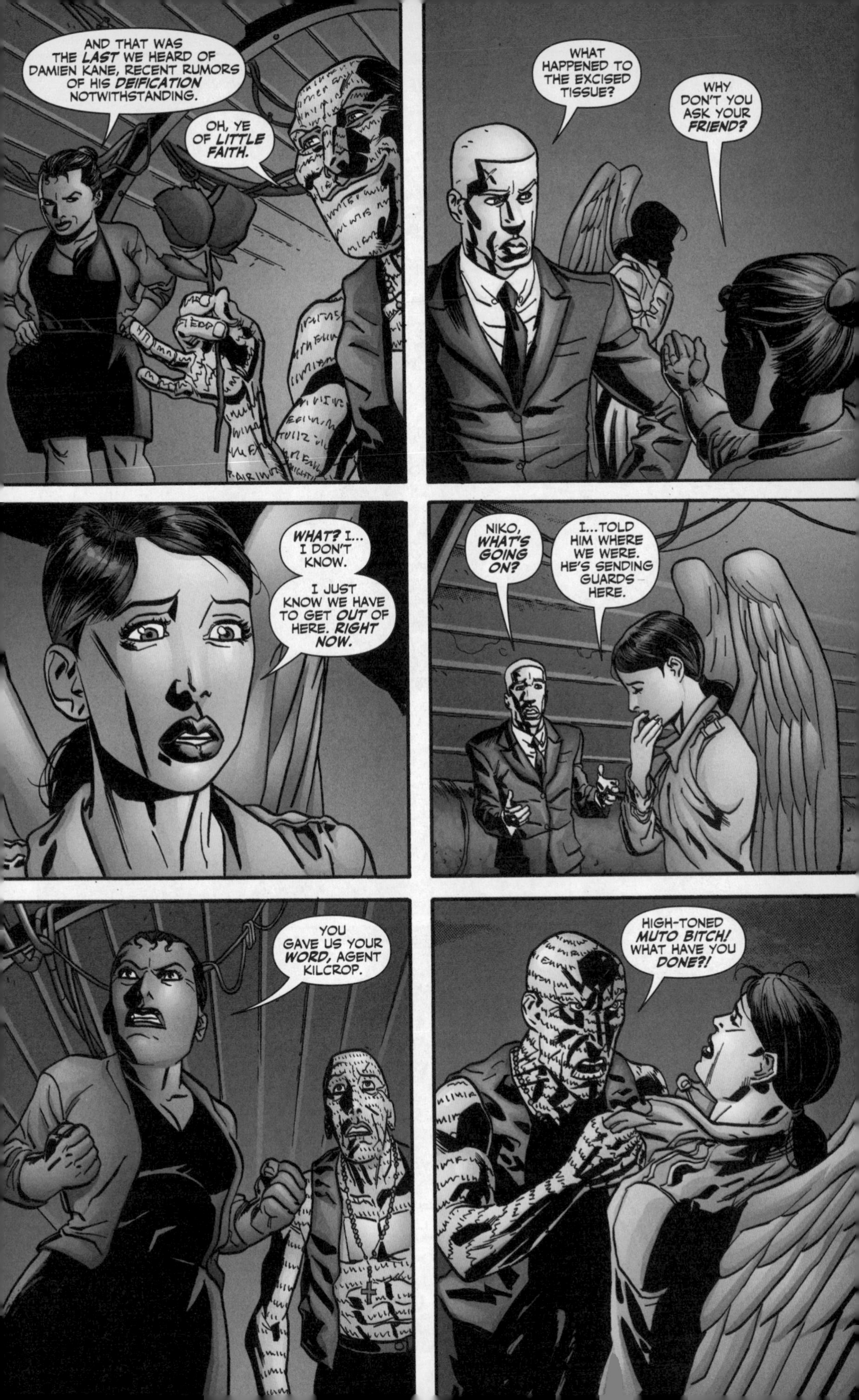
AND THAT WAS THE LAST WE HEARD OF DAMIEN KANE, RECENT RUMORS OF HIS DEIFICATION NOTWITHSTANDING.
OH, YE OF LITTLE FAITH.
WHAT HAPPENED TO THE EXCISED TISSUE?
WHY DON'T YOU ASK YOUR FRIEND?
WHAT? I... I DON'T KNOW.
I JUST KNOW WE HAVE TO GET OUT OF HERE. RIGHT NOW.
NIKO, WHAT'S GOING ON?
I...TOLD HIM WHERE WE WERE. HE'S SENDING GUARDS HERE.
YOU GAVE US YOUR WORD, AGENT KILCROP.
HIGH-TONED MUTO BITCH! WHAT HAVE YOU DONE?!

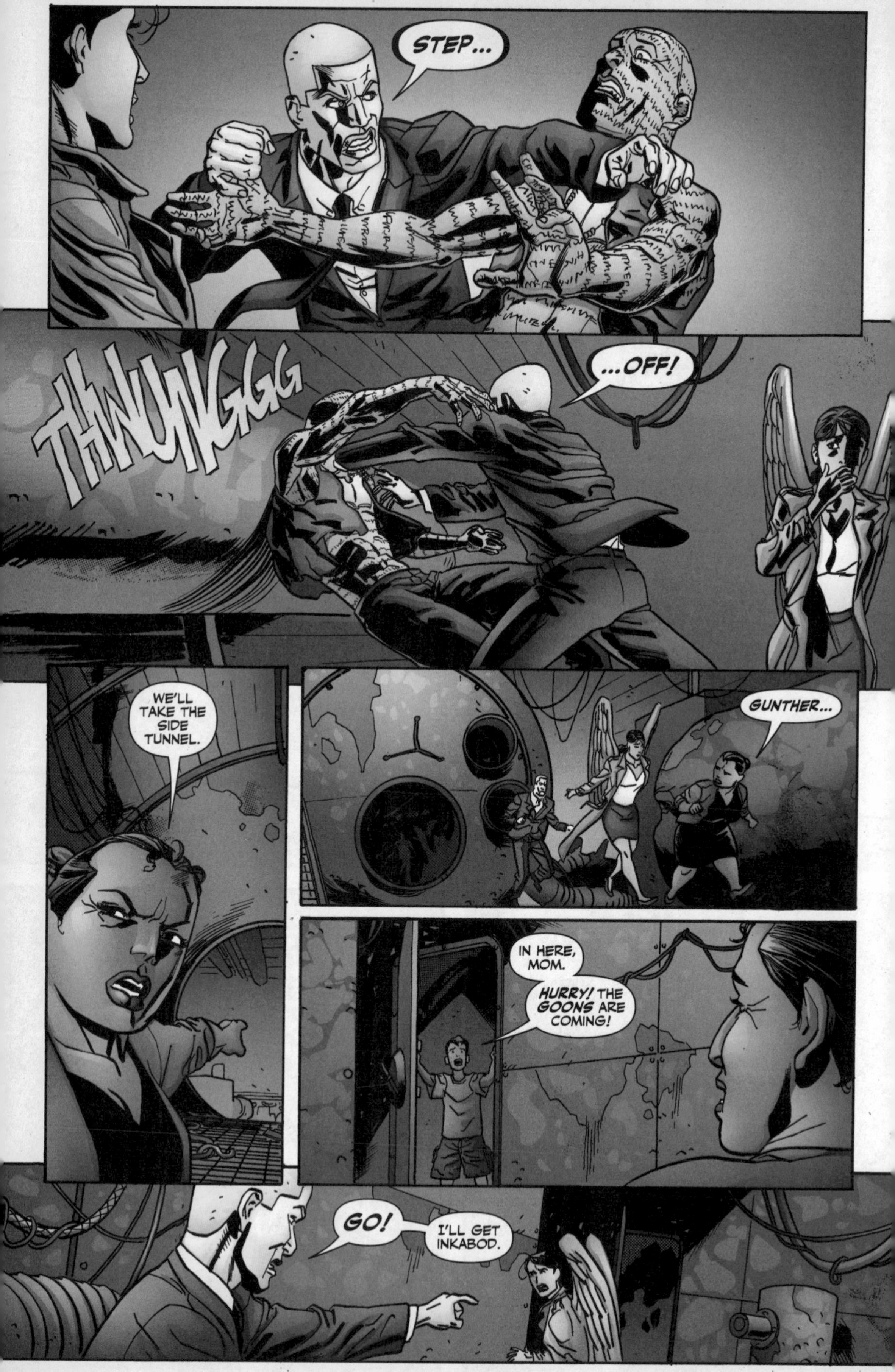
STEP...
THWUNGGG
...OFF!
WE'LL TAKE THE SIDE TUNNEL.
GUNTHER...
IN HERE, MOM.
HURRY! THE GOONS ARE COMING!
GO!
I'LL GET INKABOD.

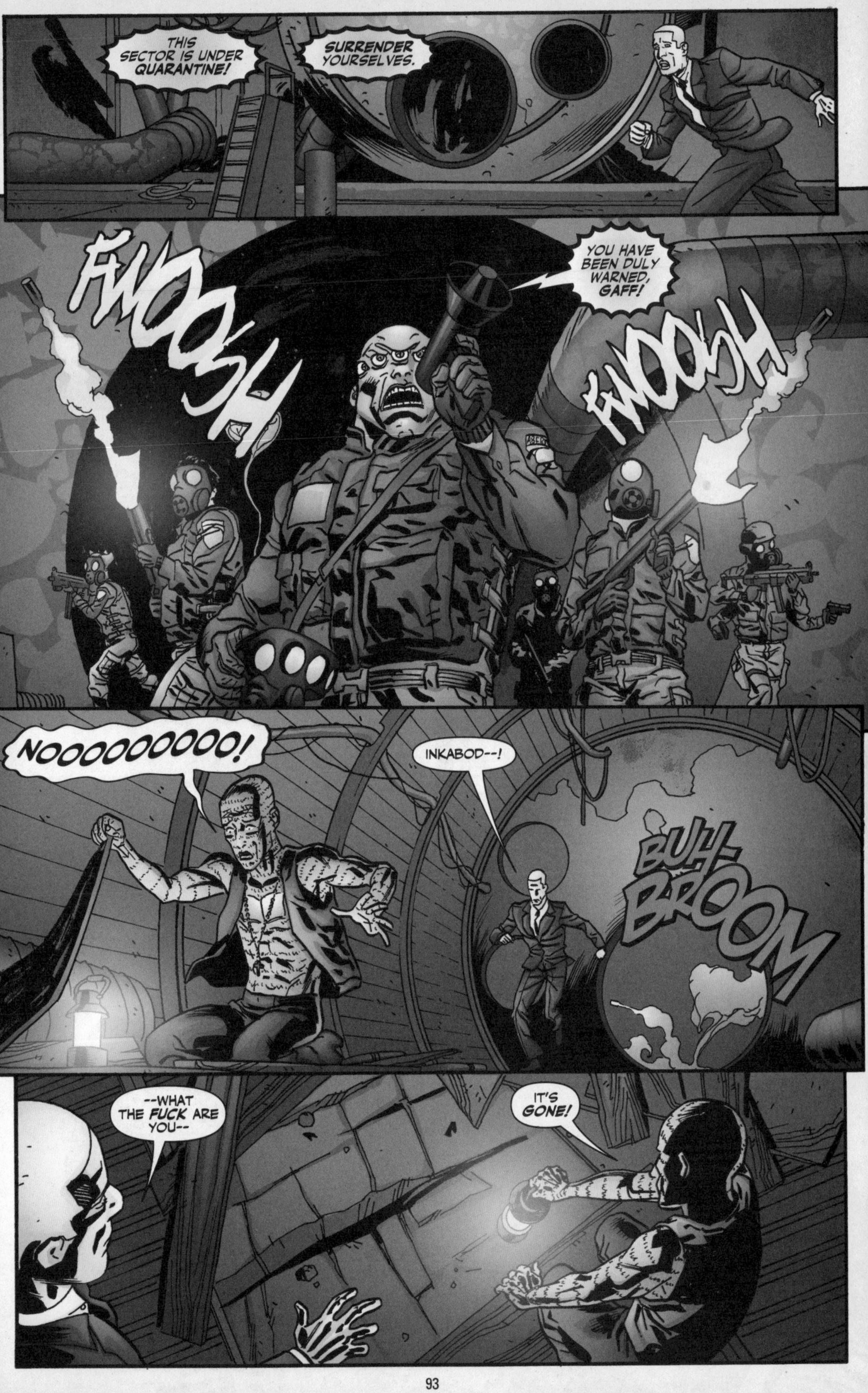
THIS SECTOR IS UNDER QUARANTINE!
SURRENDER YOURSELVES.
FWOOSH
YOU HAVE BEEN DULY WARNED, GAFF!
FWOOSH
NOOOOOOOOO!
INKABOD--!
BUH-BROOM
--WHAT THE FUCK ARE YOU--
IT'S GONE!

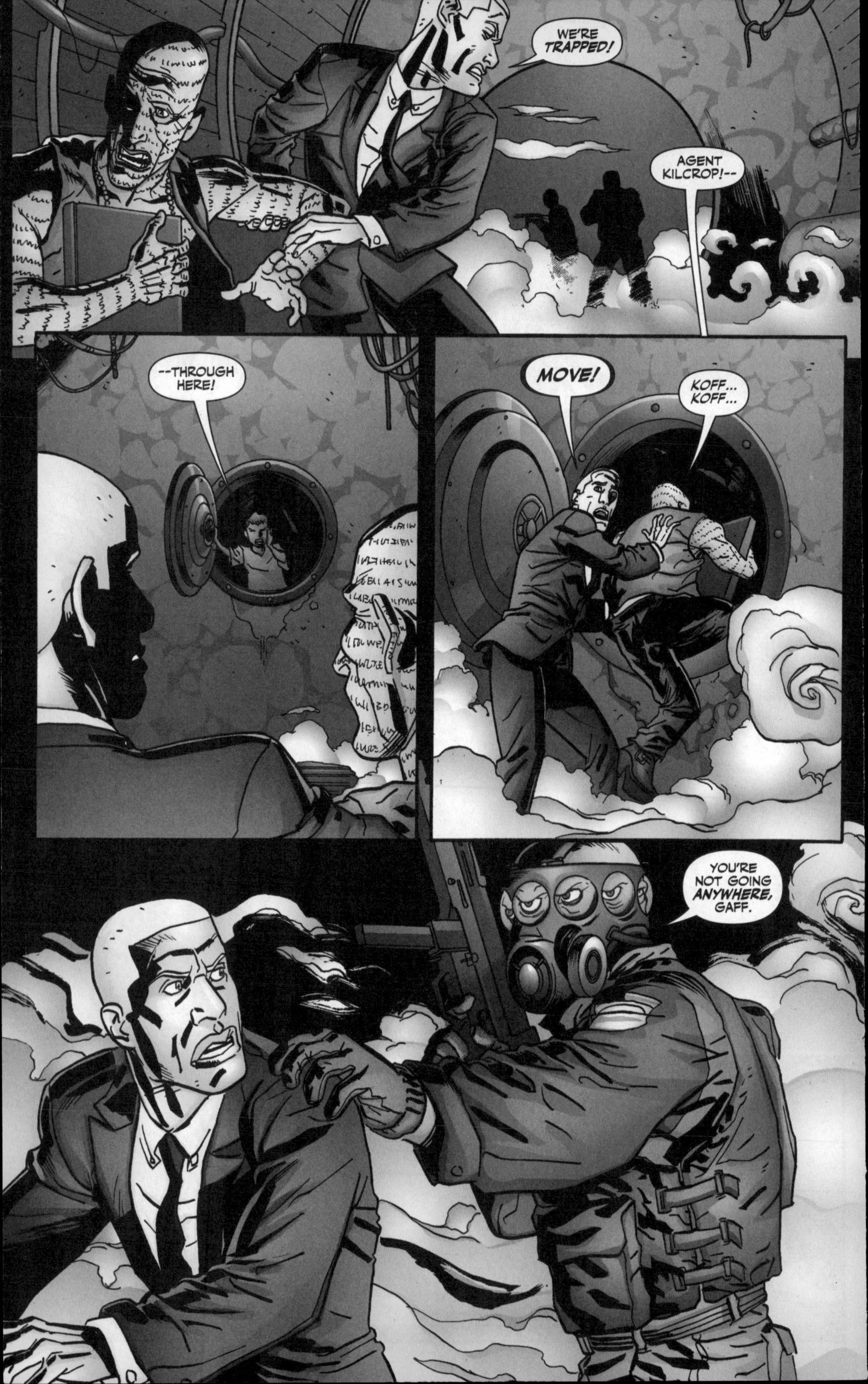
WE'RE TRAPPED!
AGENT KILCROP!--
--THROUGH HERE!
MOVE!
KOFF... KOFF...
YOU'RE NOT GOING ANYWHERE, GAFF.

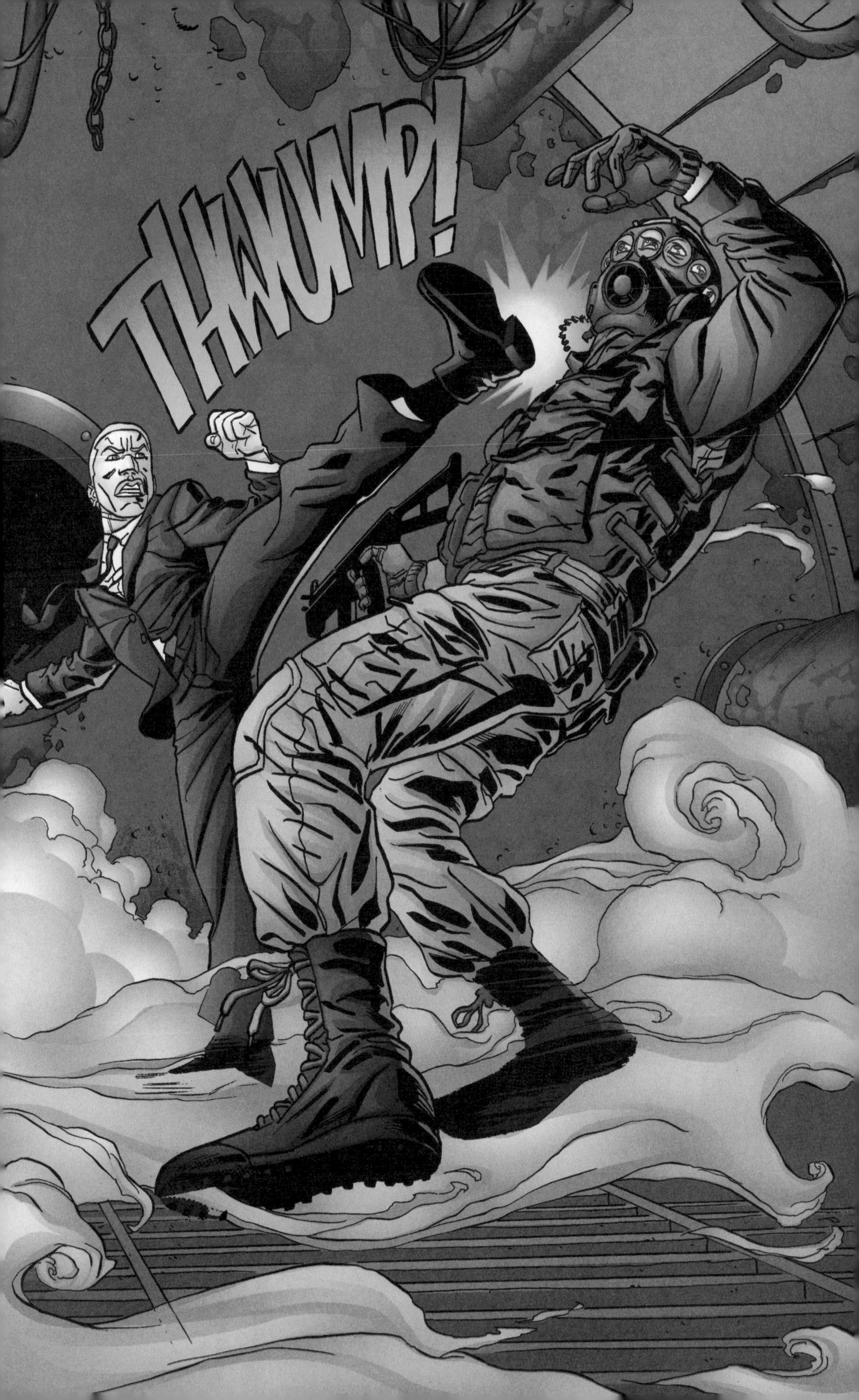
THWUMP!

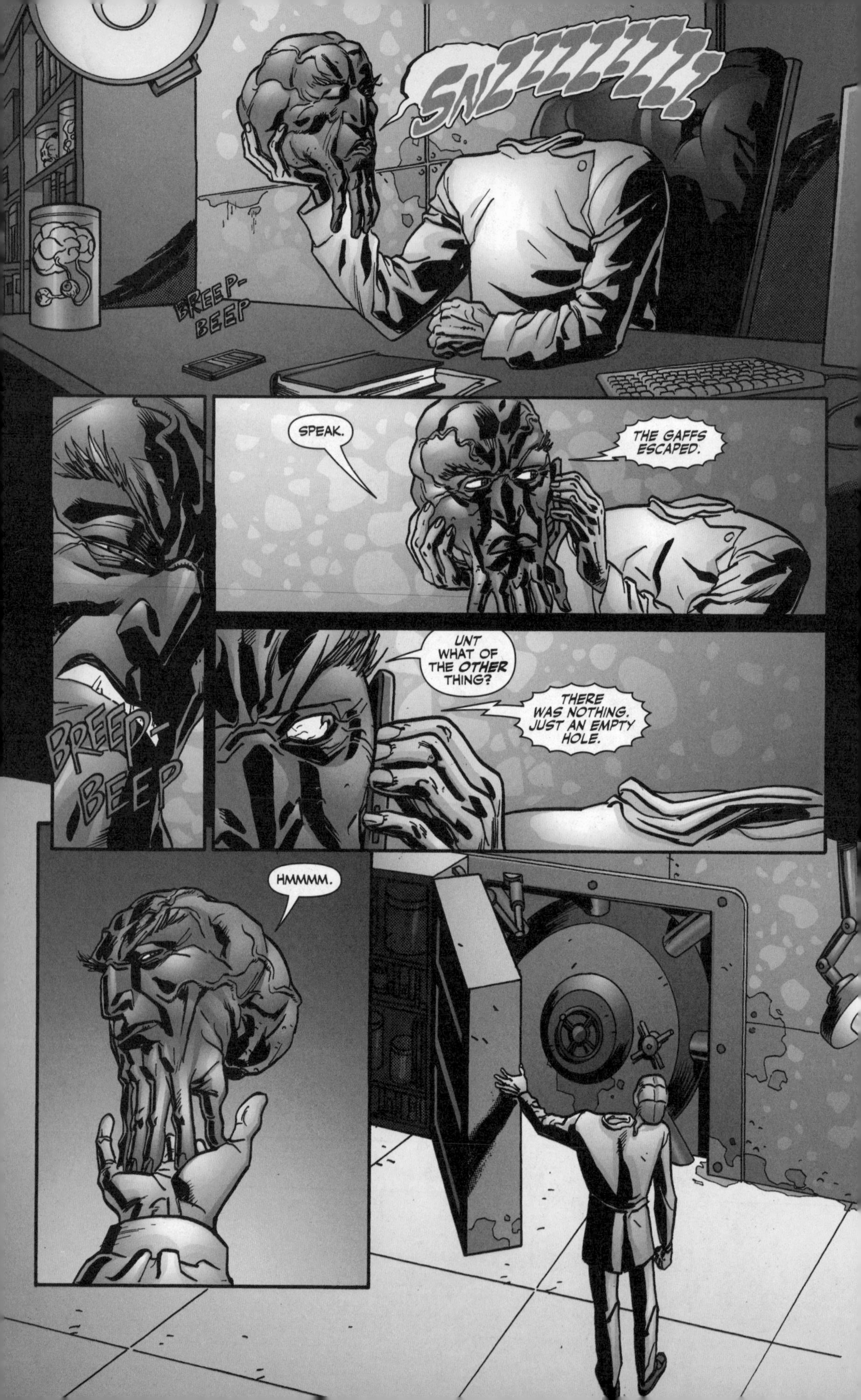
SNZZZZZZZZZ
BREEP-BEEP
SPEAK.
THE GAFFS ESCAPED.
BREEP-BEEP
UNT WHAT OF THE OTHER THING?
THERE WAS NOTHING. JUST AN EMPTY HOLE.
HMMMM.

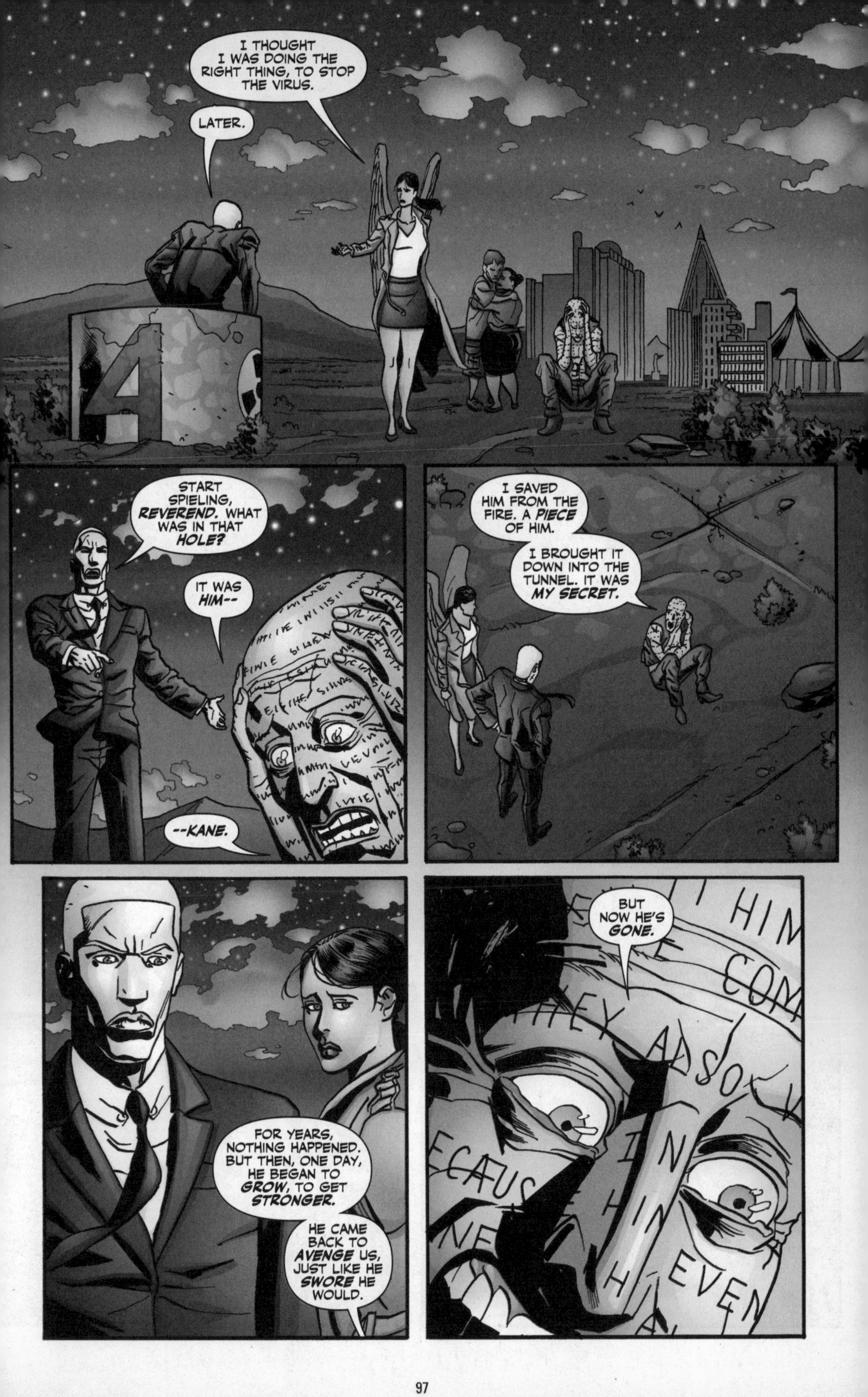
I THOUGHT I WAS DOING THE RIGHT THING, TO STOP THE VIRUS.
LATER.
START SPIELING, *REVEREND.* WHAT WAS IN THAT *HOLE?*
IT WAS *HIM--*
--KANE.
I SAVED HIM FROM THE FIRE. A *PIECE* OF HIM.
I BROUGHT IT DOWN INTO THE TUNNEL. IT WAS *MY SECRET.*
FOR YEARS, NOTHING HAPPENED. BUT THEN, ONE DAY, HE BEGAN TO *GROW,* TO GET *STRONGER.*
HE CAME BACK TO *AVENGE* US, JUST LIKE HE *SWORE* HE WOULD.
BUT NOW HE'S *GONE.*

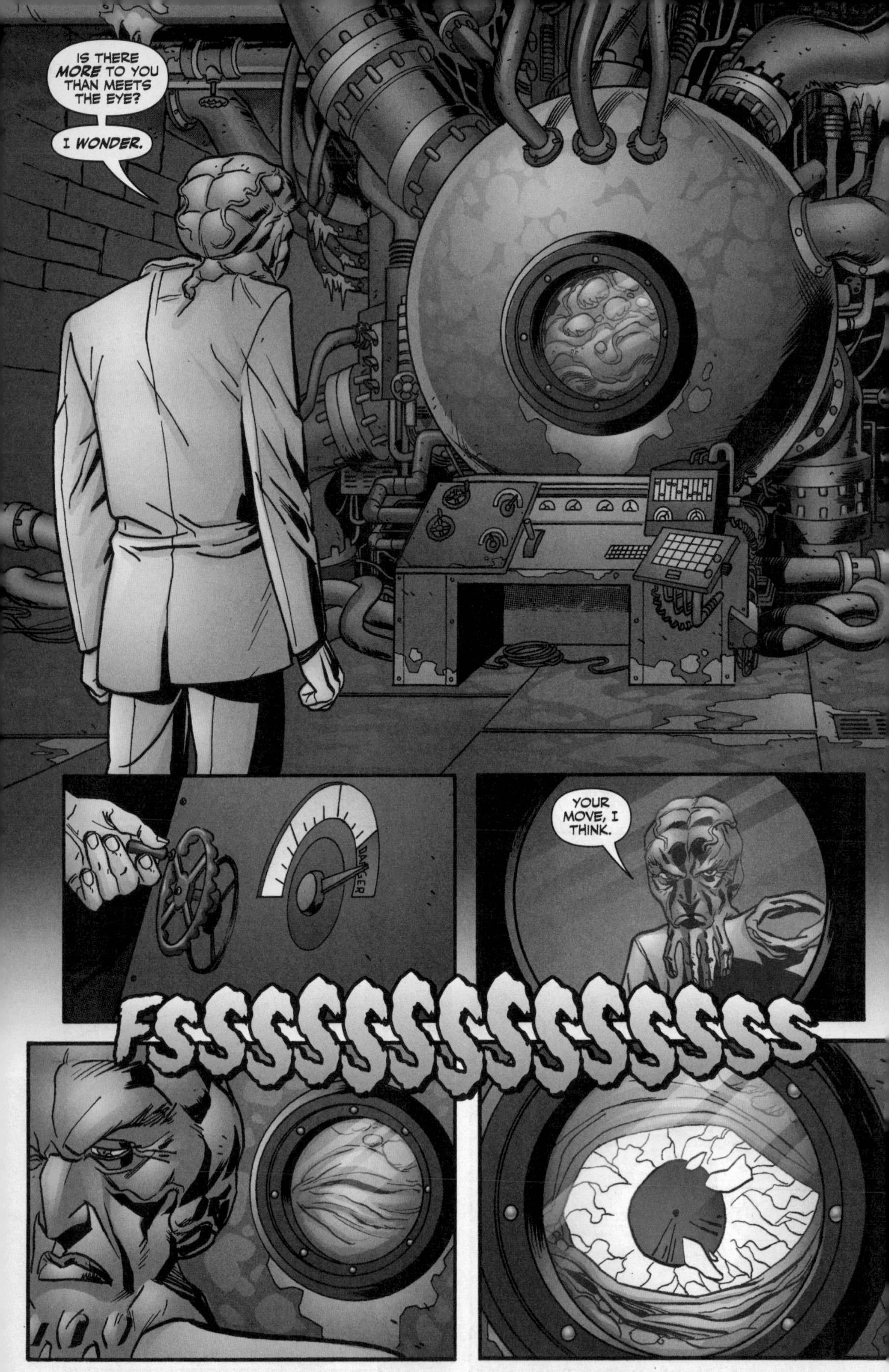
IS THERE MORE TO YOU THAN MEETS THE EYE?
I WONDER.
DANGER
YOUR MOVE, I THINK.
FSSSSSSSSSSSSSSSS

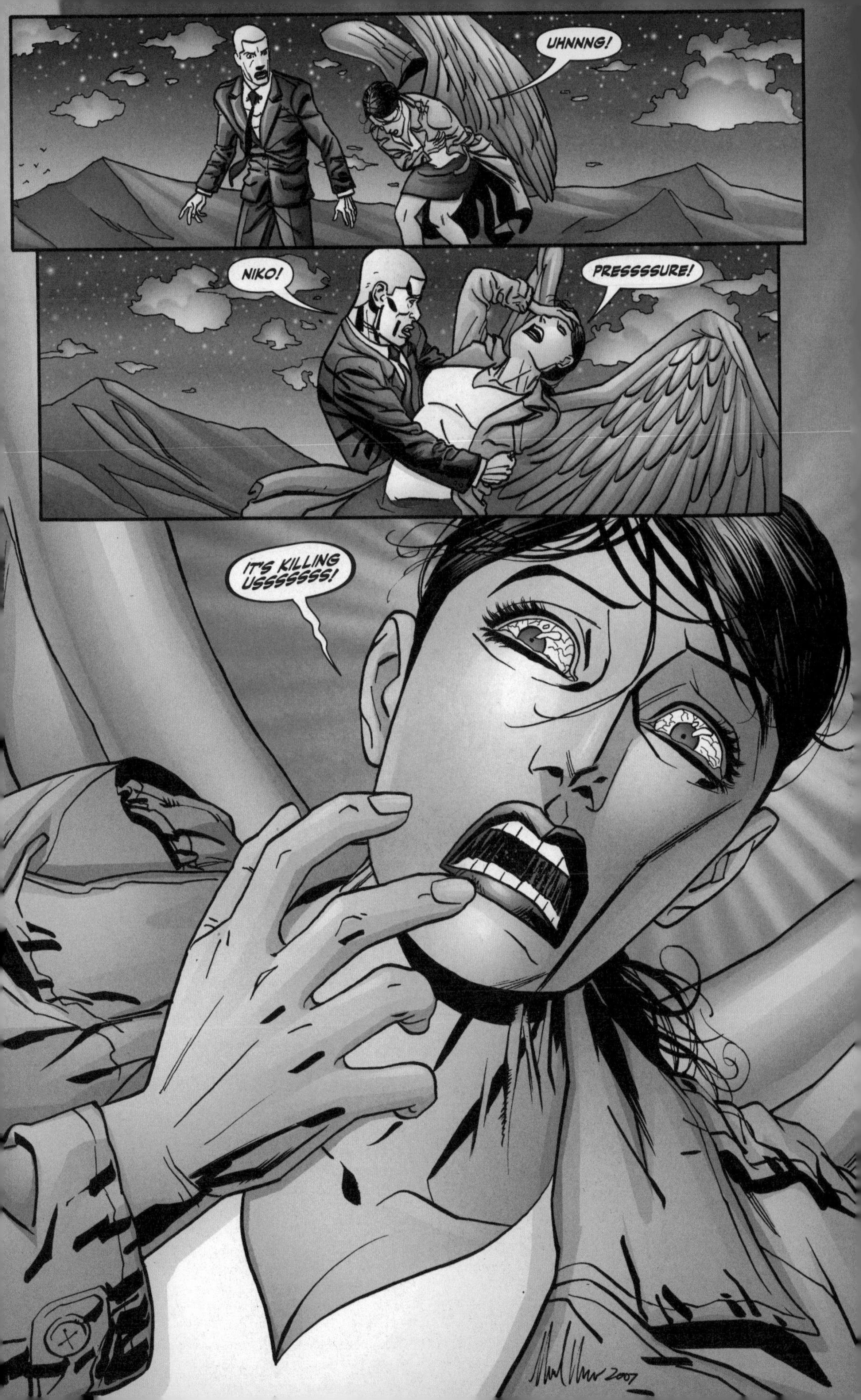
UHNNNG!
NIKO!
PRESSSSURE!
IT'S KILLING USSSSSSS!

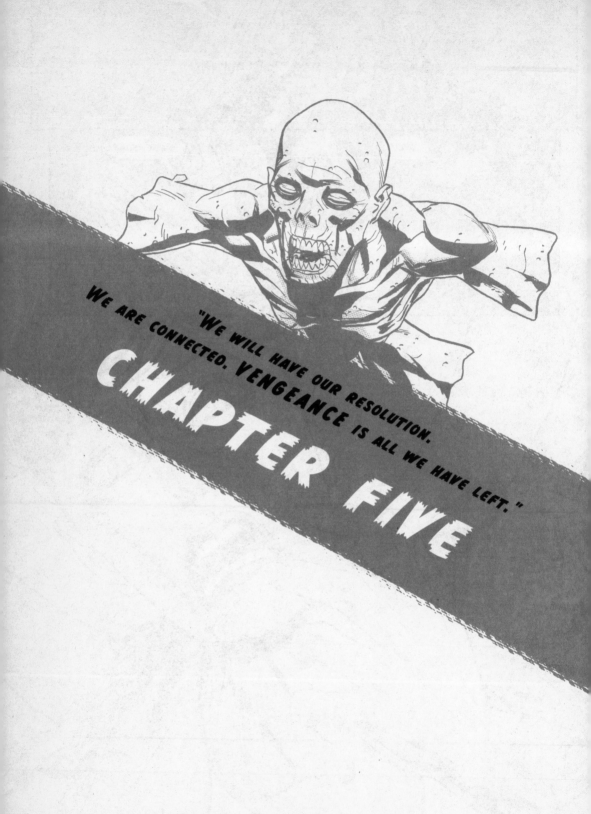

"WE WILL HAVE OUR RESOLUTION. WE ARE CONNECTED. VENGEANCE IS ALL WE HAVE LEFT."

CHAPTER FIVE

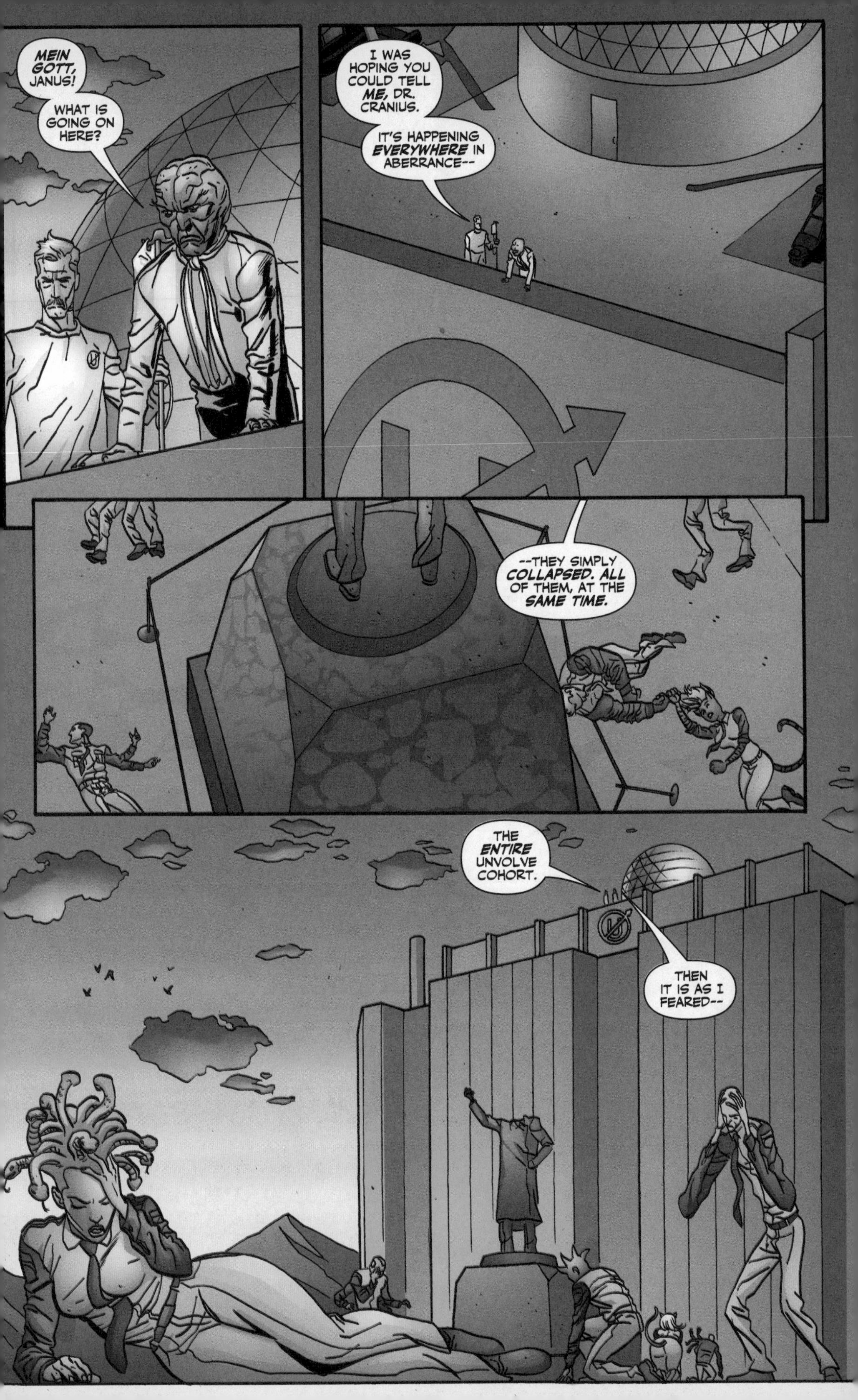
MEIN GOTT, JANUS!
WHAT IS GOING ON HERE?
I WAS HOPING YOU COULD TELL ME, DR. CRANIUS.
IT'S HAPPENING EVERYWHERE IN ABERRANCE--
--THEY SIMPLY COLLAPSED. ALL OF THEM, AT THE SAME TIME.
THE ENTIRE UNVOLVE COHORT.
THEN IT IS AS I FEARED--

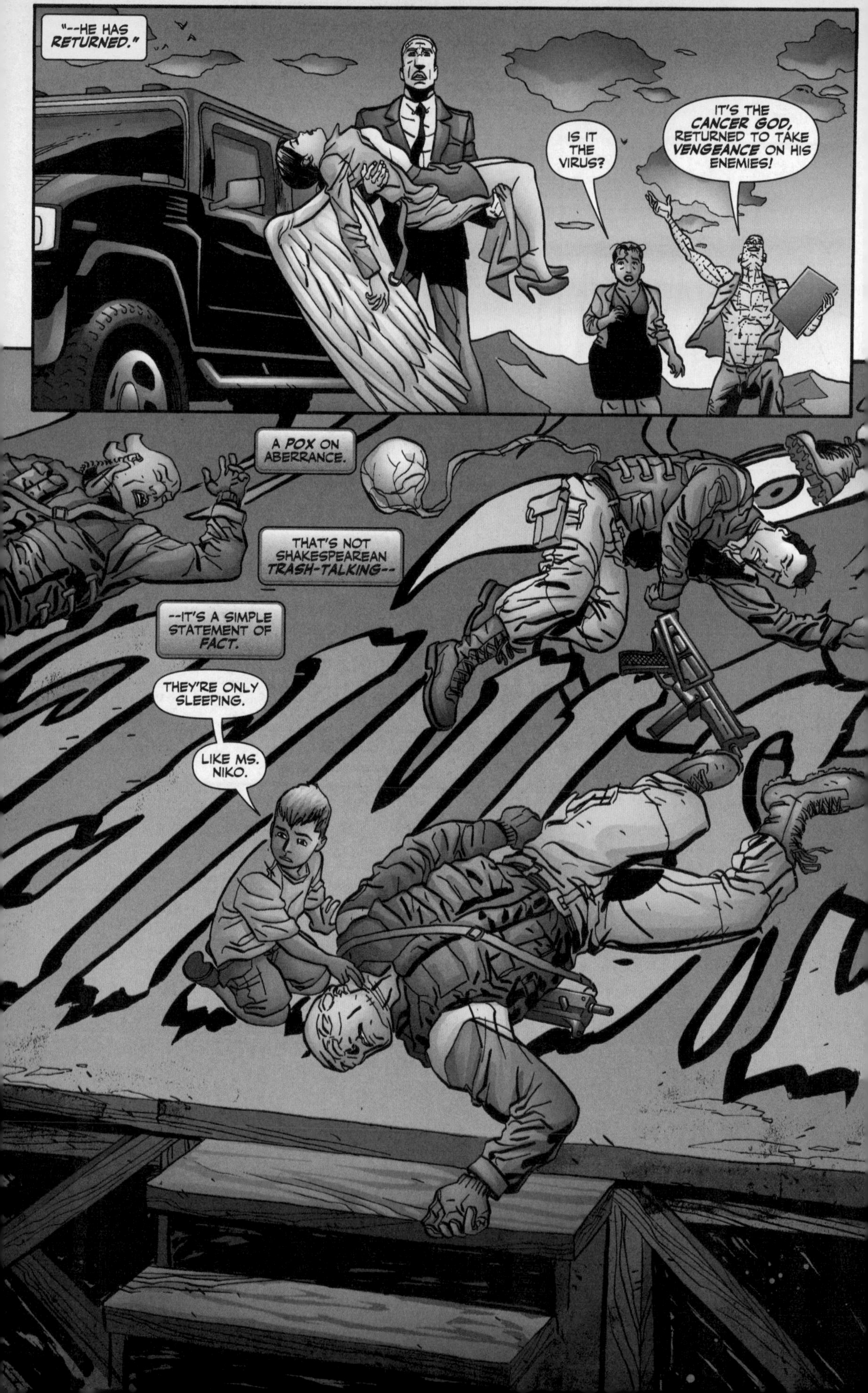
"--HE HAS RETURNED."
IS IT THE VIRUS?
IT'S THE CANCER GOD, RETURNED TO TAKE VENGEANCE ON HIS ENEMIES!
A POX ON ABERRANCE.
THAT'S NOT SHAKESPEAREAN TRASH-TALKING--
--IT'S A SIMPLE STATEMENT OF FACT.
THEY'RE ONLY SLEEPING.
LIKE MS. NIKO.

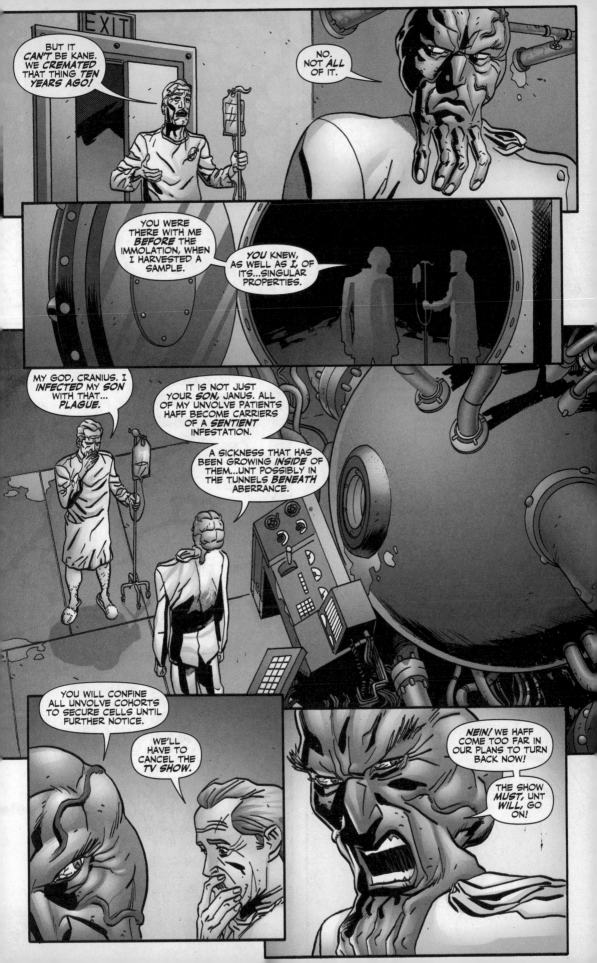

BUT IT *CAN'T* BE KANE. WE *CREMATED* THAT THING *TEN YEARS AGO!*

NO. NOT *ALL* OF IT.

YOU WERE THERE WITH ME *BEFORE* THE IMMOLATION, WHEN I *HARVESTED* A SAMPLE.

YOU KNEW, AS WELL AS *I,* OF ITS...SINGULAR PROPERTIES.

MY GOD, CRANIUS. I *INFECTED* MY *SON* WITH THAT... *PLAGUE.*

IT IS NOT JUST YOUR *SON,* JANUS. ALL OF MY UNVOLVE PATIENTS HAFF BECOME CARRIERS OF A *SENTIENT* INFESTATION.

A SICKNESS THAT HAS BEEN GROWING *INSIDE* OF THEM...UNT POSSIBLY IN THE TUNNELS *BENEATH* ABERRANCE.

YOU WILL CONFINE ALL UNVOLVE COHORTS TO SECURE CELLS UNTIL FURTHER NOTICE.

WE'LL HAVE TO CANCEL THE *TV SHOW.*

NEIN! WE HAFF COME TOO FAR IN OUR PLANS TO TURN BACK NOW!

THE SHOW *MUST,* UNT *WILL,* GO ON!

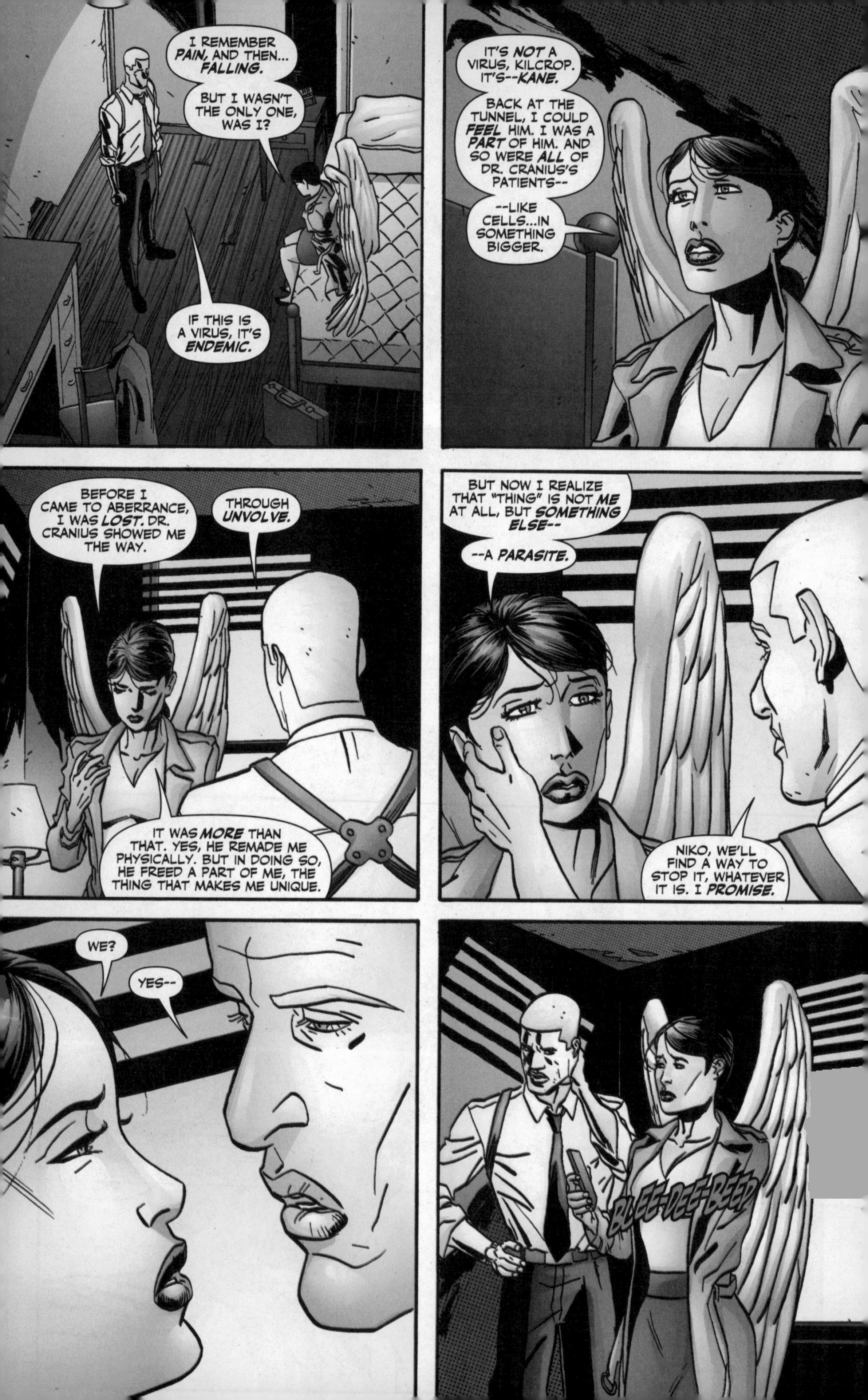
I REMEMBER PAIN, AND THEN... FALLING.
BUT I WASN'T THE ONLY ONE, WAS I?
IF THIS IS A VIRUS, IT'S ENDEMIC.
IT'S NOT A VIRUS, KILCROP. IT'S--KANE.
BACK AT THE TUNNEL, I COULD FEEL HIM. I WAS A PART OF HIM. AND SO WERE ALL OF DR. CRANIUS'S PATIENTS--
--LIKE CELLS...IN SOMETHING BIGGER.
BEFORE I CAME TO ABERRANCE, I WAS LOST. DR. CRANIUS SHOWED ME THE WAY.
THROUGH UNVOLVE.
IT WAS MORE THAN THAT. YES, HE REMADE ME PHYSICALLY. BUT IN DOING SO, HE FREED A PART OF ME, THE THING THAT MAKES ME UNIQUE.
BUT NOW I REALIZE THAT "THING" IS NOT ME AT ALL, BUT SOMETHING ELSE--
--A PARASITE.
NIKO, WE'LL FIND A WAY TO STOP IT, WHATEVER IT IS. I PROMISE.
WE?
YES--
BLEE-DEE-BEEP

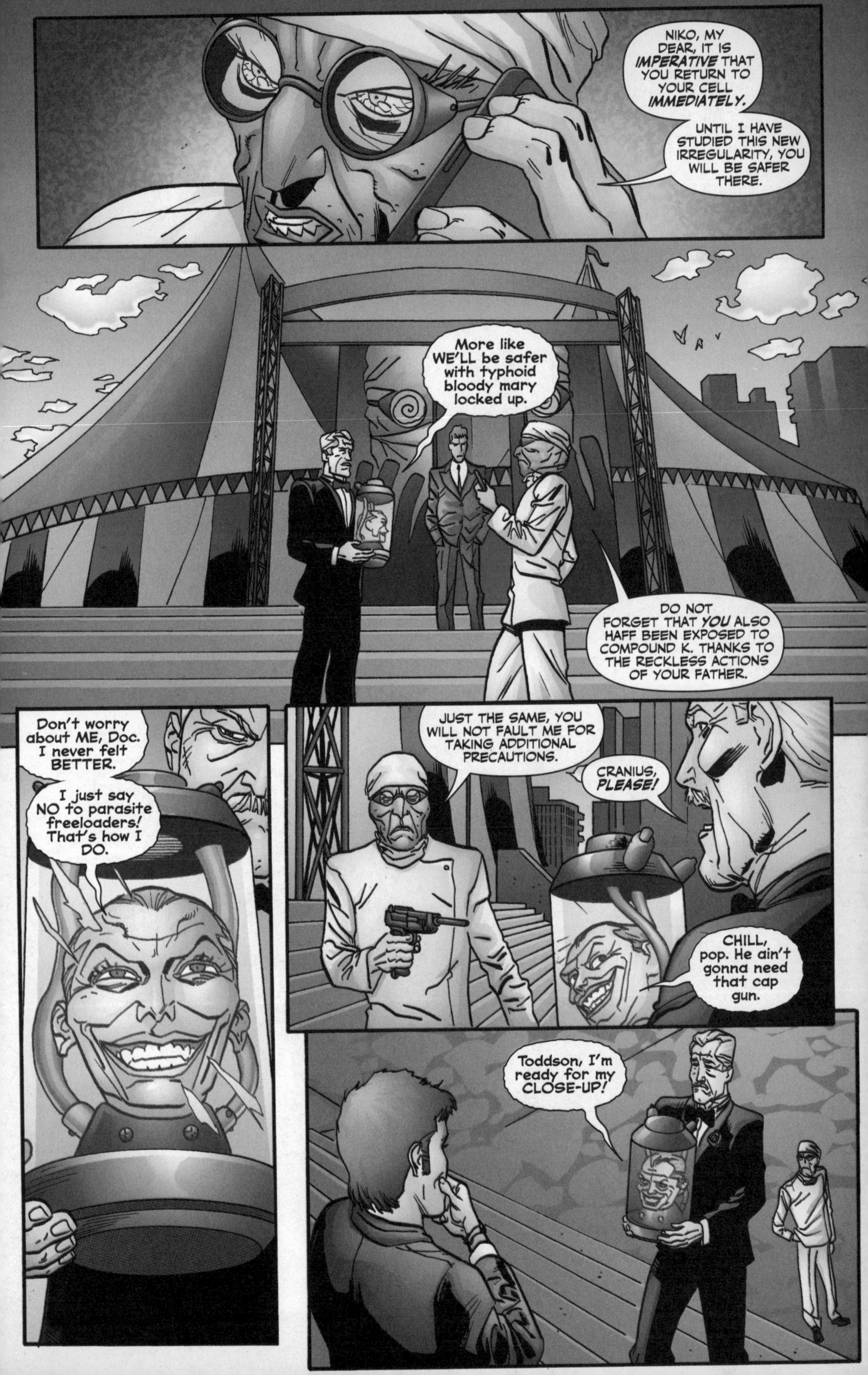
NIKO, MY DEAR, IT IS *IMPERATIVE* THAT YOU RETURN TO YOUR CELL *IMMEDIATELY.*
UNTIL I HAVE STUDIED THIS NEW IRREGULARITY, YOU WILL BE SAFER THERE.
More like WE'LL be safer with typhoid bloody mary locked up.
DO NOT FORGET THAT *YOU* ALSO HAFF BEEN EXPOSED TO COMPOUND K. THANKS TO THE RECKLESS ACTIONS OF YOUR FATHER.
Don't worry about ME, Doc. I never felt BETTER.
I just say NO to parasite freeloaders! That's how I DO.
JUST THE SAME, YOU WILL NOT FAULT ME FOR TAKING ADDITIONAL PRECAUTIONS.
CRANIUS, *PLEASE!*
CHILL, pop. He ain't gonna need that cap gun.
Toddson, I'm ready for my CLOSE-UP!

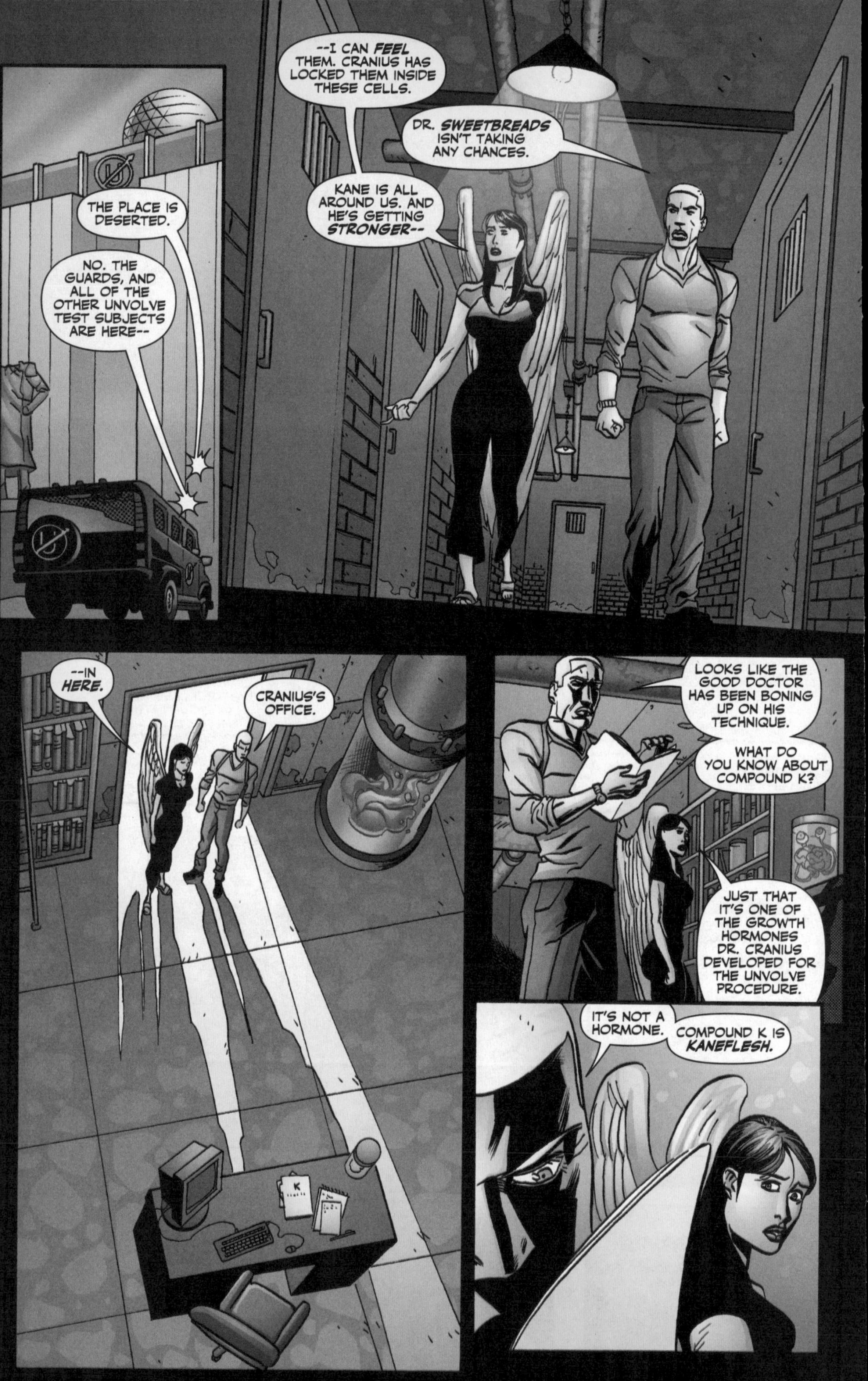
THE PLACE IS DESERTED.
NO. THE GUARDS, AND ALL OF THE OTHER UNVOLVE TEST SUBJECTS ARE HERE--
--I CAN FEEL THEM. CRANIUS HAS LOCKED THEM INSIDE THESE CELLS.
KANE IS ALL AROUND US. AND HE'S GETTING STRONGER--
DR. SWEETBREADS ISN'T TAKING ANY CHANCES.
--IN HERE.
CRANIUS'S OFFICE.
LOOKS LIKE THE GOOD DOCTOR HAS BEEN BONING UP ON HIS TECHNIQUE.
WHAT DO YOU KNOW ABOUT COMPOUND K?
JUST THAT IT'S ONE OF THE GROWTH HORMONES DR. CRANIUS DEVELOPED FOR THE UNVOLVE PROCEDURE.
IT'S NOT A HORMONE.
COMPOUND K IS KANEFLESH.

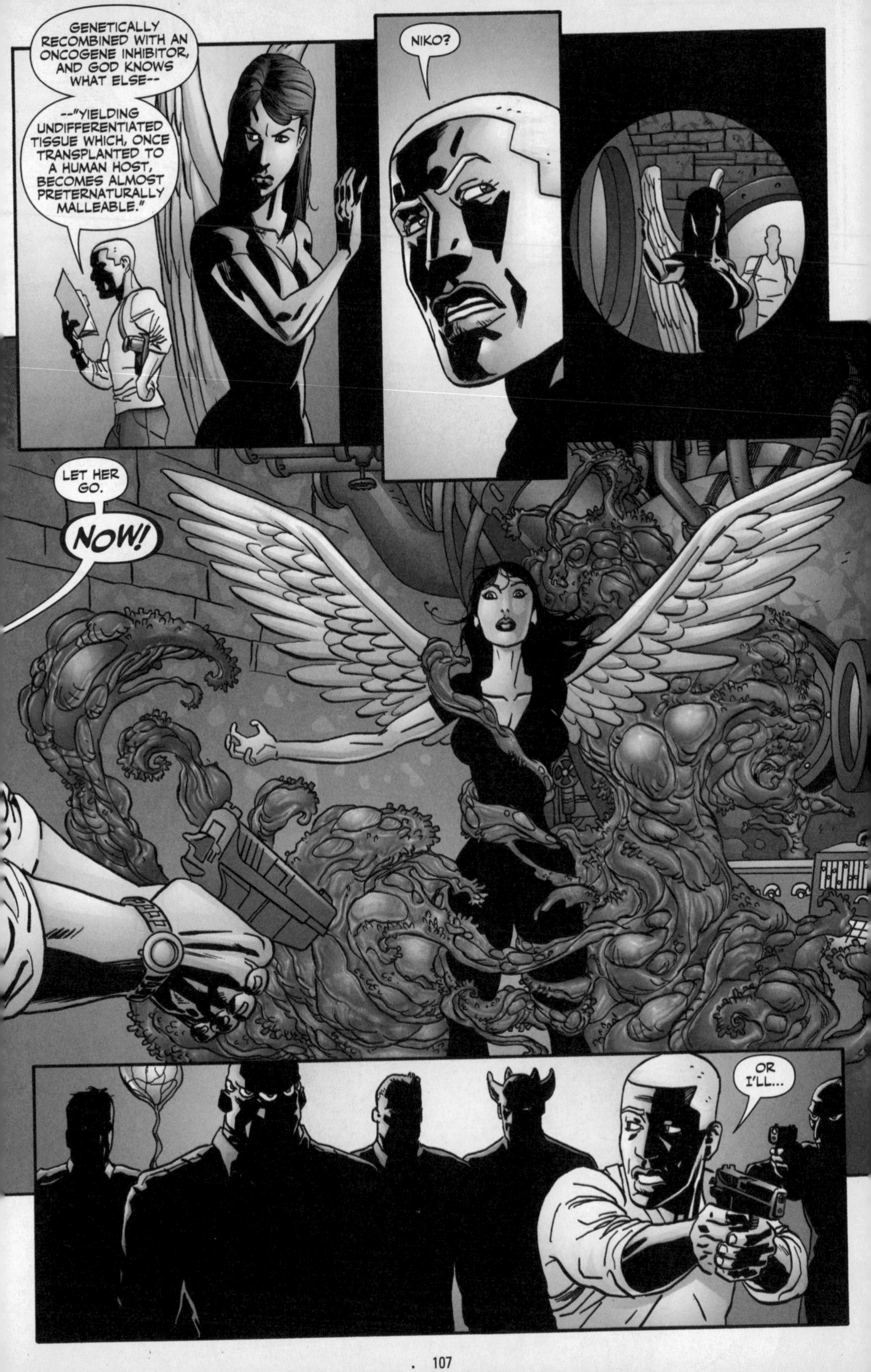
GENETICALLY RECOMBINED WITH AN ONCOGENE INHIBITOR, AND GOD KNOWS WHAT ELSE--
--"YIELDING UNDIFFERENTIATED TISSUE WHICH, ONCE TRANSPLANTED TO A HUMAN HOST, BECOMES ALMOST PRETERNATURALLY MALLEABLE."
NIKO?
LET HER GO.
NOW!
OR I'LL...

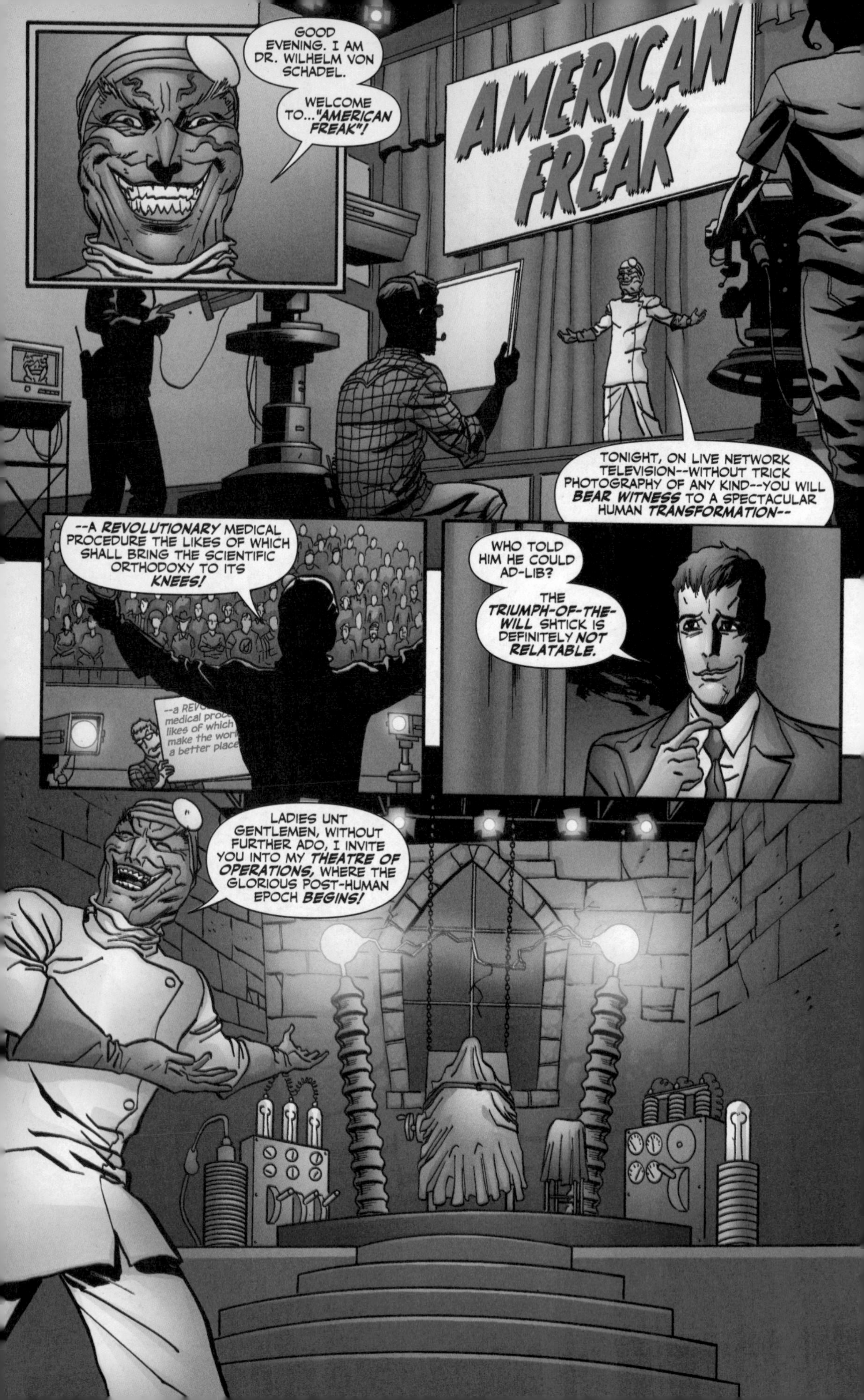

GOOD EVENING. I AM DR. WILHELM VON SCHADEL.
WELCOME TO..."AMERICAN FREAK"!
AMERICAN FREAK
TONIGHT, ON LIVE NETWORK TELEVISION--WITHOUT TRICK PHOTOGRAPHY OF ANY KIND--YOU WILL BEAR WITNESS TO A SPECTACULAR HUMAN TRANSFORMATION--
--A REVOLUTIONARY MEDICAL PROCEDURE THE LIKES OF WHICH SHALL BRING THE SCIENTIFIC ORTHODOXY TO ITS KNEES!
WHO TOLD HIM HE COULD AD-LIB?
THE TRIUMPH-OF-THE-WILL SHTICK IS DEFINITELY NOT RELATABLE.
LADIES UNT GENTLEMEN, WITHOUT FURTHER ADO, I INVITE YOU INTO MY THEATRE OF OPERATIONS, WHERE THE GLORIOUS POST-HUMAN EPOCH BEGINS!

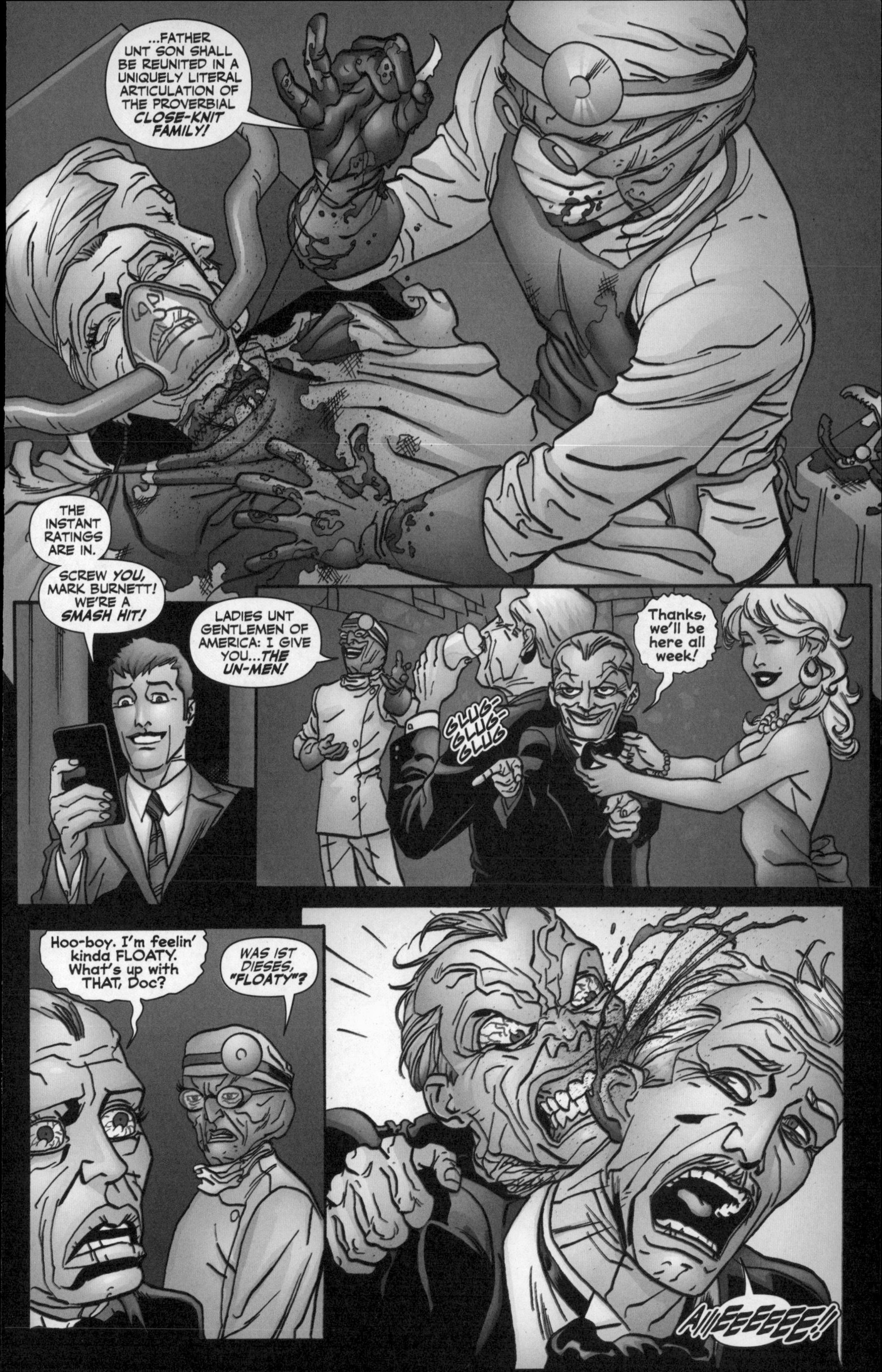
...FATHER UNT SON SHALL BE REUNITED IN A UNIQUELY LITERAL ARTICULATION OF THE PROVERBIAL CLOSE-KNIT FAMILY!
THE INSTANT RATINGS ARE IN.
SCREW YOU, MARK BURNETT! WE'RE A SMASH HIT!
LADIES UNT GENTLEMEN OF AMERICA: I GIVE YOU...THE UN-MEN!
GLUG-GLUG-GLUG
Thanks, we'll be here all week!
Hoo-boy. I'm feelin' kinda FLOATY. What's up with THAT, Doc?
WAS IST DIESES, "FLOATY"?
AIIEEEEEE!!

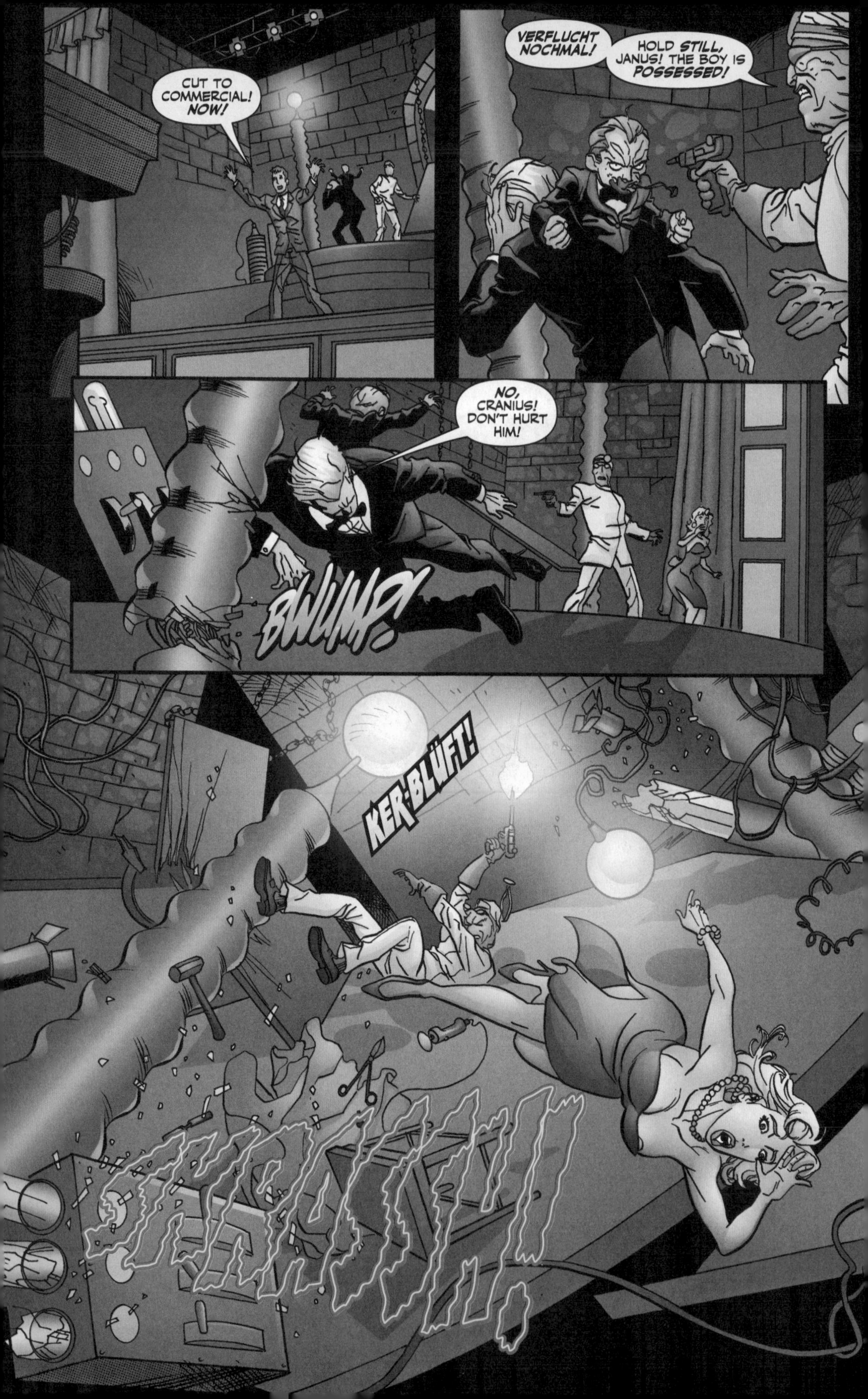
CUT TO COMMERCIAL! NOW!
VERFLUCHT NOCHMAL!
HOLD STILL, JANUS! THE BOY IS POSSESSED!
NO, CRANIUS! DON'T HURT HIM!
BWUMP!
KER-BLÜFT!

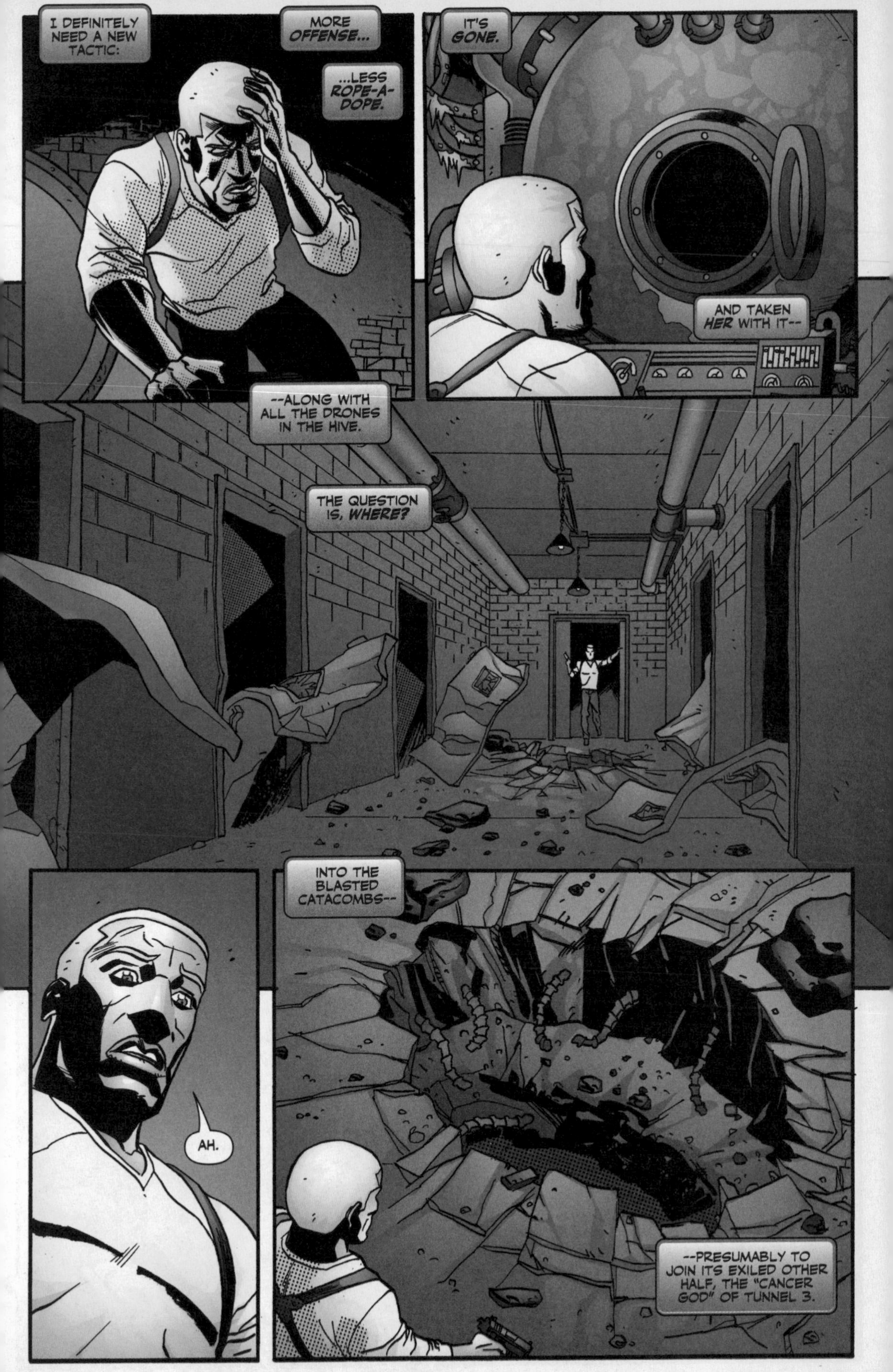
I DEFINITELY NEED A NEW TACTIC:
MORE OFFENSE...
...LESS ROPE-A-DOPE.
IT'S GONE.
AND TAKEN HER WITH IT--
--ALONG WITH ALL THE DRONES IN THE HIVE.
THE QUESTION IS, WHERE?
AH.
INTO THE BLASTED CATACOMBS--
--PRESUMABLY TO JOIN ITS EXILED OTHER HALF, THE "CANCER GOD" OF TUNNEL 3.

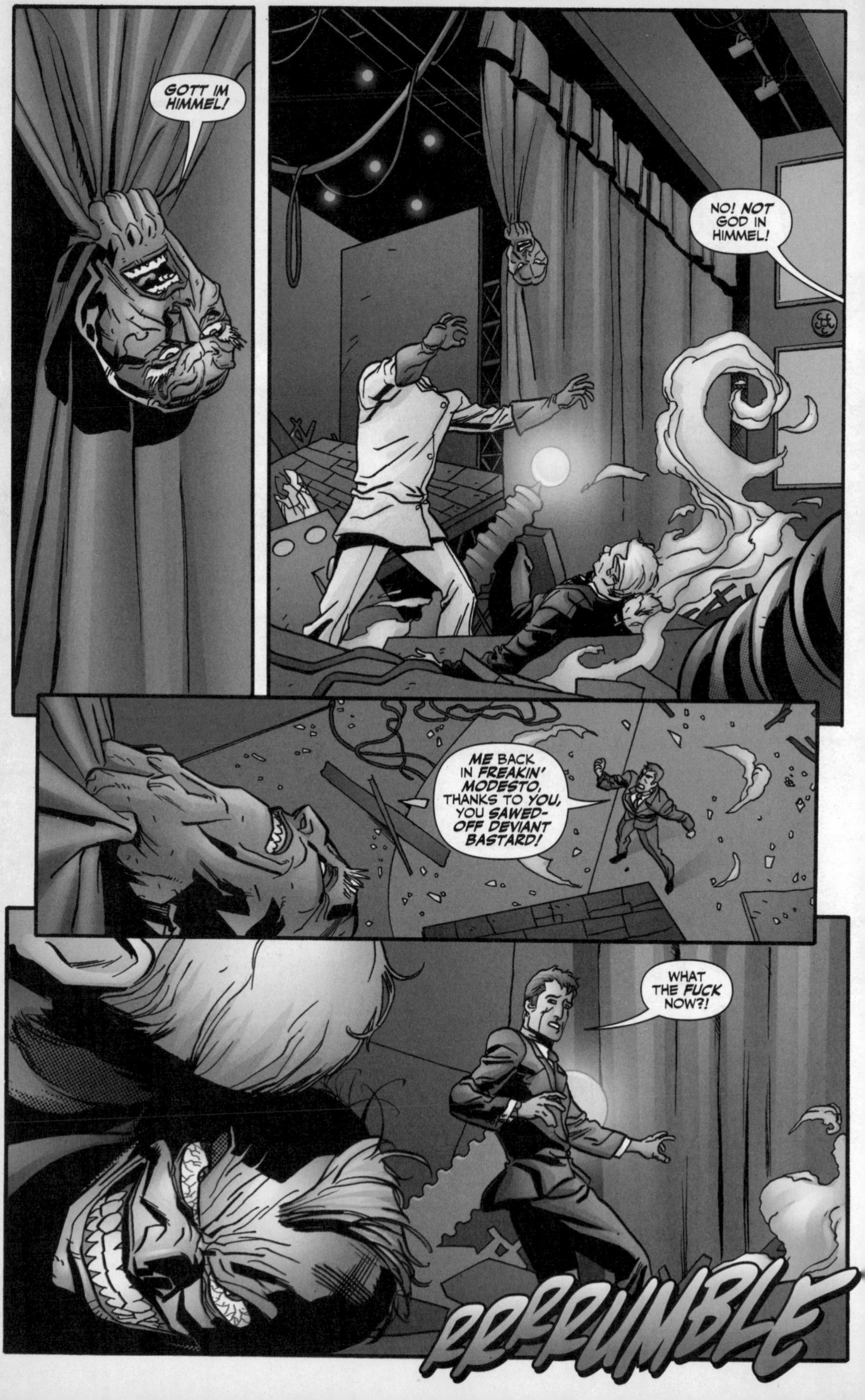
GOTT IM HIMMEL!
NO! NOT GOD IN HIMMEL!
ME BACK IN FREAKIN' MODESTO, THANKS TO YOU, YOU SAWED-OFF DEVIANT BASTARD!
WHAT THE FUCK NOW?!
RRRRUMBLE

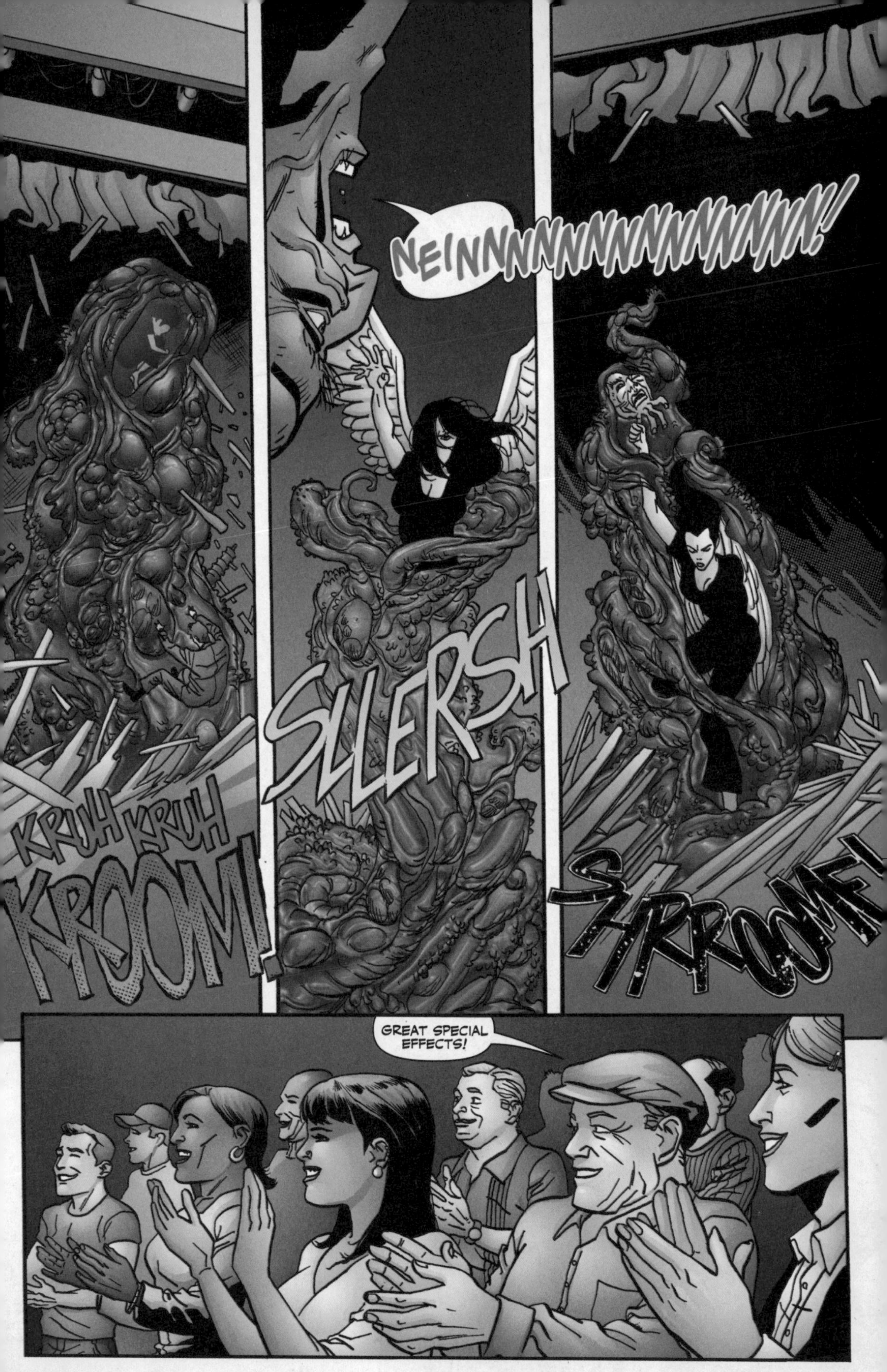
KRUH KRUH
KROOM!
NEINNNNNNNNNNNNNNN!
SLLERSH
SHRROOMF!
GREAT SPECIAL EFFECTS!

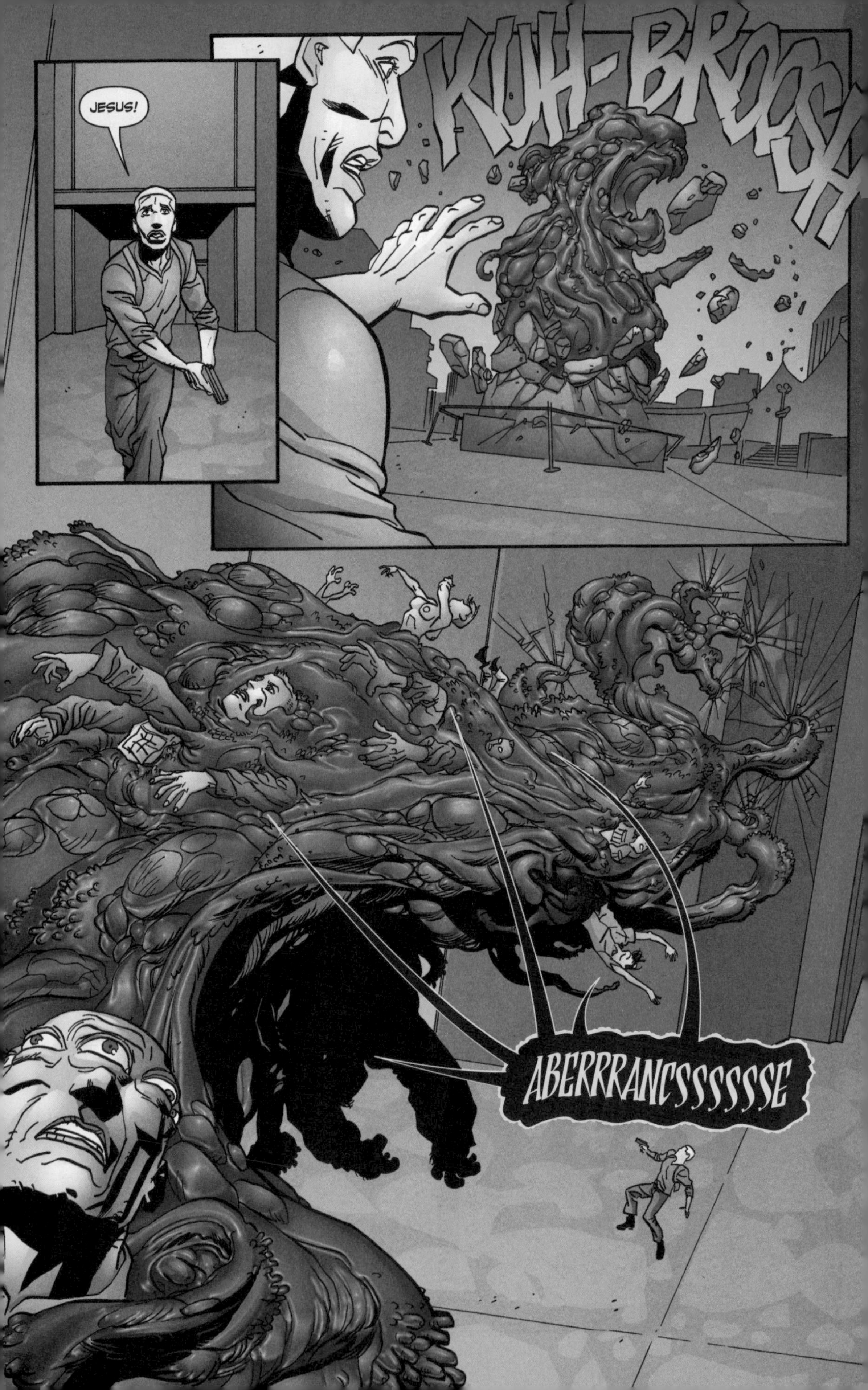
JESUS!
KUH-BROOSH!!
ABERRRANCSSSSSSE

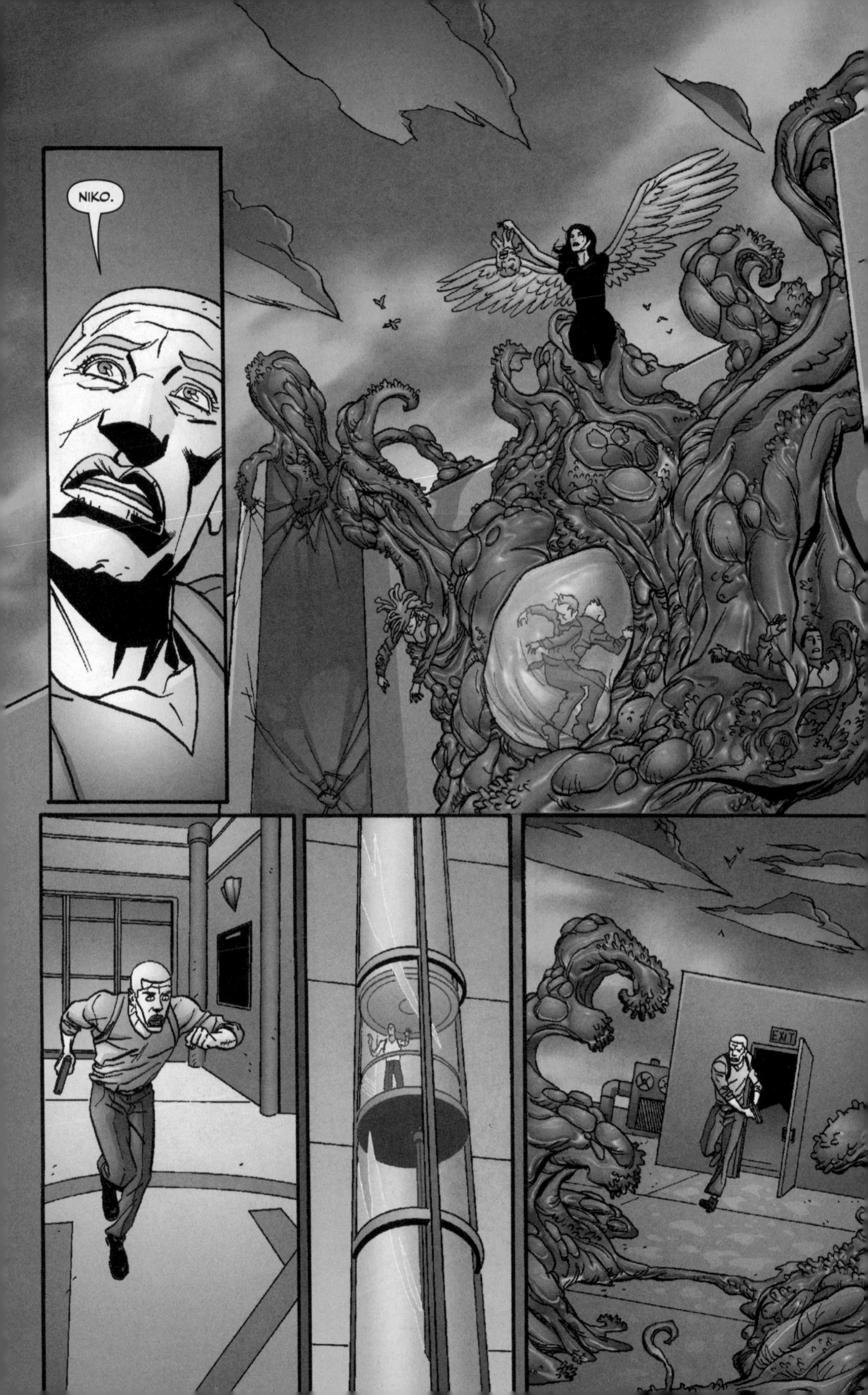
NIKO.
EXIT

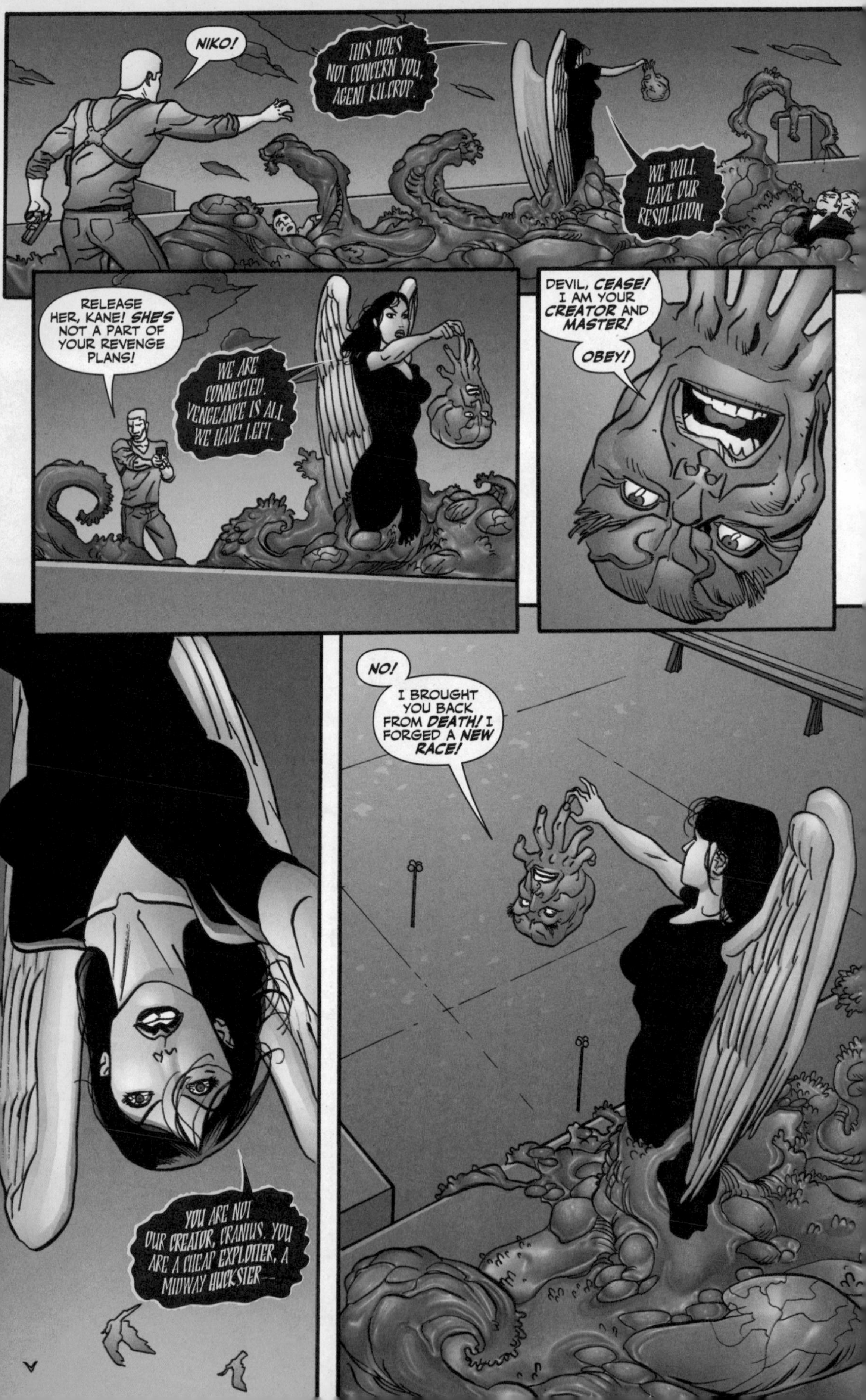

NIKO!
THIS DOES NOT CONCERN YOU, AGENT KILCROP.
WE WILL HAVE OUR RESOLUTION.
RELEASE HER, KANE! SHE'S NOT A PART OF YOUR REVENGE PLANS!
WE ARE CONNECTED. VENGEANCE IS ALL WE HAVE LEFT.
DEVIL, CEASE! I AM YOUR CREATOR AND MASTER!
OBEY!
YOU ARE NOT OUR CREATOR, CRANIUS. YOU ARE A CHEAP EXPLOITER, A MIDWAY HUCKSTER--
NO!
I BROUGHT YOU BACK FROM DEATH! I FORGED A NEW RACE!

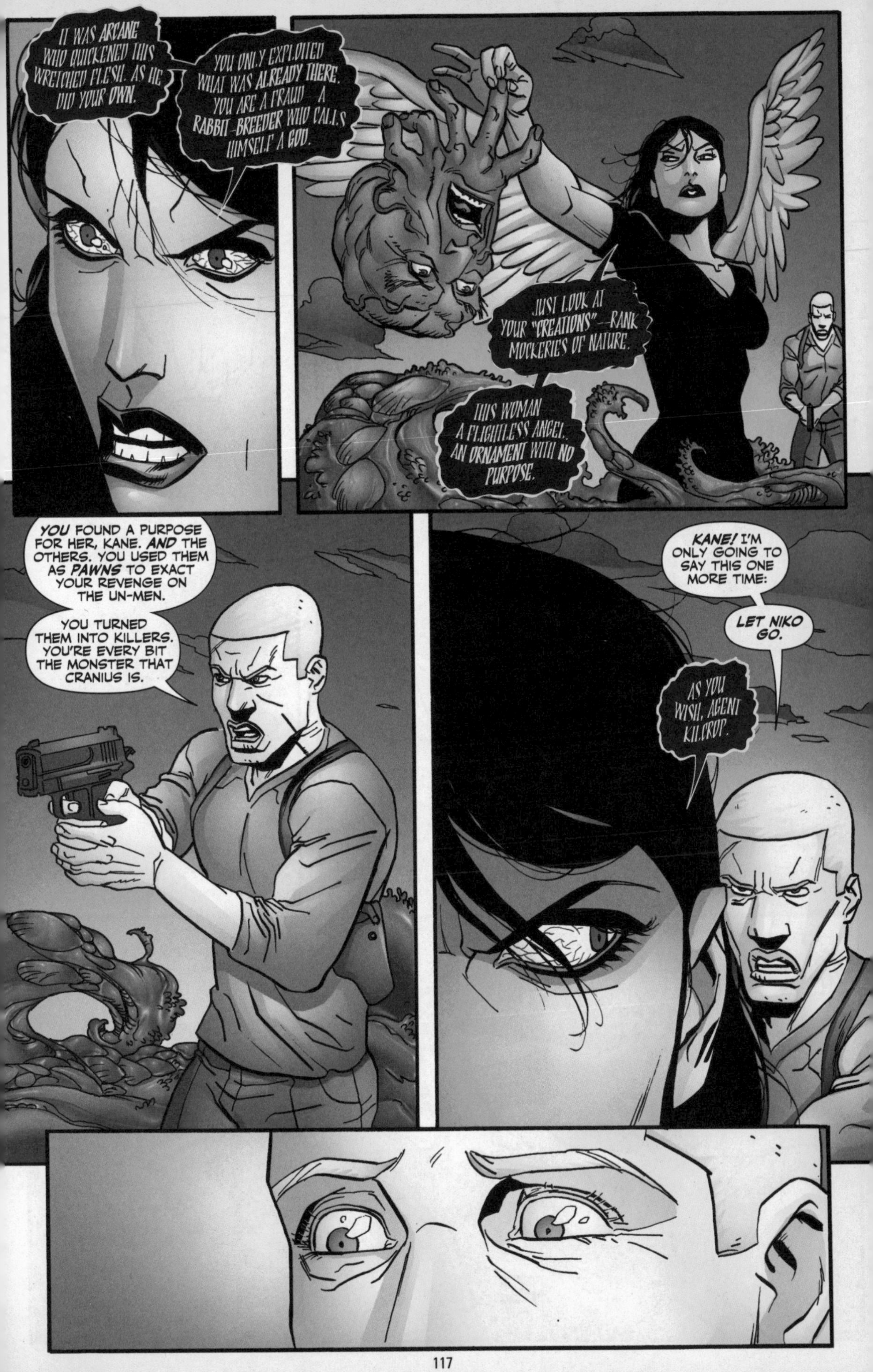
IT WAS ARCANE WHO QUICKENED THIS WRETCHED FLESH, AS HE DID YOUR OWN.
YOU ONLY EXPLOITED WHAT WAS ALREADY THERE. YOU ARE A FRAUD-- A RABBIT-BREEDER WHO CALLS HIMSELF A GOD.
JUST LOOK AT YOUR "CREATIONS"--RANK MOCKERIES OF NATURE.
THIS WOMAN A FLIGHTLESS ANGEL. AN ORNAMENT WITH NO PURPOSE.
YOU FOUND A PURPOSE FOR HER, KANE. AND THE OTHERS. YOU USED THEM AS PAWNS TO EXACT YOUR REVENGE ON THE UN-MEN.
YOU TURNED THEM INTO KILLERS. YOU'RE EVERY BIT THE MONSTER THAT CRANIUS IS.
KANE! I'M ONLY GOING TO SAY THIS ONE MORE TIME:
LET NIKO GO.
AS YOU WISH, AGENT KILCROP.

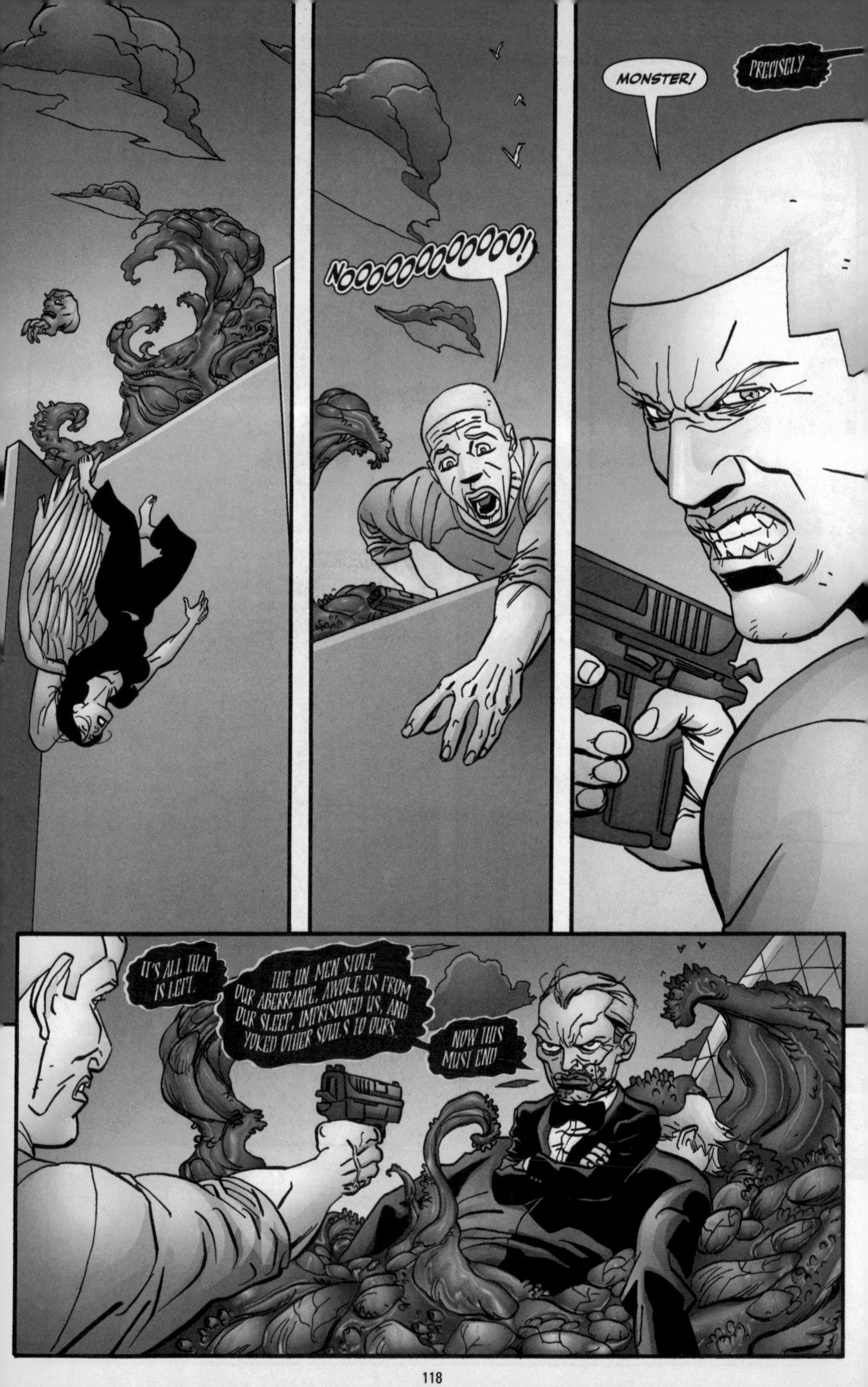
NOOOOOOOOOOOO!
MONSTER!
PRECISELY.
IT'S ALL THAT IS LEFT.
THE UN MEN STOLE OUR ABERRANCE, AWOKE US FROM OUR SLEEP, IMPRISONED US, AND YOKED OTHER SOULS TO OURS.
NOW THIS MUST END.

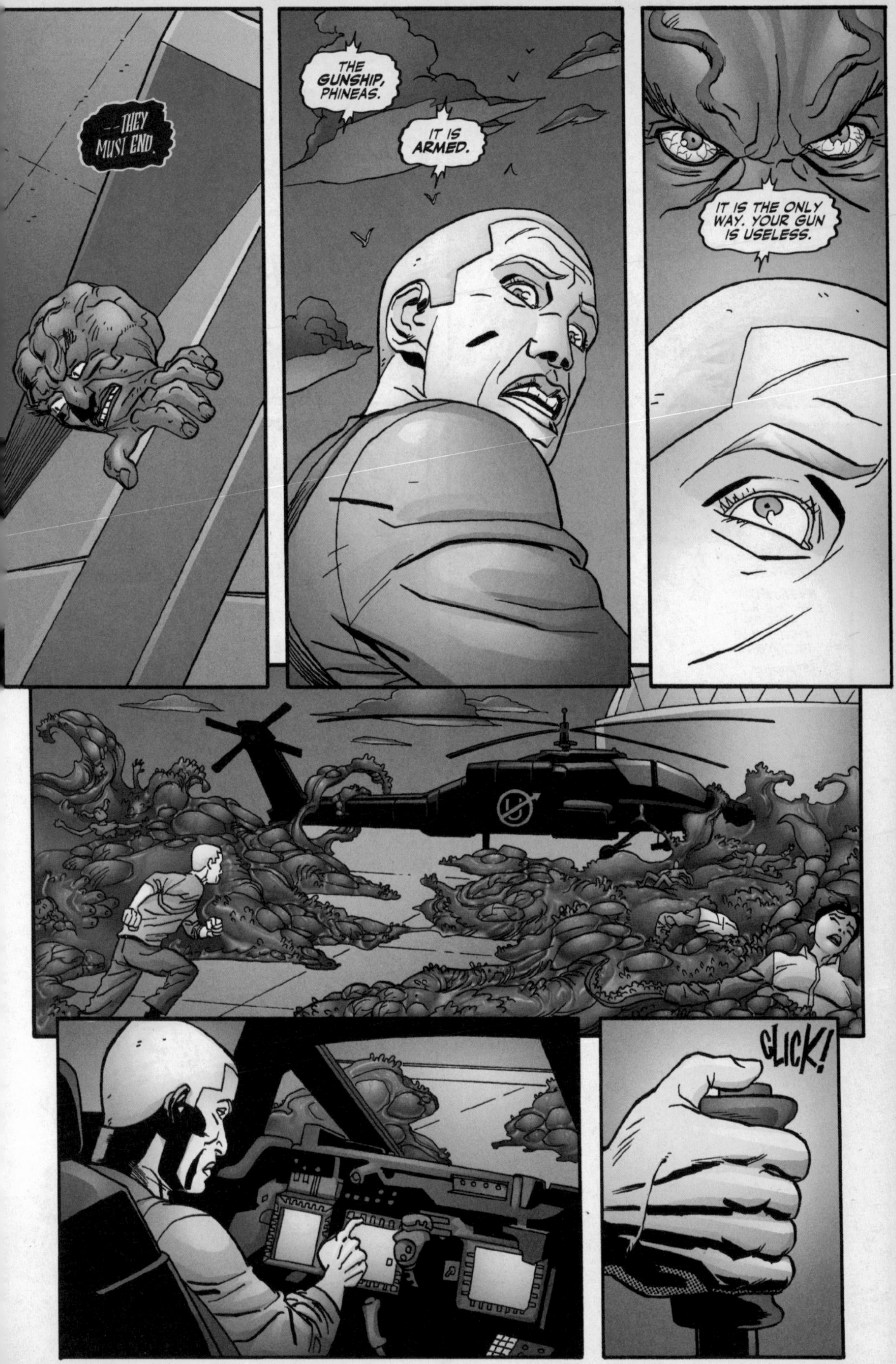
--THEY MUST END.
THE GUNSHIP, PHINEAS.
IT IS ARMED.
IT IS THE ONLY WAY. YOUR GUN IS USELESS.
CLICK!

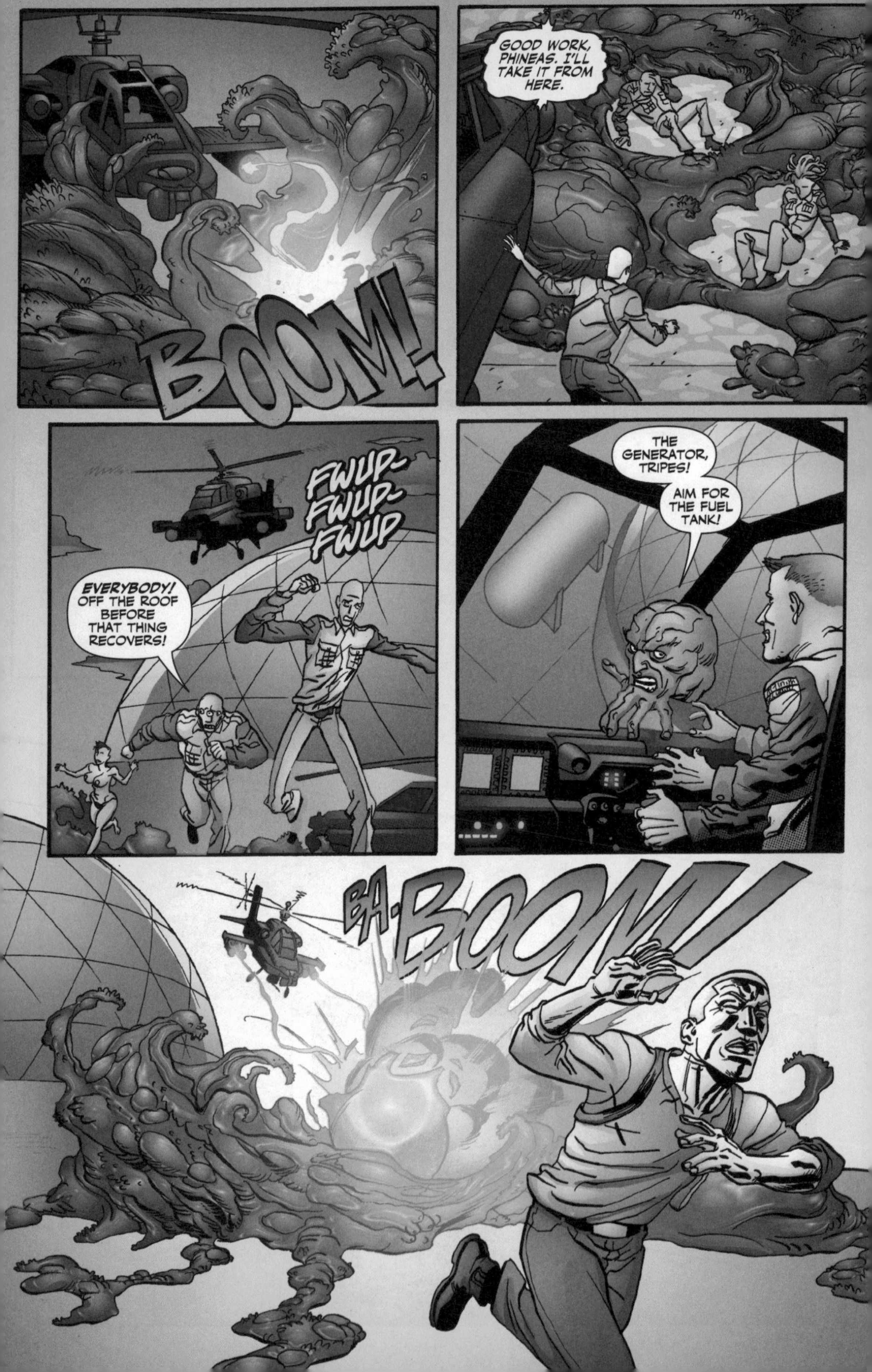
BOOM!
GOOD WORK, PHINEAS. I'LL TAKE IT FROM HERE.
FWUP-FWUP-FWUP
EVERYBODY! OFF THE ROOF BEFORE THAT THING RECOVERS!
THE GENERATOR, TRIPES!
AIM FOR THE FUEL TANK!
BA-BOOM!

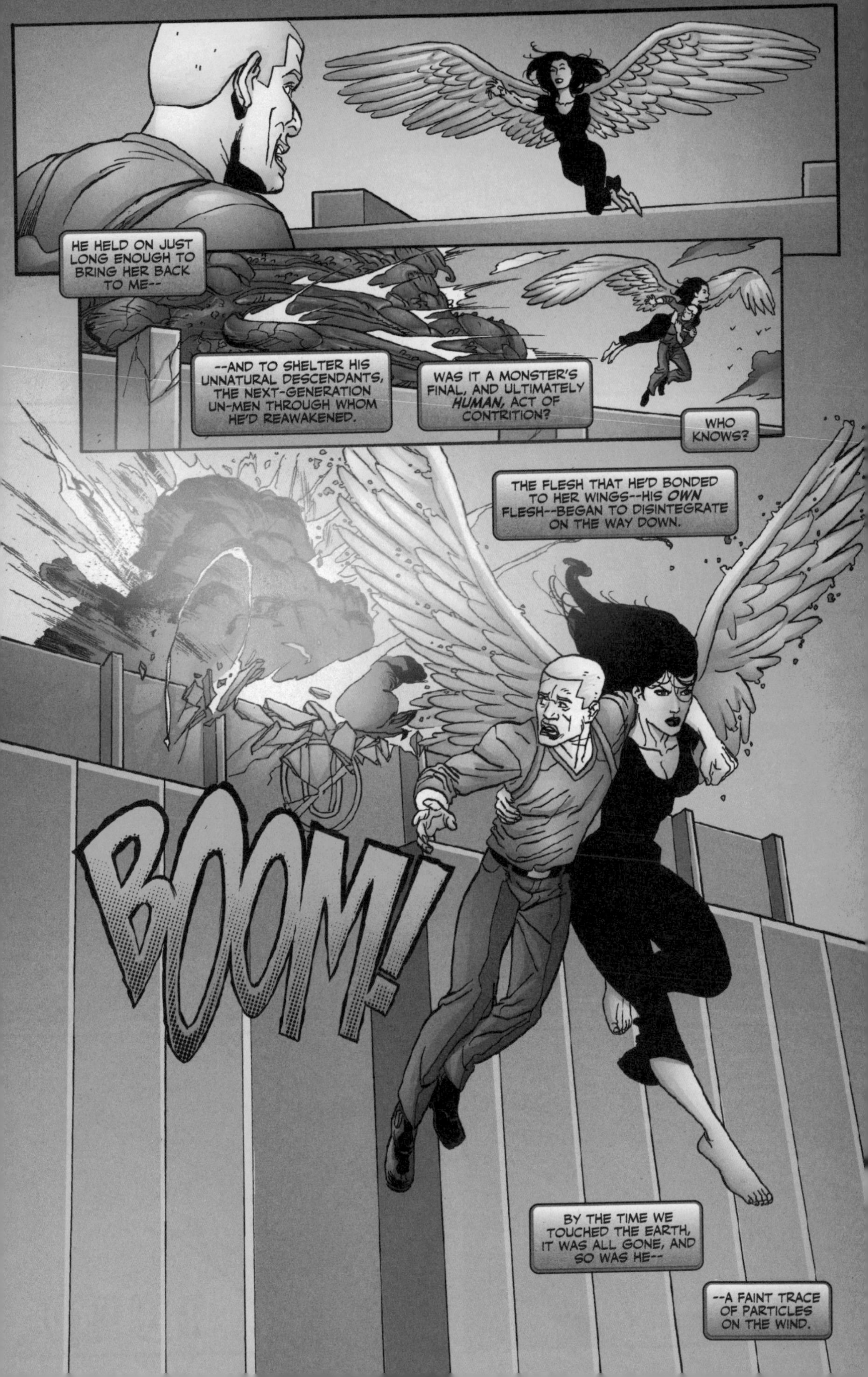
HE HELD ON JUST LONG ENOUGH TO BRING HER BACK TO ME--
--AND TO SHELTER HIS UNNATURAL DESCENDANTS, THE NEXT-GENERATION UN-MEN THROUGH WHOM HE'D REAWAKENED.
WAS IT A MONSTER'S FINAL, AND ULTIMATELY *HUMAN,* ACT OF CONTRITION?
WHO KNOWS?
THE FLESH THAT HE'D BONDED TO HER WINGS--HIS *OWN* FLESH--BEGAN TO DISINTEGRATE ON THE WAY DOWN.
BOOM!
BY THE TIME WE TOUCHED THE EARTH, IT WAS ALL GONE, AND SO WAS HE--
--A FAINT TRACE OF PARTICLES ON THE WIND.

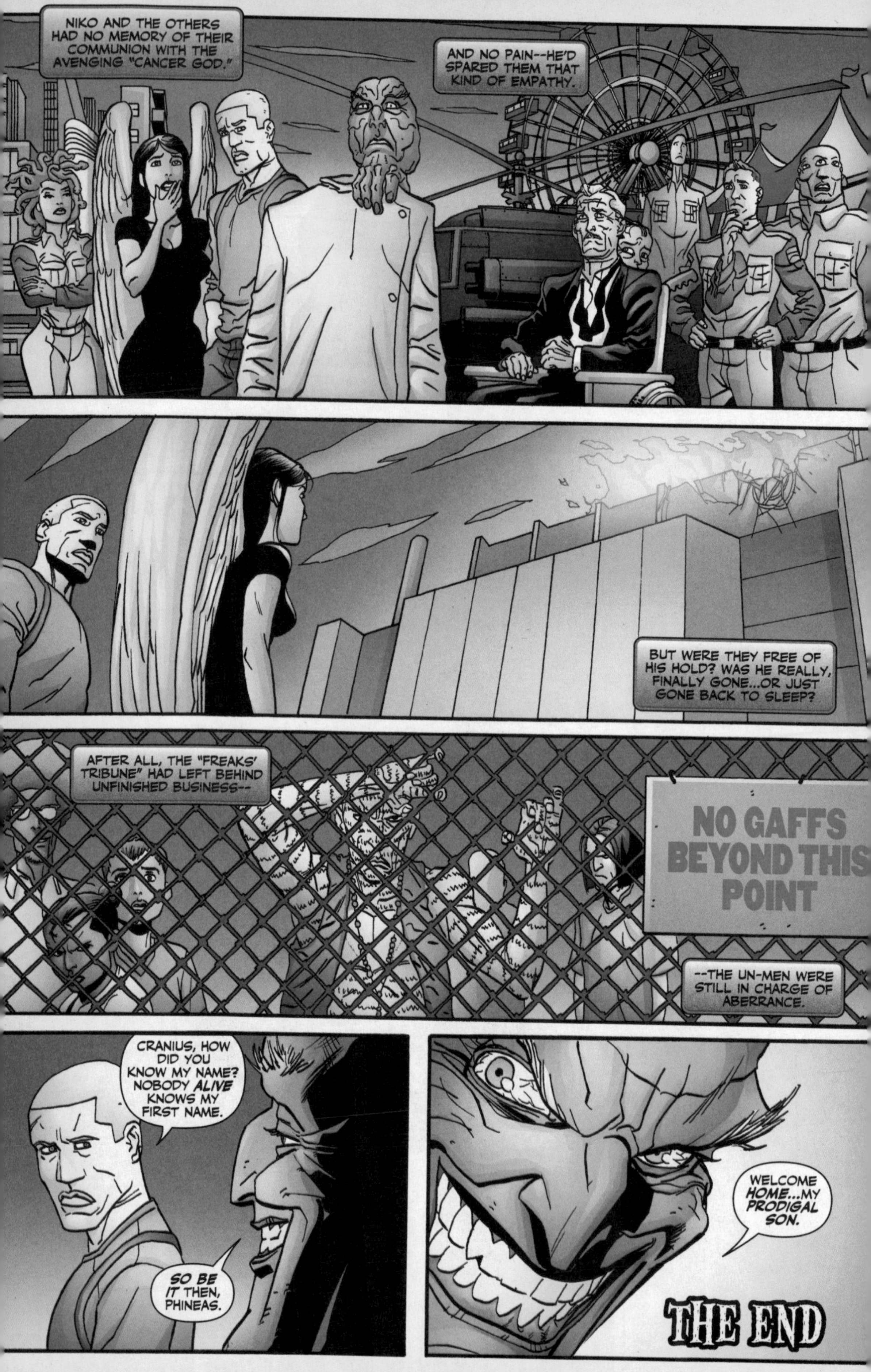
NIKO AND THE OTHERS HAD NO MEMORY OF THEIR COMMUNION WITH THE AVENGING "CANCER GOD."
AND NO PAIN--HE'D SPARED THEM THAT KIND OF EMPATHY.
BUT WERE THEY FREE OF HIS HOLD? WAS HE REALLY, FINALLY GONE...OR JUST GONE BACK TO SLEEP?
AFTER ALL, THE "FREAKS' TRIBUNE" HAD LEFT BEHIND UNFINISHED BUSINESS--
NO GAFFS BEYOND THIS POINT
--THE UN-MEN WERE STILL IN CHARGE OF ABERRANCE.
CRANIUS, HOW DID YOU KNOW MY NAME? NOBODY *ALIVE* KNOWS MY FIRST NAME.
SO BE IT THEN, PHINEAS.
WELCOME *HOME*...MY *PRODIGAL* SON.
THE END

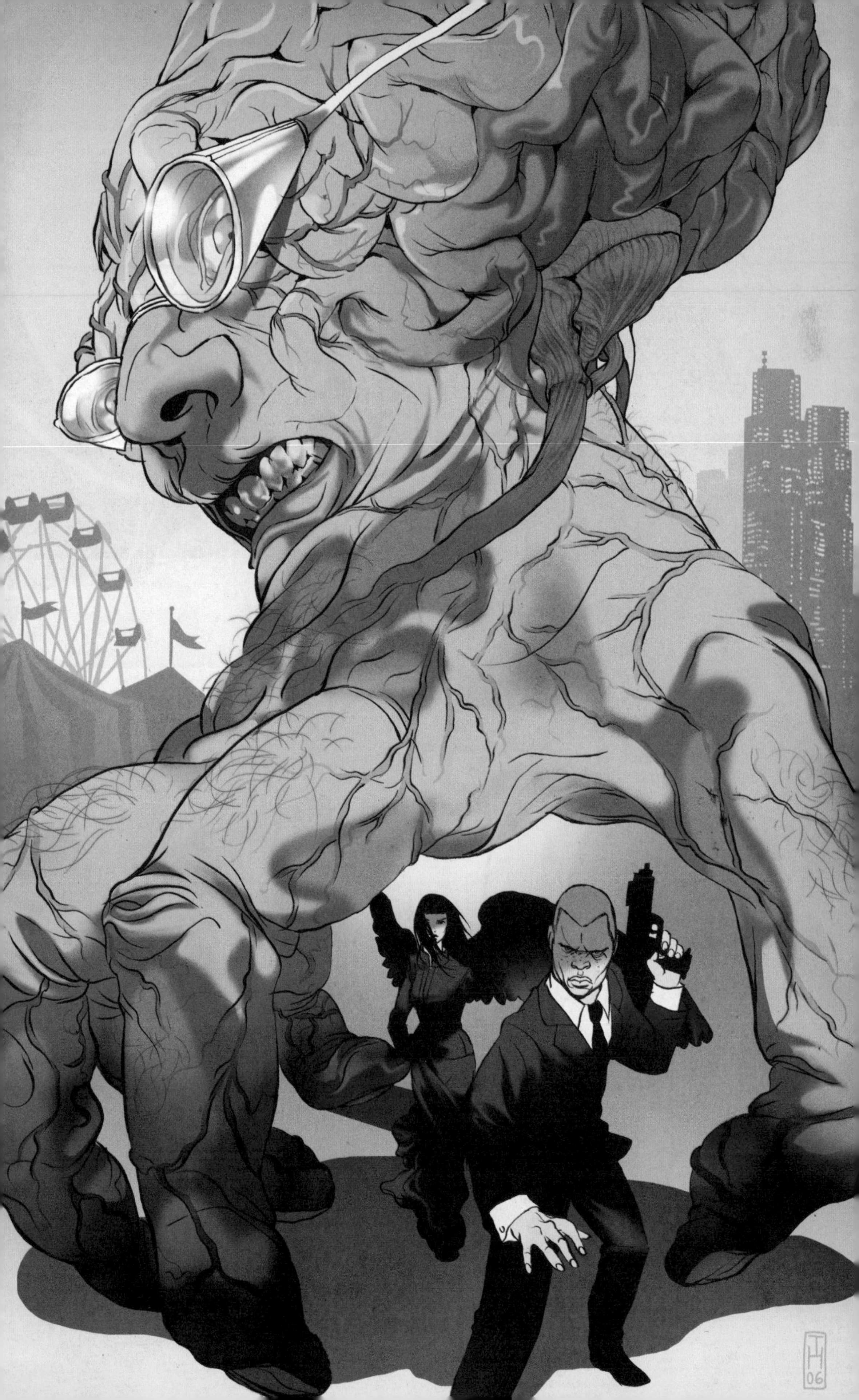

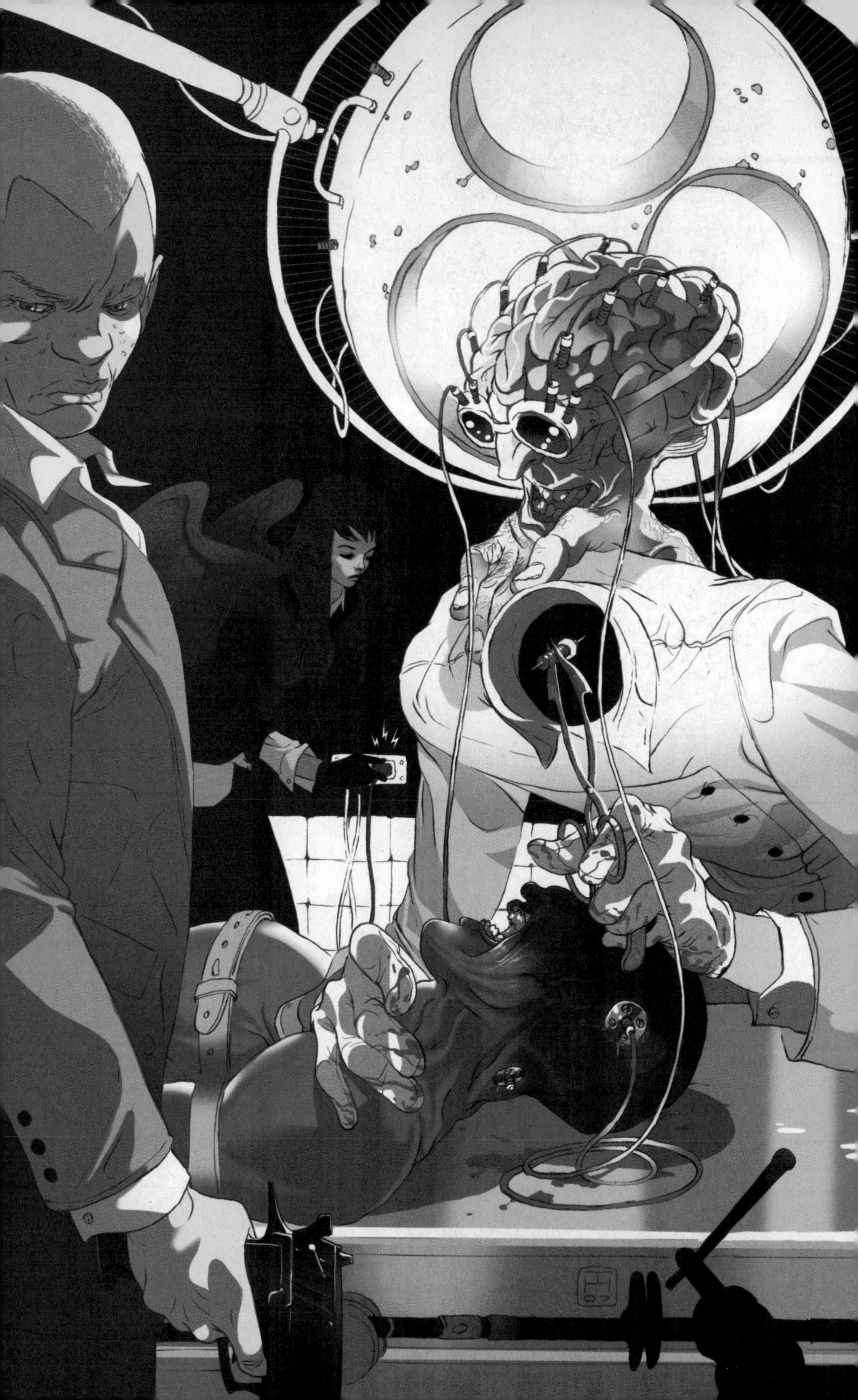

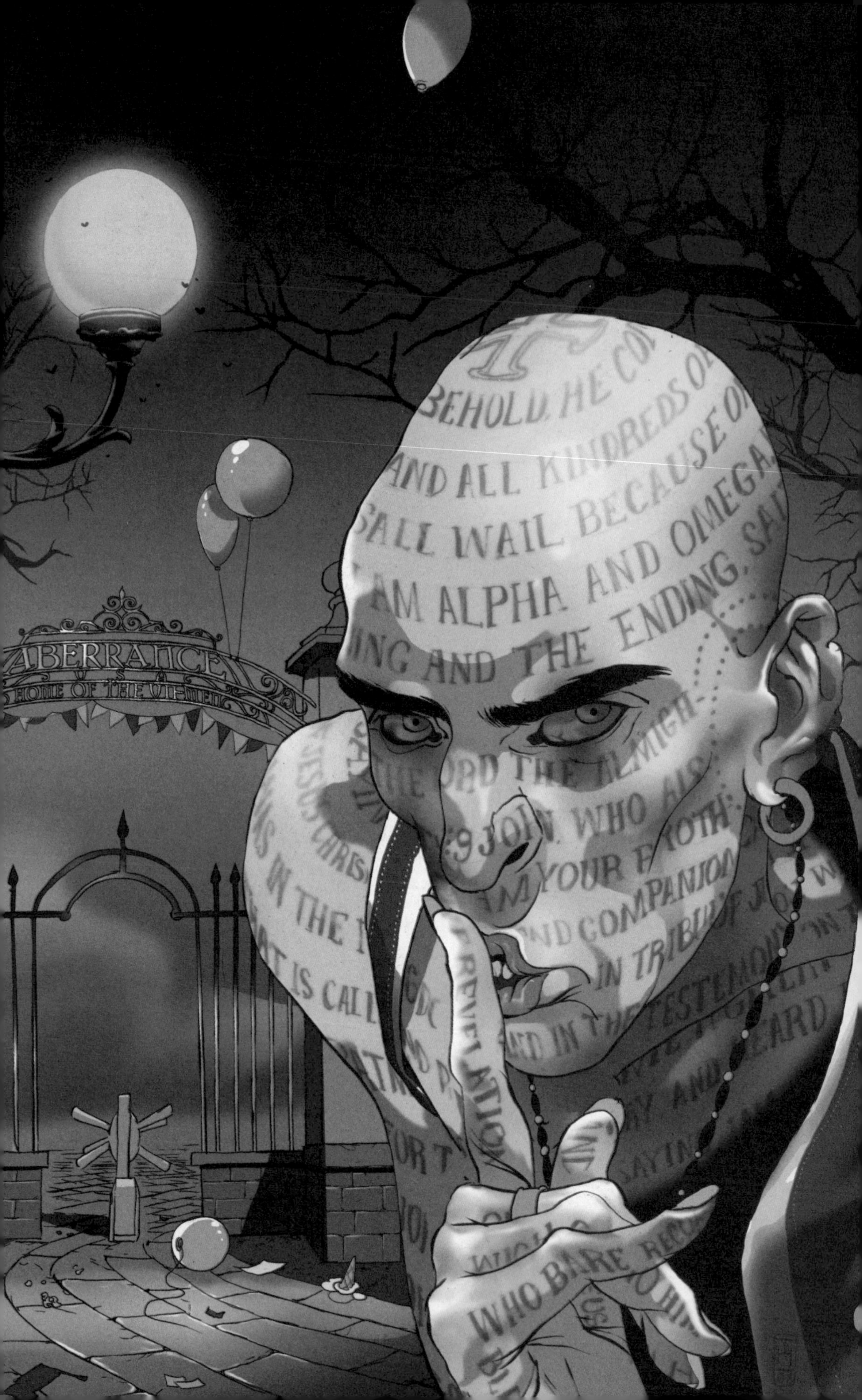

ABERRANCE
U S A
BEHOLD, HE CO
AND ALL KINDREDS OF
SALL WAIL BECAUSE OF
AM ALPHA AND OMEGA,
ING AND THE ENDING, SA
COMPANION
WHO BARE RECO

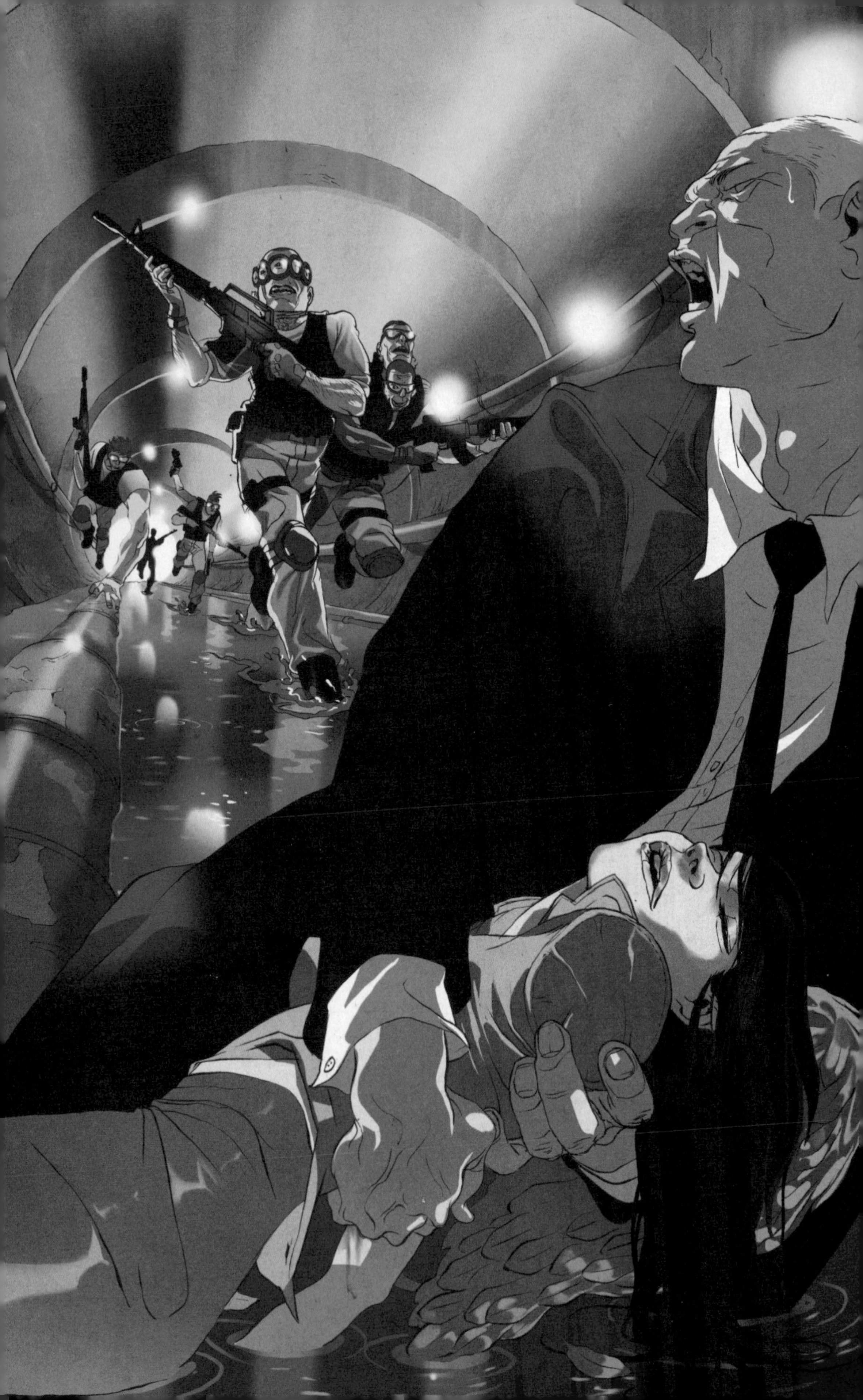